NAVIGATING NUMERACIES

Navigating Numeracies
Home/School Numeracy Practices

by

BRIAN STREET
King's College London, London, U.K.

DAVE BAKER
Institute of Education, London, U.K.

and

ALISON TOMLIN
King's College London, London, U.K.

🐎 Springer

A C.I.P. Catalogue record for this book is available from the Library of Congress.

ISBN 10 1-4020-3676-0 (HB)
ISBN 13 978-1-4020-3676-7 (HB)
ISBN 10 1-4020-3677-9 (e-book)
ISBN 13 978-1-4020-3677-4 (e-book)

Published by Springer,
P.O. Box 17, 3300 AA Dordrecht, The Netherlands.

www.springeronline.com

Printed on acid-free paper

Printed in the Netherlands.

CONTENTS

MARGARET BROWN

FOREWORD

Abstract. This introduction sets the scene for the remainder of the book by considering first the international context of widespread concern about the improvement of numeracy skills. This is related to reform movements in the UK, the US and other countries aimed at modernising primary (elementary) school mathematics curricula. A detailed account is given of the National Numeracy Strategy in England, a systemic government-imposed response to concern about standards implemented in 1999/2000. This includes a discussion of the alternative meanings of numeracy. An earlier initiative sponsored by a UK charitable trust reacting to concern about primary numeracy was the Leverhulme Numeracy Research Programme. This large-scale longitudinal study and linked set of case-study projects, focusing on reasons for low attainment, took place during 1997-2002. This book, and each other in the same series, is based on results of that research. The timescale fortuitously enabled the research team to also report on some effects of the systemic reform in the National Numeracy Strategy.

1. THE INTERNATIONAL CONTEXT

In many countries, there are recurring periods of national concern about the low standards of calculation skills shown by children in primary (elementary) schools. Recently these concerns have become more urgent and more political with the publication of international comparisons of mathematical achievement, first at secondary and more recently at primary level (e.g. Lapointe, Mead et al. 1992; Mullis et al., 1997). Dismay at a low position in the international league tables has in some cases triggered a programme of systemic reform (National Commission for Excellence in Education, 1983; Brown, 1996).

A further reason for government concern over mathematical standards is the realisation that countries in the developed world will require a highly skilled numerate workforce to maintain their economic competitiveness, while developing nations will need to improve the mathematical skills of their population as a basis for building technical and financial capacity. South Korea, a country which is close to the top of every mathematical league table, provides an example to demonstrate that high attainment is possible, even for countries with relatively low Gross National Product.

In many English-speaking countries, and some others, the concern over low attainment in number skills has led to a desire by governments for increasing control of the content, teaching and assessment of primary mathematics. In some countries such increasing government control has come after, and to some extent as a response to, curriculum changes aimed at modernising the primary curriculum and emanating from mathematics educationists and teachers.

For example in the United States the National Council of Teachers of Mathematics Standards (1989; 2000) authorised a primary curriculum which was broad, going well beyond number to statistics and geometry, and emphasised problem-solving, reasoning and mathematical communication. Understanding and appreciation of numbers and number operations, mental strategies and the ability to estimate, i.e. 'number sense' (Reys, Reys et al., 1993) were seen as more important than proficiency in pencil-and-paper algorithms in a society which had ready access to calculators and computers. Informed by constructivist (e.g.Carpenter and Peterson 1988; Steffe and Gale, 1995; Davis, 1984; Maher and Davis, 1990) and social constructivist (e.g. Cobb and Bauersfeld, 1995) results and beliefs about learning, 'reform' initiatives incorporating the Standards have aimed at making learning more participatory and discussion-based, and teachers more knowledgeable about, welcoming of, and responsive to, pupils' own methods and ideas. Such reform initiatives in fact built on a variety of earlier projects since the 1950s, aimed at active and investigatory learning, including problem-solving. Although evaluation of children's learning in the various reform projects has been overwhelmingly positive, there has been some vocal opposition among religious fundamentalists, conservative mathematicians and other right wing groups which has given rise to the 'math wars'. Such groups, who saw the changes as undermining social control and traditional computational standards, have won control in some states, and have persuaded the federal government to impose a comprehensive programme of statewide recurrent testing of mathematical standards.

A very similar pattern has taken place in the UK. A series of initiatives from the 1950s onwards, led by people such as Edith Biggs, Geoffrey Matthews with the Nuffield Project, Elizabeth Williams and Hilary Shuard, were aimed at broadening the primary curriculum and making it more child-centred and investigatory. Changes had been at least partially implemented in most schools by the mid-1980s, encouraged by the relatively progressive report of the national Cockcroft Committee (Department of Education and Science/Welsh Office, 1982). Hilary Shuard's work in the 1980s on the Calculator Aware Number (CAN) curriculum, which emphasised investigation, mental strategies and calculator methods and avoided pencil-and paper algorithms, received international recognition. However after further panic about the role of mathematical standards in industrial decline in the 1980s, and concern that the Cockcroft Committee, set up originally to investigate this, had been subverted by educationist agendas, further moves were made towards government control. These included the imposition of a national curriculum in 1989 followed by a programme of national testing (Department of Education and Science/Welsh Office, 1988). In spite of government pressure, educationists responsible for the detail maintained a broad and modern curriculum and testing programme with only minor concessions in the direction of pencil-and-paper calculation.

However in the 1990s government control tightened once again through publication of test results in league tables, a programme of frequent inspections by the Office for Standards in Education (Ofsted) which put pressure on all schools, but especially those with poor test results. As in the US such schools were initially entitled to additional support but could in the long term be closed. A desire to focus on number skills and revert to traditional teaching methods culminated in the National Numeracy Strategy which, because it forms an important part of the context of the research reported in this book, is described in detail later in this chapter.

As in the US, these moves towards greater government control have been followed by teacher shortages, especially in London and the prosperous South East of England. Vacant posts are sometimes filled by teachers on temporary contracts from private employment agencies, who are often recruited from other countries.

In Australia and New Zealand similar moves were made by governments, first imposing a national curriculum which was relatively vague and progressive, and then with a further tightening and re-focusing on number. Nevertheless the moves have stopped well short of the degree of government control that has occurred in the US and UK, and have involved much greater co-operation with educationists in developing new programmes which are research-based and properly evaluated

It is interesting to compare these changes with national reform of the primary mathematics curriculum and assessment in Holland. Here the 'Realistic Maths' programme, developed by the Freudenthal Institute (Streefland, 1991; Treffers 1991; Gravemeijer, 1997) has many features in common with reform programmes in other countries but with a greater emphasis on the development of mathematics out of models of real world situations. Perhaps because of good performances in national tests, the programme seems to have been allowed to go ahead with minimal political interference, and has achieved a coherence of vision that is probably unique. It has also influenced developments in several other countries, such as the US and UK, and South Africa.

It should be noted that some other countries which have had a tradition of a much greater degree of government control are moving in the opposite direction. Countries like Singapore, Japan and China where there has been great emphasis on number skills are trying to shift the focus to individual creativity and problem-solving skills.

Thus it is clear that all over the world governments and educationists are examining their curricula and teaching methods in primary mathematics and comparing them with those in other countries to see if higher standards in a range of objectives can be achieved.

This means that although this series of books deals with research from the UK, the results are likely to be of interest and use in many other countries, whether they are like other Anglophone countries already moving in similar directions or whether they are simply considering a range of alternative models.

2. THE MEANING OF NUMERACY

In some countries numeracy is a synonym for mathematical literacy, and hence includes areas of mathematics beyond number, for example, geometrical properties, algebra and logical reasoning. In this book however we will restrict numeracy to dealing only with numbers and operations on numbers, recognising that this to some extent includes application of number in work on measures, statistics and metric geometry.

Numeracy is now generally understood as a competence in interpreting and using numbers in daily life, within the home, employment and society. Thus the meaning of numeracy must relate to the social context of its use and the social practices that are adopted in that context (Baker, 1999). The definition of numeracy therefore must be relative and differ not only between different national cultures, but between different subcultures and local circumstances within the same national culture. For example within one household numeracy might be judged by the ability to purchase appropriate quantities of materials and successfully complete household decorations and repairs, such as constructing and putting up a set of book shelves, whereas in the next door household numeracy might be conceptualised in relation to ability to participate intelligently in a family discussion of changes in government economic policy. It is even clearer that different forms of employment involve different practices. Moreover the mathematics underlying employment practices such as those used by nurses can be subtle and difficult to ascertain (Noss, 1997). And even participation as an active citizen in a democratic society might be thought to range from the ability to interpret bar graphs of mean income by region presented in the popular media, to the ability to critique government scientific policy, for example on genetic modification of crops, with reference to papers in scientific journals.

Thus it is not easy for those with the power to make to decisions over mathematics curricula and assessment, whether in schools, local areas, states or countries, to agree what constitutes a minimal competence in numeracy required for social survival, what should be expected of most citizens and what additional aspects of numeracy over and above this level should be aimed for.

It was accepted by educational policymakers in the UK that numeracy was to be defined broadly as the competence and inclination to use number concepts and skills to solve problems in everyday life and employment. Nevertheless it was felt necessary, for political and educational reasons, that the aspect of numeracy to be newly emphasised at primary level should be proficiency in a culturally neutral context-free set of number skills, underpinned by abstract visual models, such as the number line (Department for Education and Employment, 1998). In contrast to 1980s developments, there is now little reference in the primary numeracy guidance to applications or problem-solving, and those which occur are mainly traditional 'word-problems', with artificial contexts.

Because this series of books concerns numeracy in English primary schools in the period 1997-2002, we will generally use numeracy in this narrow and traditional sense. However this usage does not reflect the beliefs of the authors.

3. THE NATIONAL NUMERACY STRATEGY

The Conservative UK Government of 1992-97 had taken 'back to basics' as one of its slogans in education as in other policy areas. As part of this theme high profile National Literacy and National Numeracy Projects were launched in 1996, each in a group of local education authorities which mainly had poor results in national tests. The Labour Party under the leadership of Tony Blair fought the 1997 election with an education policy which differed little from that of the Conservatives, and again emphasised the need to raise standards of basic skills in primary schools, with specific targets for national test results in 2002.

The Labour Party when elected already had plans to extend the National Literacy Project into a National Literacy Strategy to be implemented in all schools in England during the school year 1998/9. They had also set up a Task Force to plan during 1997/8 the details of a National Numeracy Strategy, probably to be based on the National Numeracy Project, to be introduced in all primary schools in England during 1999/2000. This decision was made before any formal evaluation of the National Numeracy Project was available, although informally it was known to be welcomed by teachers and headteachers.

The key features of the National Numeracy Strategy were:

- *an increased emphasis on number and on calculation*, especially mental calculation, including estimation, with pupils being encouraged to select from a repertoire of mental strategies. Written calculation was postponed but informal and later standard written procedures were to be introduced. Calculators were discouraged, although use of them was to be taught in specific lessons starting from Year 5 (age 9/10)
- *a three-part template for daily mathematics lessons*, starting with 10-15 minutes of oral/mental skills practice, then direct interactive teaching of the whole class and groups, and finally 10 minutes of plenary review
- *detailed planning using a suggested week-by-week set of objectives*, specified for each year group. The objectives were listed, with detailed examples to explain them in a key document 'The Framework for Teaching Mathematics from Reception to Year 6' (Department for Education and Employment, 1999). This covered areas of mathematics other than number, but introduced many mental strategies earlier than previously. Teachers were expected to reduce their dependency on text books, using the Framework document as a day-to-day reference point and referring to published text book schemes only as a source of examples
- *a systematic national training programme* based on standard packages of training materials, providing timetables, overhead transparencies to illustrate key points, and videos to demonstrate 'best practice'. Training in each Local Education Authority was organised for teachers from each school by newly appointed trainers acting as consultants and working to regional directors, under a national director. In all schools the training was run by school mathematics co-ordinators, with additional support from consultants for low-performing schools, both in-school and via local courses.

Although not legally imposed, the Numeracy Strategy has been almost universally implemented, and is being extended in a slightly modified form to secondary schools. Most teachers and headteachers have welcomed the Strategy, although teachers found it very hard work to implement, since it required them to plan new introductions to many topics and to prepare new teaching material for each lesson. Previous to this many had been following either commercially produced textbook schemes directly or schemes-of-work written in the school which made reference to published schemes. Many publishers worked hard to issue new textbook schemes to match the Framework but few were ready in time for the first year of the implementation.

Ministers expressed disappointment that national test results for children at age 11 in 2000 and 2001 failed to improve as much as expected after the introduction of the Strategy in the school year 1999/2000. (The proportion gaining the expected result for this age-group, Level 4, had gone from 69% in 1999 to 72% in 2000 and dropped back to 71% in 2001, against a national target of 75% in 2002.) Hence during 2001/2 detailed lesson plans were developed by the central team for all lessons in Years 4 and 6 (pupils aged 8-9 and 10-11 years) and were circulated to all teachers. These were later extended to include Year 5 (pupils aged 9-10 years) and piloted for Years 1 to 3 (pupils aged 5-8 years). While again there was no requirement to implement these, it was known that inspectors would expect teachers to be teaching from these plans and that they would need to provide a sound explanation if they chose alternatives. In fact teachers welcomed the plans as they saved a lot of preparation time and were generally felt to be of good quality.

The Numeracy Strategy was highly resourced in terms of training and training materials with an initial funding of £55 million and a later supplement of £25 million for the first three years. The initial training just prior to the school year 1999/2000 was a Three-day course run out-of-school by the local consultants for mathematics co-ordinators (subject leaders), headteachers, one other teacher from each school and a school governor. The co-ordinator was required to 'cascade' this training for other teachers and assistants in the school during three training days during 1999/2000. Additional training and support, in the form of both school visits by the consultant and a Five-day external course for two teachers, was given to schools identified as in need of 'intensive' support. This support was extended in subsequent years to a wider range of schools.

Some local teachers were designated as 'leading mathematics teachers' and given additional training and release time; teachers from their own and other schools were invited to observe them teach and discuss the lesson and other points with them afterwards.

Schools were provided with some additional money for resources but expected to spend it on equipment which was promulgated by the Strategy and shown in videos e.g. small white boards, number fans and digit cards for each pupil, 100-squares, counting rods, number lines and place value cards. They were also expected to provide release time for their mathematics co-ordinators to work with colleagues.

More details about the Strategy are available from its central offices (e-mail: nnswebeditor@cfbt-hq.org.uk) and from reports by the official evaluators (Earl et al., 2000; Earl, Levin, Leithwood, Fullan & Watson, 2001) and from the inspectorate (Office for Standards in Education, 2000a; 2000b; 2001)

4. THE LEVERHULME NUMERACY RESEARCH PROGRAMME

The national concern about standards of numeracy in England in the late 1990s also led the Trustees of the Leverhulme Trust, a charitable foundation, to offer to fund a £1 million 5-year study on low attainment in basic skills at primary level. The competition for the funding was won by a team based at the Department of Education and Professional Studies, King's College London, for research focused on numeracy. The resulting programme, known as the Leverhulme Numeracy Research Programme, ran from 1997 to 2002 with the aim:

> • to take forward understanding of the nature and causes of low achievement in numeracy
>   and provide insight into effective strategies for remedying the situation.

We wanted to examine the contribution of many different factors to low attainment, in individual children, classes, schools or population groups, by studying, on both a large and small-scale, cases in which these factors varied. Two intervention studies were also planned as part of the Programme.

The research design, which included a large-scale longitudinal study (the Core Project) and five focus projects, is outlined below. (Further detail of data collection and analysis procedures on individual projects which contribute to the research reported in each book in the series is provided in the Annexes at the end of each volume. Findings are reported elsewhere.)

4.1. The Core Project: Tracking numeracy (Margaret Brown, Mike Askew, Valerie Rhodes, Hazel Denvir, Esther Ranson, Dylan Wiliam, Helen Lucey and Tamara Bibby; 1997-2002)

Aim: To obtain large-scale longitudinal value-added data on numeracy to:
  • inform knowledge about the progression in pupils' learning of numeracy throughout the primary years, and
  • to assess relative contributions to gains in numeracy of the different factors to be investigated in the programme.

Methods: Data on pupil attainment was gathered twice a year for 4 years, on two longitudinal cohorts each of about 1600 pupils, one moving from Year 1 (age 5-6 years) to Year 4 (age 8-9 years) and the other from Year 4 to Year 7 (age 11-12 years). Each cohort included all children of the appropriate age in 10 primary schools in each of 4 varied local education authorities (two groups of over 70 classes). Only a small subset of 180 pupils in seven secondary schools, including at least one in each of the four local education authorities, were followed into Year 7 and were tested only at the end of the year, because of the logistic problems of observing lessons and testing specific children in large numbers of secondary schools. Detailed data was collected annually on pupils, teachers and schools including lesson observations, teacher questionnaires and interviews with teachers, mathematics co-ordinators and headteachers. (This data relates also to the younger cohort in the Reception year (ages 4-5) although it was not practicable to test the pupils at that age). Many instruments were modifications of those designed for our 'Effective Teachers of Numeracy' project (Askew et al., 1997). This data formed the basis for both statistical and qualitative analysis to investigate the relative contributions of different factors.

The core study provided a base for the case-study investigations in the focus projects, and both generated hypotheses to be explored in the focus projects and allowed hypotheses arising from those to be checked on a larger sample.

4.2. Focus Project: Case-studies of pupil progress (Mike Askew, Hazel Denvir, Valerie Rhodes and Margaret Brown; 1997-2002)

Aim: To obtain a clear and detailed longitudinal picture of the numeracy development of a range of pupils taught in a varied set of schools and to examine this in the light of their classroom experiences, to ascertain what works, what goes wrong, and why.

Methods: This project explored the classroom practice factors influencing pupil attainment, including school, teacher, teaching, curriculum and individual pupil factors. From the longitudinal core sample we selected 5 schools which presented interesting contrasts. In each of these schools we selected children of varied attainment, six from a Reception (age 4-5 years) and six from a Year 4 class (age 8-9 years) to provide longitudinal case study data, plotting progression in learning over 4 or 5 years. Children were observed and informally interviewed in two blocks of five lessons each year, and their written work collected. Longer interviews concerning perceptions of progress, attitudes and home support, and involving assessment questions, occurred at the end of Years 3 and 6.

4.3. Focus Project: Teachers' knowledge, conceptions and practices and pupils' learning (Mike Askew, Alison Millett & Shirley Simon; 1999-2002)

Aim: To investigate the relationships between teachers' beliefs about, knowledge of and practices in teaching numeracy and whether changes in beliefs, knowledge and/or practices raise standards.

Methods: The project followed twelve teachers before, during and after their experience of a short course of professional development as part of the National Numeracy Strategy. We adapted the methods of eliciting teachers' subject knowledge and beliefs in a series of interviews from our earlier work (Askew et al., 1997) in order to construct teacher profiles. Changes in teachers' practices were monitored using video recording of lessons, and changes in pupils' attainment by using the tests developed for the core project. The teachers' profiles, their classroom practices and their pupils' attainment were monitored over three years.

4.4. Focus Project: Whole school action on numeracy (Alison Millett & David Johnson; 1997- 2001)

Aim: To identify whole-school and teacher factors which appear to facilitate or inhibit the development of strategies for raising attainment in numeracy.

Methods: This research focused on six schools as they each experienced an inspection and then implemented the National Numeracy Strategy. Each school had identified the need for improvements in their teaching of numeracy and we have collected data both on the strategies schools used to develop the teaching of numeracy and the effect of these strategies on pupils' attainment. The research investigated the complex interplay of school factors, such as school policies and leadership, and teacher factors involved in the implementation of change over four years. The research used documentary analysis, observation in classrooms and at meetings, and interviews with a range of informants (headteachers, mathematics co-ordinators, classroom teachers, governors and parents).

4.5. Focus Project: School and community numeracies (Brian Street, Alison Tomlin, Dave Bake and Helen Lucey; 1998 - 2002)

Aim: To refine and establish the meanings and uses of numeracy in home and school contexts; to establish differences between practices in the two environments and to draw inferences for pedagogy.
Methods: This project investigated the influence of social factors on attainment, in particular differences between numeracy practices, and the linguistic practices associated with them, in the pupils' home and school contexts. Three schools were selected to provide a range of home cultures. Case-study pupils were then chosen from Reception classes (age 4-5 years) and followed through Year 1 (age 5-6 years) and into Year 2 (age 6-7 years). We used ethnographic methods including participant observation of classrooms and of informal situations in and out of school, and interviews with teachers, parents and pupils. The study extended previous work on literacy practices (Street, 1999) into numeracy, but retained a comparative element between the two.

4.6. Focus Project: Primary CAME (Cognitive Acceleration in Mathematics Education) (David Johnson, Mundher Adhami, Michael Shayer, Rosemary Hafeez, Sally Dubben, Ann Longfield & Jeremy Hodgen; 1997-2000)

Aim: To investigate the effect on the development of numeracy of managed cognitive challenge/conflict designed to encourage verbal interactions and metacognitive activity in whole-class and various small group arrangements of children in Year 5 (age 9-10 years) and Year 6 (age 10-11 years).
Methods: An experimental design was used to investigate whether intervention in classroom practices aimed at promoting intellectual development could be effective. It extended our earlier work on CAME (Cognitive Acceleration in Mathematics Education) in secondary schools (Adhami et al., 1998) which used Piagetian and Vygotskian paradigms. The research team, including teacher-researchers in each of two laboratory schools, first devised and trialled a sequence of mathematical problem situations designed to challenge children, and to promote teacher-child and child-child discussion in cooperative small group work and whole-class discussion. This led to the main fieldwork involving research with teachers in a further 8

schools, with the teacher-researchers as tutors. We used systematic observation of lessons and professional development sessions, and pre- and post- intervention pupil assessments of cognitive development and mathematical attainment. A linked study has demonstrated how this intervention acted as a basis for teachers' continuous professional development.

4.7. Relation to the National Numeracy Strategy

When the Leverhulme proposal was written it could not have been anticipated that a new government would quickly implement the National Numeracy Strategy. Clearly this affected the Leverhulme Programme as the implementation of the Strategy in schools occurred in the middle year (1999/2000) of the 5-year research programme. For example it meant that curriculum objectives, teaching sequence and aspects of teaching methods no longer varied between classes, and thus the effects of differences in these could only be perceived in data from the early years of the project. The original plan for a intervention project concerning teacher professional development (*Teachers' Knowledge, Conceptions and Practices*) also had to be modified to fit with the Strategy training courses, since schools would not have been able to support additional training in the year of implementation of the Strategy.

The Leverhulme work addressed fundamental issues in primary numeracy and was by no means merely an evaluation of the implementation of the Numeracy Strategy. Indeed there was a government authorised evaluation which was carried out, with the parallel Literacy Strategy, by a Canadian team (Earl et al., 2000; 2001). But our data was used to inform this evaluation and, as well as tackling its own wider brief, was able to illuminate some effects of a particular attempt at systemic reform.

4.8. Coherence of themes

Although the structure of the Leverhulme Programme has been described as six projects, there has been great added benefit in the projects being part of the larger programme. The results of the programme were first analysed separately for each project and then integrated into a sequence of four common linked themes, to each of which several projects contribute.
- children's learning and progression
- teachers and teaching
- home, culture and school
- professional development of teachers.

These four themes are the topics of the four books in this current series. The first two themes are combined into two books, the first addressing generic features of teaching and learning numeracy and the second examining teaching and learning in different numeracy topics. The third and fourth themes form a book each. Thus the four titles in the series are:
- Teaching and learning about number: interactions in primary lessons and pupil progression

- Teaching, learning and progression in key numeracy topics
- Numeracy practices at home and at school
- Primary Mathematics and the Developing Professional

5. REFERENCES

Adhami, M., Johnson, D. & Shayer, M. (1998). *Thinking Maths: The Programme for Accelerated Learning in Mathematics*. Oxford: Heinemann Educational Books.

Askew, M., M. Brown, et al. (1997). *Effective Teachers of Numeracy: Report of a study carried out for the Teacher Training Agency*. London, King's College, University of London.

Baker, D. (1999). "What does it mean to understand maths as social." *Paper presented at the British Congress of Mathematics Education, 15 -17 July 1999 University College Northampton*.

Brown, M. (1996). The context of the research - the evolution of the National Curriculum for mathematics. In D. C. Johnson & A. Millett (Eds.), *Implementing the mathematics National Curriculum: policy, politics and practice* (pp. 1-28). London, UK: Paul Chapman.

Carpenter, T. P. and P. L. Peterson (1988). "Learning through instruction: The study of students' thinking during instruction in mathematics." *Educational Psychologist* **23**(2): 79-85.

Cobb, P. and H. Bauersfeld, Eds. (1995). *The emergence of mathematical meaning: interaction in classroom cultures*. Hillsdale, NJ, Lawrence Erlbaum Associates.

Davis, R. B. (1984). *Learning Mathematics: The Cognitive Science Approach to Mathematics Education*. London, Croom Helm.

Department for Education and Employment (DfEE) (1998). *The implementation of the National Numeracy Strategy: The final report of the Numeracy Task Force*. London, UK, DfEE.

Department for Education and Employment (DfEE) (1999). *The National Numeracy Strategy: Framework for teaching mathematics from Reception to Year 6*. London, UK, DfEE

Department of Education and Science/Welsh Office. (1982). *Mathematics Counts: report of the Committee of Inquiry into the Teaching of Mathematics in Schools*. London, UK: Her Majesty's Stationery Office.

Department of Education and Science/Welsh Office. (1988). *Mathematics for ages 5-16*. London: Department of Education and Science.

Earl, L., Fullan, M., Leithwood, K., Watson, N., with Jantzi, D., Levin, B., & Torrance, N. (2000). Watching and Learning. OISE/UT Evaluation of the implementation of the National Literacy and Numeracy Strategies. First annual report. Toronto: OISE/UT.

Earl, L., Levin, B., Leithwood, K., Fullan, M., & Watson, N. (2001). Watching & Learning 2: OISE/UT Evaluation of the Implementation of the National Literacy and Numeracy Strategies. Second Annual Report. Toronto: OISE/UT.

Gravemeijer, K. (1997). Instructional design for reform in mathematics education. *The Role of Contexts and Models in the Development of Mathematical Strategies and Procedures*. M. Beishuizen, K. Gravemeijer and E. C. D. M. Van Lieshout. Utrecht: Freudenthal Institute.

Lapointe, A., N. Mead, et al. (1992). *Learning mathematics (Report of the IAEP 1990/1 survey)*. Princeton, NJ: Educational Testing Service.

Maher, C. and R. B. Davis (1990). Teachers' learning: building representations of children's meanings. *Constructivist views on the teaching and learning of mathematics*. R. B. Davis, C. A. Maher and N. Noddings. Reston VA, National Council of Teachers of Mathematics.

Mullis, I. V. S., Martin, M. O., Beaton, A. E., Gonzalez, E. J., Kelly, D. L., & Smith, T. A. (1997). *Mathematics Achievement in the Primary School Years: IES's Third Mathematics and Science Study*. Massachusetts: Boston College.

National Commission for Excellence in Education (1983) *A Nation at Risk: the imperative for educational reform*. Washington, DC: US Government Printing

National Council of Teachers of Mathematics. (1989). *Curriculum and evaluation standards for school mathematics*. Reston, VA: National Council of Teachers of Mathematics.

National Council of Teachers of Mathematics. (2000). *Principles and Standards for School Mathematics*. Reston VA: National Council of Teachers of Mathematics.

Noss, R. (1997). *New cultures, new literacies*. London: Institute of Education.

Office for Standards in Education. (2000a). *The National Numeracy Strategy: an interim evaluation by HMI*. London: Office for Standards in Education.

Office for Standards in Education. (2000b). *The National Numeracy Strategy: the first year*. London: Office for Standards in Education.

Office for Standards in Education. (2001). *the National Numeracy Strategy: the second year*. London: Office for Standards in Education.

Reys, B. J., R. E. Reys, et al. (1993). "Mental computation: a snapshot of second, fifth and seventh grade student performance." *School Science and Mathematics*.

Steffe, L. P. and J. Gale, Eds. (1995). *Constructivism in education*. Hilldale, NJ: Lawrence Erlbaum Associates.

Streefland, L., Ed. (1991). *Realistic mathematics education in primary schools*. Utrecht: Freudenthal Institute, Utrecht University.

Street, B. (1999). Literacy 'events' and literacy 'practices': theory and practice in the 'New Literacy Studies'. *Multilingual literacies: comparative perspectives on research and practice*. K. Jones and M. Martin-Jones. Amsterdam: John Benjamin.

Treffers, A. (1991). Didactical background of a mathematics program for primary education. *Realistic mathematics education in primary schools*. L. Streefland. Utrecht: Freudenthal Institute, Utrecht University.

BRIAN STREET DAVE BAKER ALISON TOMLIN

INTRODUCTION TO THE BOOK

1. RATIONALE

Our aim in writing this book and in the research on which it is based is to widen the range of explanatory factors in addressing children's low achievement in numeracy in primary schools. Research on, and educational policy for, raising achievement in numeracy, particularly in the UK, has recently focused more on school factors in attainment, such as teacher subject knowledge, pedagogy (pace, style, whole class teaching, setting, calculators, homework), schools (leadership, effective management, policies), and educational structures (assessment regimes and systems, local/regional education authorities). In the UK the National Curriculum has been founded on such approaches, (cf Levin, 1999; DfEE, 1999), Studies of 'effectiveness' have attempted to identify key factors that correlate with attainment (Galton et. al. 1980/1999).

> " .. there is a strong relationship between children's performance in maths and reading
> tests between the ages of six and eight and their parents' earnings, with the children of
> higher earning parents performing better." (HM Treasury, March 99, p 29 drawing on
> data from the National Child Development Survey 1991).

'Teacher effects' research has listed 'expectations', 'classroom management', 'curriculum pacing' etc., using multilevel analyses to identify significant factors (Muijs and Reynolds, 2001) whilst the Oracle studies identified different 'teaching styles' and offered 'parameter estimates' of likely student responses (Bennett, 1976; Galton et. al., 1980/1999).

Few factors in such studies attain real numerical significance and the approach can be criticised for over technicism and for failing to recognise the integrated and holistic character of teaching and learning that a more qualitative approach entails. The Leverhulme Programme instead adopted a longitudinal approach, developing ways of measuring pupil progression across a five year span (see Books 1-3 of this series). Recognising, then, the difficulties with the 'school effect' approach, the School and Community focus of the Leverhulme Numeracy Research Programme sought to shift the emphasis to the relationship between home and school. As we show in Chapter 1, there is considerable evidence for the effect of non-school factors on attainment and outcomes of school numeracy (cf Feinstein,L 2003) We sought understandings and explanations for such correlation and influences.

The aims and objectives of the research team, then, were to refine and establish the meanings and uses of numeracy in school and community contexts and to establish the links between the two environments in order to further understanding of pupils' achievement in numeracy in the school context. The project aimed to investigate the influence of social factors, in particular the pupils' home contexts, on numeracy attainment in school. The research built upon previous projects in which members of the team had been involved, including research on formal and informal numeracy practices in a UK primary school (Baker, 1996) and on everyday literacy practices in and out of schools in the UK and in the US (Street & Street, 1991) and also in international contexts (Street, 1995; 2000). The present project looked at actual uses and meanings of numeracy in and out of school, amongst children based in a number of UK Primary schools. A further focus was the language practices - reading, writing, speaking and listening - associated with numeracy, a theme connected with the Leverhulme funded Home-School Literacy project in which the researchers were also involved (Gregory et. al., 2004). The Project was based on the belief that many children bring positive resources with them from their home environments and that these are important for understanding how they perform in class.

2 METHODS

The methods employed were designed as congruent with these aims and objectives, involving mainly observation of selected schools and classrooms and of informal situations in and out of school; interviews with teachers; visits to see children at home, observations of them at home and at school and interviews with their parents/carers;   analysis of texts, including commercially produced textbooks designed for home use, official curriculum documents, school policy documents, schemes of work, homework, teacher feedback etc. Fieldwork within the research was ethnographic in style (cf. Bloome and Green, 1996). It was conducted in three schools, Mountford, Rowan and Tarnside, which provided contrastive, 'telling' cases (Mitchell, 1984) to cover, where possible, a range of schooling and the main dimensions of suspected heterogeneity in the population e.g. class, ethnicity, urban/ suburban (See Appendix for details about the fieldwork and the schools cf. also articles by the authors listed in the Bibliography). The researchers conducted longitudinal case studies in one class in each of the three schools, from Reception (1999/2000) through to Year 2 (2001/2002), focusing on about four children in each, and following them through to their homes where both observations and informal interviews were conducted. The team of three researchers between them made a total of 100+ visits to schools, 50+ visits to homes and conducted 20+ interviews with heads, teachers and parents. In addition members of other teams within the Leverhulme Programme collected data on children's home background, including postcode information correlated with such social indicators as free school meals, ethnicity and class, and we are able also to draw on data drawn on this and on other teams' interviews with teachers and children and classroom observations.

The team drew up 'frameworks' documents as terms of reference for jointly developing questions, check lists for interviews and observations, etc (see Appendix and Chapter 3). The three main researchers conducted observation on three cohorts of pupils as they passed through three levels of Primary School – Reception, Year 1 and Year 2 in the three schools. The researchers tracked selected children from these classes back into their homes and conducted observations and interviews with parents and other carers in home environments, regarding numeracy events and numeracy practices (see Chapter 2 for conceptual apparatus) and parents' perceptions of school work. Analysis has followed ethnographic-style approaches in which initial concepts were revised in the light of data and new questions generated as the researchers and the participants reflected upon findings (see Chapter 3 on Methodology). A major component of the presentation of this material is through case studies of the home/ school relations focussing on individual target children and on each school as a basis for thematic accounts across cases (see Section 3).

3 THE 'SOCIAL' IN NUMERACY

The research was founded on a model of what the social means when looking at numeracy. In Chapter 2 we explain this use of social and we draw on the research as an illustration of these ideas in both the case studies and the thematic sections of the book. Our view of the 'social' in mathematics and mathematics education has some overlaps with that of other mathematics education researchers and theorists, whose work we describe briefly in Chapter 2, including for example Paul Ernest, Jo Boaler, Ubiratan d'Ambrosio, Steve Lerman, Pollard with Filer,. (1996, 2000), Guida de Abreu, Martin Hughes, Ole Skovsmose, and Carol Aubrey etc. The present account, however, is unusual in its foundation in ethnographic research methods and its close relation to recent developments in literacy and literacy education research (Barton,, Hamilton, & Ivanic, 2000; Baynham & Baker 2002; Collins and Blot 2002; Hull & Schultz, 2002; Heath. and Mangiola,L 1991; Street, B & J 1991; Street, 2003; Villegas, 1991). It is timely we believe to try to offer explanations for low achievement in numeracy based on a broader perspective on the 'social', of the kind familiar in much of this literature on literacy as social practice and being applied by some researchers to children's and adults' maths practices.

A key question for this volume, then, is how useful it might be to develop such concepts and insights in studying numeracy at home and at school. In the work we report on here, we seek to develop a language of description and to refine the lenses for viewing mathematics or numeracy practices in social contexts that might complement and enrich the current tools for description available in the field. By describing and understanding different meanings that pupils bring to their encounters with schooled mathematics/numeracies, including meanings derived from broader contexts, we hope to offer different explanations for low achievement than those which are currently dominant.

The book is aimed at policy makers, teacher trainers and teachers as well as education students on MA and research courses, who have an interest in explanations for children's low achievement in numeracy. Researchers in other countries, interested in comparative studies of children's numeracy may also find sufficient documentation here on practices in the UK to be interested in taking the material up for their own research practice – as indeed teams in the US, South Africa and Australia have recently done (refs). Those interested in the field of literacy studies will also be interested to follow through the implications of adapting their perspectives to the numeracy field.

4 SYNOPSIS OF CHAPTERS AND SECTIONS

The book had been organised into four sections. In Section 1 we introduce the research itself and outline the theoretical and methodological principles underlying the approach. We put the study into broader perspective, considering other research on issues of class, poverty, ethnicity and pupil attainment and relating it to both our own data and to that collected by colleagues in other strands of the Leverhulme Programme. For instance, quantitative data on pupils' attainment from the tests set in the 50+ schools in the Leverhulme Programme each year have been correlated with data on gender, ethnicity, English fluency, and their relationship to such factors as postcodes, free schools meals and single parent families (cf Brown et. al. 2004 – book 2 of the present series).These data suggest a significant relationship between class, poverty and pupil attainment, although little relationship between social variables and pupil gains. The quantitative data are used to put into broader perspective the qualitative data based on in-depth case studies from which most of the accounts in the present volume are drawn. With respect to gender, we acknowledge its significance, especially with respect to such quantitative measures, but our qualitative data does not focus on this aspect specifically and we do not feel we have sufficient significant data to contribute at this stage to debates about gender issues and numeracy attainment.

In Section 2 we elaborate on the distinctive theoretical perspective and methodology that inform the accounts presented here, Chapter 2 develops the implications of viewing numeracy as a 'social practice': drawing, amongst other sources, on research in the field of literacy as a social practice, we attempt to follow through the implications of such a perspective both for addressing the broader questions outlined above and more precisely for generating and analysing our own data regarding the numeracy practices at home and at school of selected children. We outline here the main concepts drawn upon in the rest of the book – numeracy as social practice, numeracy events and numeracy practices. We ask 'how have children's relative attainment in numeracy been described and in what ways does a 'social' approach force us to revise some dominant assumptions?'. This will be followed in Chapter 3 by an account of the ways in which we approached the collection, analysis and representation of the data. Our methodological focus is on case studies as offering 'analytic induction' – ways of articulating and analysing the issues raised at a theoretical level and thereby contributing to conceptual understanding and, we hope, clarity (Mitchell, 1984). We suggest ways of exploring the relationship between home and school via case studies and Mitchell's notion of 'telling cases'.

Section 3 consists of such 'case studies' – of both selected children and of schools – and aims to provide ethnographically rich accounts of the everyday practices of children in and out of school, and this deliberately takes up a significant proportion of the book..

We then offer in Section 4, some interpretation of the themes that the case studies raise, also weaving in further data from home and school taken from our field notes. In Chapter 6 we address in-school aspects of numeracy practices, under the headings of 'engagement' and 'switching'. Chapter 7 shifts the focus to home numeracy practices, looking in particular at 'cultural resources'. In Chapter 8 we consider the relation between the two domains and sites, home and school. Finally, in the Conclusion, we suggest some implications for theory, policy, research and practice

LIST OF TABLES

SECTION ONE: THE CONTEXT

In this section we set the context and scene of the research and of the book. The section consists of two chapters. The first is the introduction to the book, which outlines the research aims and synopsis of the book. We provide the rationale for our approach, explain our methods and how they differ from much recent research in this field and then offer an initial exposition of our use of the concept of 'social', which is developed further in Chapter 2 and then runs throughout the book. We then provide a synopsis of the chapters of the book to give the reader an overall map of the design. The second part of this Section consists of chapter 1, in which we discuss the educational background and debates that surround current explanations for low achievement in numeracy in schools and we outline alternative ways that the research and the book approach these issues. In particular we indicate our shift from the dominant explanation focused on 'school effect' to looking at the implications of 'home effect', citing literature from studies in various countries. We describe some of the alternative models that have been proposed to either the deficit or the social engineering models for enhancing the schooled performance of children from 'non-traditional' backgrounds and offer a bridging position. Finally we locate the study in the broader context of the Leverhulme funded research programme at King's College London, that has also provided the basis for other volumes in this series.

CHAPTER ONE: EXPLANATIONS FOR UNDERACHIEVEMENT

Class, Poverty, Ethnicity

1. THE CONTEXT

Consideration of the effect of 'social' factors in explaining children's under achievement in numeracy, has tended to be marginalised in recent years, at the expense of attention to school factors, such as teacher subject knowledge, pedagogy, school leadership, effective management etc. This shift from home effect to school effect, however, runs counter to much of the research and evidence across the same period that demonstrated the continuing significance of out of school factors, whether defined in terms of 'socio-economic status, 'poverty, relative wealth etc. For instance, a UK Treasury report recently drew attention to macro visible social factors like relative poverty which their findings suggested do play a large role in educational achievement:

> " .. there is a strong relationship between children's performance in maths and reading tests between the ages of six and eight and their parents' earnings, with the children of higher earning parents performing better." (Her Majesty's Treasury, March 99, p 29 drawing on data from the National Child Development Survey 1991).

This is further emphasised in the UK Government's commissioned evaluation of the National Numeracy and National Literacies Strategies, by Ontario Institute for Studies in Education/University of Toronto (OISE), which says:

> "outcomes of schooling are heavily influenced by non-school factors especially family background .. School outcomes have higher correlations with family variables than with any factor in the school" (Levin, 1999 p 4).

The Final OISE Report states even more strongly:

> "As is appropriate, the main focus through NLS and NNS has been on the school – what schools can do to improve pupil learning through improved teaching practice. To close the gap between high and low performing children, however, may require more attention to out-of-school influences on pupil attainment. If this is the case, government efforts to strengthen the connections between education and other policy areas that support families and communities will be crucial" (OISE Jan 2003, p. 8)

In similar vein, Feinstein (2003) drew upon the 1970 Cohort data to develop an index of development for 1292 UK children assessed at 22, 42, and 120 months. The

3

B. Street, D. Baker and A. Tomlin (eds.), Navigating Numeracies, 3-11.
© 2005 *Springer. Printed in the Netherlands.*

paper discusses the importance of these early scores as measures of human capital formation and argues that they can provide insights for growth or labour economists as well as those concerned with social equity. Position in the distribution of this index at 22 months (in 1972/3) is shown to predict final educational qualifications at age 26 (1996). The position at 22 months is shown to be related to family background. However, the children of wealthy parents who scored poorly in the early years, had a tendency to catch up and overtake the children of less well off parents who scored well in the early years. Whereas children of worse off parents who scored poorly were extremely unlikely to catch up and are clearly shown to be an at-risk group. As children mature and do more discriminating tests, the family background association strengthens.

Feinstein concludes from this that: "children are already stratified by social class in standard tests of intellectual and personal development at 22 months" (p 85/6). and

> "There is no evidence here that entry into schooling in any way overcame the polarisation [by social class] of children in the late 1970s. The most generous statement that may be made for schooling is that it may or may not have minimised the deepening effects of parental background" Feinstein (2003, p 85)

This is remarkably similar to the findings of Ginsberg et al (1997) across a number of countries; namely that children may start school in relatively different positions that relate directly to their socio-economic background, but that these differences, which may not always be great at early years, tend to widen as children progress through schooling. That is, whatever differences were found at the outset are 'perhaps amplified in some way by the process of schooling'. This paper links with previous work by Ginsberg and others in attempting to address the question of whether children from different national and ethnic backgrounds arrive at school more or less prepared for schooled numeracy. He addresses speculations regarding the relationship between such 'readiness' and children's home language. For example some languages, like Japanese, seem to make it easier to handle 'teen' numbers for instance, having the 'benefit of transparent base-ten structure'. He also looks at relationships between class (usually defined in US studies as based on Socio Economic Status (SES) and grossed out as poverty/ middle and upper income groups) and attainment. Studies had tended to show that US students were behind Asian ones in maths but that white USA children were ahead of African-Americans and USA Hispanics and the aim of the research reported in 1997 was to attempt to identify patterns across these groupings and to suggest some explanations for differences where they were significant.

Ginsberg's study focused on the concept of 'informal mathematical knowledge' which they conjectured:

> "can be a useful foundation for mathematics learning in school and that deficiencies in informal knowledge may interfere with schooling". (Ginsberg 1997, p 166)

Informal mathematical knowledge was to be identified through a series of assessments in 'everyday' contexts of children's 'basic concepts' regarding counting, addition and ordering.

Whilst there are contestations about the nature of such 'basic skills' there are some similarities between the concepts employed by Ginsberg and our own focus on out of school numeracy practices (see Chapter 2). There are also some methodological differences in that Ginsberg and his colleagues employed experimental methods whilst the research described in this volume was mostly ethnographic-style. Nevertheless, the overall concern for the role of out of school factors in school attainment is common and we draw attention to their work at this stage in order to locate our own approach within the larger framework of 'home effects' studies. The actual study by Ginsberg and his colleagues involved a 'Birthday Party' game in which puppets and toys were used to set four year olds from the various groups tasks concerning: a range of mathematical skills concepts. These included: Finger Displays of Number; Production from 10; Counting by Ones; Comparison of Number; Concrete Addition; Digit-Span Memory; Concrete Subtraction; Informal Subtraction; Informal Addition. These were seen, according to the authors, as the 'basic cognitive skills' in mathematics that school children would need in order to develop schooled maths. The tests were administered, in their home languages, to children from China, Colombia, Japan, Korea and the US. In the latter case, the children were divided between White, African-American and Hispanic groups. Class factors were not controlled for and some ethnic groups contained mixes of lower and upper SES.

The results were slightly surprising to the authors in that they appeared to indicate less significant variation at the beginning of schooling than had been attested by other studies. There was certainly a clear ranking of the pupils according to their 'success' on the tests, with China top, Colombia bottom and the US in the middle. However, some of the Chinese had been exposed to pre-school instruction in numeracy and when this group was excluded, the Chinese did no better that the US children. Likewise, although the Colombians ranked generally bottom on most tasks, the group actually included some upper class children whose performance was as good as those of the higher ranked countries. Class, then, did seem to be a factor, although statistical significance was not always apparent. Likewise, the range of attainment by children from different groups overlapped considerably, so that some children from the lowest ranking group might perform better than some from the highest ranking. The most striking features of the findings overall were that:

> "Informal mathematical abilities are widespread at the pre-school level. .. Children from various racial and ethnic groups and from various countries exhibit competence in informal mathematics." (Ginsberg 1997, p 201)

Despite the evident economic disadvantage of many of the African-Americans and the general assumption that East Asians performed better in maths,, 'In general despite confounding of race and class, the differences among the Whites, African-Americans and Korean (Americans) were not large' (Ginsberg et al 1997, p. 198). At this early stage of pre-school, most children appeared to 'possess basic counting and to understand the rudiments of addition', they were 'intellectually "ready" to learn basic arithmetic as it is usually taught in school' (Ginsberg et al 1997, p. 199).

Whilst differences between such groups have been identified as children grow older, they were not very great at the point when children began school:

"Whatever academic differences emerge later on they cannot be explained by USA deficiencies at the pre-school level. African-Americans, Korean-Americans and whites all seem to possess key informal mathematical skills. Thus at the age of 4 before entrance into elementary school, these groups of children possess basic counting and to understand the rudiments of addition, they were intellectually 'ready' to learn basic arithmetic as it is usually taught in school" (Ginsberg et. al., 1997, p 199)

2 EFFECT OF HOMES

The question this raises then is not simply the familiar one of why/ how home background disadvantages some groups, since it is evident than some children start school from relatively lower positions in terms of schooled numeracy, but rather why some groups fall behind once they are in school. For instance, 'initial differences between African-Americans and Whites are relatively small and increase in school,(p. 199). Ginsberg and colleagues (1997) cite here similar findings for early reading cf Raz and Bryant (1990) on Great Britain: 'socially disadvantaged children did not fall behind the middle class children in phonological awareness until they went to school'. A recent article by Gee (2001) on the results of literacy surveys in the US reinforces this point, citing the National Research Council Report: 'Children living in high poverty areas tend to fall further behind [by the Spring of Third Grade] regardless of their initial reading skill' (Gee, 2001, p. 12; Snow et. al., p.98). Likewise, Gee (2001) is concerned about the much-discussed 'fourth grade slump'. The NRCP Report notes: The "fourth grade slump" is a term used to describe a widely encountered disappointment when examining scores of fourth graders in comparison to younger children (Chall, et. al. 1990)' and comments 'It is not clear what the explanation is or even that there is a unitary explanation' (Snow et. al., p. 78).

We attempt here to summarise the implications of the findings of these various reports on both literacy and numeracy, in order to contextualise our own research. Our main focus is on the implications for research, but we do also draw attention to what researchers and others have had to say about the implications for policy and practice. We develop these points further in the concluding chapter after we have laid out our own findings.

The major finding of the 'home effects' literature is that, whilst differences between groups of young pre-school children in terms of initial performance on literacy and numeracy are not as different as some 'crises' accounts might suggest, that is as Ginsberg argues, initial levels of literacy and numeracy may be 'adequate' for initial schooling, nevertheless the different groups seem to pull apart as the children proceed through school. At its most benign, the picture is that such differences are 'amplified in some way by the process of schooling' (p. 199). This would appear to suggest that schooling – at least in its current form – may present a problem rather than a solution. This would also suggest, as Gee argues, that strategies for improving literacy and numeracy which involve more of the same are not likely to deal with such problems as the 'fourth grade slump' since they may have been a causal factor of the problem in the first place.

Explanations for this damaging effect of schooling are many. Ginsberg et al propose 'socialisation' as a factor and cite research that shows how different cultures may socialise children into different orientations – e.g. "person-oriented versus problem oriented" (Puerto Rican studies by Hertzig et al, 1968). Again cultural explanations might include the socialisation into display versus silence (a famous study by Philips (1972) of Native American socialisation reinforces this point). They also cite 'expectations', especially by teachers as a possible factor, something that Gee expands upon. Ginsberg et al started with an interest in language differences but seem to play down the advantages for mathematical work of the relative facility of Japanese and Chinese for quantitative work. Gee argues for a subtler notion of 'language abilities' that relates them more to Discourse patterns and styles, genres, social languages and cultural models amounting to 'forms of life' (pp. 21-3). Whilst avoiding suggesting that other groups are in any way in 'deficit', he shows how upper middle class professional families may inculcate in their children the same 'language abilities' as those required by schooling. For instance, 'the child's acquisition of the reader Discourse (being-doing a certain kind of reader) is simultaneously aligned with (traditional) school-based Discourses and part of his acquisition of his primary Discourse' (p. 22). The school replicates the Primary Discourse of middle class homes whilst it presents children from other backgrounds with a Secondary Discourse. In both cases, it is not just 'skills' and 'abilities' that are at play, it is issues of 'identity, class, race, gender, privilege, equity and access' that are called up even when apparently technical issues, such as reading levels (or we might add, mathematical procedures) are taught and tested.

Further explanations of a more sociological kind are also worth noting here, though Ginsberg et al tend to stop short of more elaborate conceptions of the 'social' and there are limits to how far we can apply their US-based data to the situation in the UK. Reay and Lucey (2000), for instance, reporting on UK research, take Gee's position a step further and argue that the middle class have not just conveniently lined up their home Discourses with those of school, but that this is a deliberate strategy. Whatever the school requires – and in the UK, this is changing in line with Government policy on 'choice' and marketisation – the middle class will do what is necessary to get their children advantage. What differentiates them from working class families may be this orientation, a disposition to take hold of the strategies and Discourses required, although it can be argued that it is easier to do so when these strategies are already closer to the children's home experience. Such Discourses, we suggest, may include numeracy as well as literacy which is more commonly taken to be the case. When Gewirtz (2001), for instance, suggests that middle class families may be characterised as 'active consumers', a disposition that comes into full play when faced with an education system that will only reward a few of its entrants, we take this to affect numeracy achievement as well as that in other areas of the curriculum. Children may, then, start relatively unequal in terms of formal skills when they enter schooling but the fact that some soon fall further behind may be more a product of middle class strategy and disposition than of working class inability or home 'deficits'. This would also explain why some working class children do well, a factor used by politicians to argue against the significance of class background: it may be that some working class homes do adopt these dispositions with the results that we have already seen for middle class families. Asian groups in the US may fall into the same category, whilst African-Americans remain resistant to the dominant Discourse and hence start to 'fall behind'. Feinstein's data for the UK suggests that certainly for poorer groups, the children are more likely to fall behind than to catch up: He says that as children mature and do more discriminating tests, the family background association strengthens, Feinstein (2003)

Gewirtz suggests that one policy response to such evidence by the Labour Government of the 1990s in the UK has been to attempt to inculcate all social groups into the Secondary Discourse of middle class schooling. Rather than adapting schooling to varied backgrounds, the aim of the Prime Minister of Great Britain and Northern Island, Tony Blair and his colleagues is to turn the working class into the active consumers they identify with the middle class and what Gewirtz terms 'the re-socialising of working parents' (2001). This is not unlike Ginsberg's analysis of the function of the US Head Start Programmes. Whereas the Programmes have been presented as helping children from 'deprived' homes to 'catch up' as they enter school, the data suggests that they are not particularly far behind at the outset anyway: 'For African-Americans, Head Start does not seem needed to compensate for initial cognitive deficits in informal mathematics. Its value must be found in other areas, like *socialization for schooling* (Ginsberg et. al., 1997, p. 199) (our italics).

3 ALTERNATIVE MODELS

What alternatives present themselves to either the deficit or the social engineering models for enhancing the schooled performance of children from 'non-traditional' backgrounds? At one extreme lies the *de-schooling* position which argues that, if school is the problem then abandon it and provide other means of supporting and enhancing people's learning. If the informal mathematics of four year olds is sufficient for their life practices, then why intervene: if it isn't, then at appropriate points in life when they meet situations that need enhancement of their mathematics, inputs and support can be provided. Whether it could be provided across the age range is a huge conceptual and logistical issue. The 'anthropological' response, following the insights offered by Gee (2001), Heath (1983), Moll et. al., (1992), Philips,(1972) and others regarding cultural models and 'forms of life', has been to propose a kind of Vygotskyan solution: to build upon the skills and knowledge that children bring from home and to loosen the school's own insistence on only one form of Discourse as appropriate. This is what Larson and her colleagues (2001) have argued, looking to 'scaffold' children to standard requirements whilst also incorporating some of their home skills into the formal sector. Likewise, Heath in an application of her ethnographic research principles to the classroom commissioned by the National Council for Teaching of English in the USA (NCTE) (Heath & Mangiola, 1991), tries to show how 'children of promise' can be helped with school literacies with reference to their home literacies.

What scope is there for comparison of the research outlined above with the research reported in this volume? Ginsberg et. al., for instance, suggest that attention to class differences could be expanded: 'It would be interesting to obtain comparable class data on poor White children in the US' (p. 198). We might add: 'and in the UK': to some extent the data cited above from Feinstein, Levin, Machin etc. does complement that of the USA. However, in the UK case the data were collected on the basis of cohort studies rather than using experimental methods, of the kind applied by Ginsberg et al. Likewise, the suggestion that 'socialization for schooling' may be a significant factor in schooled achievement may also be followed up through comparisons of home/ school relations in different class/ ethnic background schools. Some of Reay and Lucey's work does address these questions, although again using case studies rather than statistical sampling.

Another key factor in the literature cited above was the extent of children's 'readiness' at school entry. Ginsberg's finding that at this stage there was not much variation even between richer and poorer groups appears to conflict with the findings of Martin Hughes and colleagues that such differences may be as much as a year at school entry.

Hughes suggested that:

> "there was a substantial difference between the middle-class children and working-class children in their overall performance (that is their total number of correct answers for all tasks combined expressed as a percentage). This difference was equivalent to about a year's difference in age" (Hughes 1986 p 32).

Our own case studies tend to bridge these two positions. On the one hand, the major participants, such as teachers and agencies entering the area of Mountford, the working class school in which we conducted research, subscribed to the dominant expectations and indeed stereotypes about low achievement by such children at school entry. Their expectations also appear at first to be supported by the baseline data for the school that shows Mountford children performing much less well than other children in the region, even those in equally poor areas elsewhere (see Chapter 5a). However, when we look more closely at these school entry tests, we find that they already presume a level of schooled discourse. Like 'Birthday Party' assessments given by Ginsberg et. al, such tests may already be more geared to schooled numeracy than to the 'everyday' numeracy practices of different families. If this is the case, then we need to differentiate between Ginsberg's notion of 'informal' numeracy, tests of which suggest more children than previously assumed may begin school 'ready' for formal numeracy; and 'everyday' numeracy practices, evidence of which might suggest a larger gap and less 'readiness' for the schooled variety. Such a distinction might help explain the differences between different research reports on children's readiness for school, ranging from the Ginsberg view of relatively small differences, to those of Hughes (1986), Machin (1999) and Feinstein (2003) all of which, as we noted above, suggest differences from a very early age, as did the pre-school test results for Mountford in the present study (see Chapter 5a). It is, then, to 'everyday' numeracy practices that the present study is addressed: we are interested in the 'effects' of home background both as children enter school and after. The studies cited above can be reconciled from this perspective, since the variation in children's home experience may help explain both relative inequality in schooled skills when they begin school and the 'amplification' of such differences as they proceed through school. Comparisons between the three schools in our research do reinforce the notion that children at the school located in a richer environment continue to improve at a greater pace than those in the school located in the poorer area (see Section 3).

4 LEVERHULME PROGRAMME RESEARCH

The Leverhulme Programme as a whole, of which the present volume reports on one strand, did collect statistical data that speaks to some of the issues raised above. This has been described and analysed in volumes 1-3 of the present series. For instance, differences in attainment in school numeracy in sub-populations is given in Book 2 of the series. The findings there demonstrate that different sub-populations which could be regarded as having some sort of disadvantage generally have mean attainment scores which are lower than those of the dominant group. This includes children from different ethnic minorities, children not fluent in English, families who live in greater poverty and single parent families. However the extent of the differences is varied; for example some ethnic groups (e.g. 'Indians') have scores which are not significantly different from the white group.

The Leverhulme Programme researchers found that differences related to poverty are generally the largest, but in no case are they larger than the equivalent of 8 months' progress (roughly the difference between the start and end of a single school year). They found a high negative correlation with mean test score ($r= -0.63$), which is in line with other data in English schools. However there was a range of attainment within groups of schools with similar proportions of children with free school meals. When they examined the gains made over the year however there was little correlation between these gains and the proportion of free school meals ($r= -0.06$). This suggested, contrary to the studies by Ginsberg and colleagues (1997) and by Feinstein (2003), on which we reported above, that schools with children from poorer backgrounds make similar annual gains to other schools but have lower scores since they started further behind. The explanation for this disparity might lie in differences between the research methodology, the indicators used, the countries studied etc, and indicate a need for further comparative research along these lines. Of course some children qualifying for free school meals in our UK data still did very well (as indeed did a few children in the US samples); in the Leverhulme data there were 4 such children in the top 56 (top 5% of the whole group). However there five times as many (20) children qualifying for free school meals in the lowest scoring 56 (lowest 5%).

The results from the Leverhulme studies suggest a significant relationship between class, poverty and pupil attainment, although little relationship between social variables and pupil gains. These data are used to put into broader perspective the qualitative data based on in-depth case studies from which most of the accounts in this volume are drawn. The research in this book, whilst located in relation to these broader debates and issues, makes its own distinctive contribution based more on in depth case studies of specific schools, children and their areas than on statistical or sampled data. Before describing that research in more detail, we go on in Chapter 2, to outline the theoretical framework and concepts we drew upon in collecting the data and analysing the findings.

SECTION TWO: THEORY AND METHODOLOGY

In this section we set the theoretical and methodological frames for the research and for the book. The section consists of two chapters. The first is largely theoretical. In it we outline what we mean by a 'social practice' approach to numeracy and in particular the central concepts of numeracy events and practices. We consider the different approaches to the concept of the 'social' in numeracy research and offer an 'extended' view to counteract the sometimes narrow definitions evident in the field. Our conceptions of numeracy as social have built upon and extended work in the field of literacy as social practice and we provide here a brief account of some of that work and of conceptual development in that field. We then introduce our own concepts of numeracy events and practices that provided the building blocks for the research described in the rest of the book and indicate what we mean by an 'ideological model' of numeracy. We then summarise a number of other approaches to the sitedness of numeracy that we have built upon and offer a brief signalling of our distinction between site and domain that underpinned much of our data collection. The second chapter in this section is concerned with methodology. We describe here the sites we focused upon in our research and in particular the children and the schools that figure throughout the book. We justify the selections of subjects in terms of the theoretical and conceptual framework outlined in earlier chapters and explain for the reader the approaches we have used to explore relationships between home and school via case studies and critical incidents. In particular we draw upon the methodological debates in social science research to justify our emphasis upon case studies as the critical focus for data collection and analysis. We describe for the reader our working practices as a research team, indicating the dialectical process between building initial concepts and models and then, through report back and discussion of field data, how we came to modify these and to develop new categories. One such set of classifications that arose from this interaction with the data was the distinction between sites and domains and we offer here both a model and some illustrative data as a basis for the fuller accounts to which the reader will be exposed in Sections 3 and 4.

13

CHAPTER TWO: THEORETICAL POSITIONS

A 'social' approach to numeracy: Numeracy events and practices

1 NUMERACY AS 'SOCIAL' PRACTICE

This chapter indicates some of the theoretical and conceptual issues raised by the 'school and community numeracies' team's attempt to conduct 'ethnographic-style' research (Green and Bloome, 1997) in the area of numeracy at home and at school and in particular to conceptualise numeracy as a 'social practice' and with reference to literacy theory (Baker, 1996 and 1998; Street, 1984; 1995; Baker and Street; 1996, Brown et al 1998)). We begin by laying out our own assumptions regarding this field of inquiry. We take numeracy to be a powerful set of symbolic tools, concepts and representations, which can be used to serve a number of purposes. We also work with the assumption that numeration systems are as much subject to interpretative approaches concerning ideology, institutions, social relations and values as are other systems of meaning and communication that have been the subject of interpretative social science more generally. It is no more given that the study of numeracy demands a positivist epistemology or that its tools and concepts are 'universal' and 'value free', than it is for the study of literacy, from which we derive a number of our key concepts. This, then, is what is meant when we say that that in our research we viewed mathematics as social.

2 EXTENDED SOCIAL

We have found during this project that many parties and interests refer to the notion of a 'social' perspective on numeracy. These uses of the term cover many different conceptions of both numeracy and of 'social practice', not all of which we associate with the perspective being offered here. We describe some of these uses and attempt to explain how our own view differs.

Firstly by 'social', we do not mean just the social theories of learning in the sense often meant by 'sociocultural' theorists following Vygotsky and other social psychologists, a position that tends to dominate much current thinking in mathematics education theory.

Secondly we do not mean by 'social' the immediate interactions to be observed, for instance, amongst children in classrooms or conversations between learners of mathematics when doing mathematics (Baker, 1999). In research into ways of

B. Street, D. Baker and A. Tomlin (eds.), Navigating Numeracies, 15-24.

viewing mathematics as social, Baker, 1999, found that the dominant understanding of the social amongst mathematicians was very narrow. It was limited to either interactions with others when talking about mathematics or to a functional or useful role for mathematics in solving problems and denied the value laden nature of mathematics.

A third view of 'social' that we have encountered in education in our research, is what we term the 'social' as 'pedagogic', that is a view of the contribution that people's social or everyday uses of numeracy can make to children's grasp of schooled numeracy (see Chapter 5b; Chapter 8). This view is held by many teachers and is captured in the advice of the Basic Skills Agency regarding parents' talk around numeracy with their children:

> By **talking** (original emphasis) about the maths you are using as you go about your day to day routine you can help your child understand what maths is used for ... Maths is all around us not just in 'maths books'. Young children will only be able to 'do sums', later, if they know what numbers mean and what they are used for. *(BSA, accessed 10.9.2002)*

Many teachers in our research replicate this view, such as this comment by Marilyn, a teacher at Tarnside school (see Chapter 5b):

> I would imagine that on a very basic level the children who perform well in school are the ones who get any kind of extra maths practice, as it were, at home, so ..... silly things like sorting or walking along the street and noticing colours and shapes and just general conversation really, at a young age. Not those who sit down quite so formally as Rick and write numbers from one to five million. But just everyday stuff that they can then bring into school and relate to what they are doing ((AT Interview Marilyn 2nd Aug 99)

Another teacher at the same school, Thelma talks of:

> "just everyday situations, maths is everywhere isn't it? It's not a separate entity on it's own, it's just.... you know, there is so much at home they can talk about to do with number and I think it really shows the ones that do, compared to the ones that [don't]." (AT Interview Thelma 27 July 01)

This view of how parents talking with their children at home might enhance their maths 'practice' in school is what many maths educators mean by a 'social' approach to maths. When we have given talks on 'maths as social' it is often interpreted by audiences in terms of this 'pedagogic' view of the social.

Whilst the view we take in this book does include the pedagogic concern expressed here for the 'everyday' character of numeracy practices in ordinary situations, we hope that the account offered in this book will complexify the pedagogic point expressed as well as extend meanings of the social in numeracy. As we demonstrate in the case study chapters, such as Chapter 5b where we describe a number of teachers' beliefs of this kind, the relationship of everyday to schooled maths is more complex than the Basic Skills Agency point implies. For instance, the numeracy practices of home differ from those of school in significant ways; they are embedded in different relations and purposes; school uses of them tend to 'recontextualise' (Bernstein, 1996) home uses into those of school; and there is often a gap between the rhetoric of taking account of everyday numeracy and the reality of classroom practice, with its curriculum and assessment focus. So we would not wish the account of maths as social on which this book is based to be read off simply in terms of this 'pedagogic social', any more than the 'sociocultural' or the 'interactional' social cited above.

As an alternative to these views of the social in mathematics we propose a different, extended view, which sees the social in terms of context, values and beliefs, social, and institutional relations (Baker, 1999: p50), what we refer to as an 'ideological' model of numeracy (cf Baker and Street, 1996). From this perspective, social relations refer to positions, roles and identities of individuals in relation to others in terms of numeracy. Social institutions and procedures we see as constitutive of control, legitimacy, status and the privileging of some practices over others in mathematics, as evidenced through accepted and dominant paradigms and procedures in the ways that mathematics is carried out and conceptualised. Taken together, these concepts provide an alternative way of viewing mathematical practices, an alternative model. In our research we wanted to identify and make use of such a model because it may reveal complexities that are at present hidden, especially regarding context and power relations. This further enables us to acknowledge and make explicit the plurality of mathematics practices.

The wider view of 'social' theory in mathematics on which the ideological model is built has drawn upon research in ethnomathematics (e.g. (D'Ambrosio, 1997), philosophy of mathematics (e.g. Ernest, 1998), sociology of mathematics (e.g. Restivo, 1993) and critical perspectives on mathematics education (e.g. Dowling, 1998; Powell, 1997; Skovsmose, 1994). Stephen Lerman, discussing 'the social turn in mathematics education research', offers a survey of the turn from psychological to sociological perspectives on maths education, and suggests that socio-cultural theories offer a language of description for the positioning of subjects in discourses (Lerman, 2000). Whilst not discounting these perspectives, we would like to draw upon a broader tradition of social theory, of the kind already applied by some researchers to adults' mathematics practices (Baker, 1998; Coben, 2000; Civil, 2000; Evans, 2000). Such a tradition provides a broad social perspective on mathematics itself. That is to say that mathematics, as with all forms of knowledge is itself socially constructed.

This does not entail simply privileging 'everyday' mathematics or 'ethnic' mathematics or treating everything as 'social', which can be rather vacuous. Rather, it provides a vehicle for an exploratory inquiry into considering mathematics as a social practice. Such an approach allows for the identification, analysis, and comparison between numeracy practices sited in different social settings and especially those in homes and schools, an issue we develop further below and that provides the basis for substantive chapters in Section 3. For example, the concept of the broad social allows a researcher to focus on the values and beliefs that feature in choices made and on the significance of contexts in which numeracy is sited. Home and school contexts are very different and, we argue, we need to understand the extent to which the numeracy practices sited within them are different.

The narrow view of the social, based as it is on an 'autonomous' model of numeracy as described by Baker and Street (1996), (one that sees mathematics as abstract, decontextualised and value free) together with conventional pedagogy and curriculum, leads to blaming failure or low achievement in numeracy on the teacher, the child or the home and seeing them as in some sense in deficit; the teacher in terms of her subject knowledge or her use of ineffective teaching practices; the child in his lack of skills, knowledge and understandings; and the home as lacking the schooled numeracy knowledge or commitment to support the children (Freebody, Ludwig and Gunn, 1995). Our extended social model, in making the epistemological and ideological explicit (Baker and Street 1996), provides other ways of viewing and understanding low achievement and could lead to policies that go beyond access and empowerment towards transformations of curriculum and pedagogy. Instead of viewing low achievement in terms of deficit the model accepts social notions of difference and multiple practices; it seeks to represent and build upon informal numeracy practices and 'funds of knowledge' (Moll, 1992). We describe below how we link these concerns for a broad view of the social in numeracy with a conceptual apparatus adapted in part from literacy theory and that employs the terms numeracy events and practices that enable us to focus on numeracy practices in and out of school.

3 LITERACY EVENTS AND LITERACY PRACTICES

Our contribution to this 'social turn' in numeracy, then, lies in the adoption of the concepts of *numeracy events* and *numeracy practices* as analogous to *literacy events* and *literacy practices* (Street, 2000; Baker, 1996 and 1998; Baker and Street, 1996) as central concepts in our research project. A great deal of work in the field of 'social literacies' has addressed many of the issues outlined above, for instance regarding explanation for achievement/ underachievement in schooling (Barton & Hamilton, 1999; Barton Hamilton & Ivanic, 2000; Heath,S.B. 1983; Street, 1984; 1996). From this perspective, the underachievement of children from less affluent homes, for instance, may have to do with the boundaries and barriers such children face between formal and informal literacy practices, between what Street and Street (1991) and Cook-Gumperz, (1986) term 'schooled literacy practices' and out-of-school literacy practices (cf Hull & Schultz, 2002). One dimension of the research, complementary to the themes indicated in Section 4 (engagement; coding and switching between home and school; cultural resources) is to consider how far this social literacies work can be applied to the field of numeracy education and what remains distinctive to numeracy. We will explain the origins of the terms *literacy events* and *literacy practices* in literacy theory and then consider what is involved in applying them to the field of numeracy as *numeracy events* and *numeracy practices* (Baker, 1996 and 1998; Baker and Street 1996).

Shirley Brice Heath, a literacy researcher in the USA, characterised a 'literacy event' as 'any occasion in which a piece of writing is integral to the nature of the participants' interactions and their interpretative processes' (Heath, 1982, p. 93). Street argues that

> "*Literacy events* is a helpful concept, I think, because it enables researchers, and also practitioners, to focus on a particular situation where things are happening and you can see them happening. This is the classic literacy event in which we are able to observe an event that involves reading and/or writing and can begin to draw out its characteristics: here, we might observe one kind of event, an academic literacy event, and there,

another, which is quite different, such as checking timetables and catching the bus, browsing through a magazine, sitting in the barber's shop, reading signs when negotiating the road" (Street, 2000, p. 21)

However, literacy researchers have identified limitations with the concept of literacy events. As Street argues:

> But there is also a problem if we use the concept on its own that it remains descriptive and … it does not tell us how the meanings are constructed. If you were to observe a particular literacy event as a non-participant who was not familiar with its conventions you would have difficulty following what is going on, such as how to work with the text which provides the focus of the event and how to talk around it . There are clearly underlying conventions and assumptions around literacy events that make them work. (Street, 2000, p. 21)

This then brought literacy researchers to the concept of *literacy practices*. Street has employed the phrase (Street, 1984, p. 1; 1988; 2000, p. 21) as a means of focussing upon 'social practices and conceptions of reading and writing', focusing upon the social models of literacy that participants bring to bear upon those events and that give meaning to them. The concept of literacy practices attempts not only to handle the events and the patterns of activity around literacy but to *link* them to something broader of a cultural and social kind.   Part of that broadening and extending involves attending to the fact that in a literacy event we have brought to it concepts, social models regarding what the nature of this practice is and that make it work and give it meaning. Those models we cannot get at simply by sitting on the wall with a camera and watching what is happening: you can photograph literacy events but you cannot photograph literacy practices. There is an ethnographic issue here: researchers using ethnographic methods have to start talking to people, listening to them and linking their immediate experience out to other things that they do as well. That is why it is often meaningless to just ask people about literacy (or numeracy) alone, as in recent surveys (BSA, 1997; OECD, 1995) or even about reading and writing. This is because what might give *meaning* to literacy events may actually be something that is not, in the first instance, thought of in terms of literacy at all. For instance, in the case of academic practices, it may be about social relations and the academy.   Heath and McLaughlin (1993) found in discussing newspaper reading with urban adolescents in the USA that much of their activity did not count in their minds as literacy at all, so a superficial survey would have missed the significance of their actual literacy practices - their scanning of newspaper articles for references to their social group - and perhaps labelled them non-readers, or more insultingly 'illiterate' as in much press coverage of this area. So one cannot predict beforehand what will give meaning to a literacy event and what will link a set of literacy events to literacy practices. Literacy practices, then, refer to this broader cultural conception of particular ways of thinking about and doing reading and writing in cultural contexts.   One of the key issues, at both a methodological and an empirical level, is how can we characterise the shift from observing literacy events to conceptualising literacy practices.

Consideration of the relation between *literacy events* and *literacy practices* provides a useful basis from which to engage in field research on literacy as a social practice. Building on this ethnographic tradition, recent work in the UK by Hannon

(2000), and Weinberger (1995) has noted the complex overlaps and interrelations between parents' and teachers' perceptions of children's literacy in the early years. Their work, provides a helpful counter to the dominant 'deficit' model of family literacy practices (Bentley et. al.1995, for instance, counter pose this with a 'wealth' model; cf also Blackledge, 2000; Hannon and James, 1990; Pahl, 2002a and b; Tett 2000). These authors provide a basis for positive approaches to family literacy policy that builds on home strengths rather than simply attempting to overcome 'problems' in the home.

4 NUMERACY EVENTS AND PRACTICES: TOWARDS AN IDEOLOGICAL MODEL

A key question for the present research, then, is how useful it might be to develop such concepts and insights from the literacy field in studying numeracy at home and at school. By focusing on *numeracy events* as units of inquiry in both home and school, we are able to observe those 'occasions in which a numeracy activity is integral to the nature of the participants' interactions and their interpretative processes' (Baker, 1998). We have used the word numeracy to reflect the links with literacy but for the purposes of this study, as we have outlined earlier, we see numeracy and mathematics as synonymous (cf a discussion of meanings of numeracy in the introduction to this Series by Margaret Brown). We employ the notion of numeracy events as units of inquiry in both home and school, as we seek to observe, describe and analyse the ways in which numeracy has meaning for participants both in their everyday lives and within the specific institutional context of school. In describing our field work in both homes and schools, we firstly focus on numeracy events – the finger counting episode described in Chapter 6; a teacher 'switching' between one mode of representation and another – from visual to written to symbolic to oral – within a single portion of a numeracy class (Chapter 5a; a theme we explore further in Section 3 where we address the issue of 'switching' between modes, varieties and contexts); the relative 'engagement' of one of our target children, Kim in a set of tasks in class (Chapter 4b); Seth's parents' debate about the ways of managing and borrowing money and the interest rates charged (Chapter 4a). Such a focus on numeracy events provides the empirical building blocks for our accounts, especially the detailed case studies described in Section 3 and the thematic accounts in Section 4 as we move from events to practices and consider the wider social contexts and meanings in which the events are embedded.

In parallel to the shift in literacy theory to the notion of literacy practices, we have coined the term *numeracy practices* as more than the behaviours that occur when people do mathematics/numeracy - more than the events in which numerical activity is involved – instead focusing on the conceptualisations, the discourse, the values and beliefs and the social relations that surround numeracy events as well as the context in which they are located. Such a concept of numeracy practices is sited in the extended notion of the social in mathematics outlined above and is a central starting point for our research (Baker and Street, 1996) and provides a frame for the units of analysis in this research. It attempts to provide a nuanced language of description and a lens through which to view practices in different contexts. It allows us to deconstruct and classify numeracy practices and to seek qualities and characteristics of differently sited practices and then seek similarities, differences and relationships between them.

Numeracy practices then are broad notions about the ways numeracy is dealt with in different contexts and settings. As an illustration of the application of the concept in our research, we note here the differences between school and home numeracy practices. School numeracy practices, for instance, can be characterised as having educational purposes with a teacher in control of both social relations and of knowledge; for example, the consolidation and exercise of a particular skill such as 'change from 10 p' (c.f. Chapter 5a). Home numeracy practices, on other hand, can be characterised as domestic in purpose, where a child has a level of involvement or control over both social relations and knowledge. An event involving purchasing objects when shopping could be seen to be an instance of a home numeracy practice. What is seen as important at school could be different to what is valued at home. At school knowing and recalling the change from 10 p for several differently priced objects is an important skill. The teacher knows the answer and sets the questions. They are not inherently part of managing money but rather of managing classroom relations and laying the foundations for specific formal mathematical knowledge. The process of teaching money or number in school, then, is implicated in certain values, contexts, social relations and institutional relations which we see as schooled numeracy practices. However if a child went shopping to purchase an object, the exchange of money may involve change which would be part of a domestic management practice and not an educationally determined and set skill. This would be part of home numeracy practices with its own calculating procedures and processes and values, contexts and social relations.

Given the centrality of the concept of numeracy practices in our research, a key task has been to operationalise the concept by analysing it into dimensions or components. These dimensions are not seen as distinct separate aspects. They are always in interplay with each other. But an analysis of data based on such dimensions could help to provide a way of comparing and contrasting home and school numeracy practices and understandings of relationships between the different numeracy practices of/in homes and schools. At one level the classification of numeracy practices we have observed can provide a larger perspective on contrastive features of these practices. Whilst at another level we can seek finer grained contrastive features.

We provide below an outline of our attempt to operationalise this concept which draws on an earlier article (Baker, 1996) where it was proposed that numeracy practices could be seen as having four dimensions - *content, context, values and beliefs and social and institutional relations (*see tables in Chapter 8 for elaboration of these in relation to home and school sites) and in the sense indicated above that all are permeated by power.

• *Content.* We see this as including the activities, techniques, procedures and processes of numeracy that individuals engage in. This could be described as the mathematics dimension of numeracy practices and can be seen when separated from the other components to be the dominant, autonomous (abstract, decontextualised, value-free, culture free) view of numeracy, (Baker and Street, 1996; Street, forthcoming).

• *Context*. This refers to the framing of those occasions when numeracy is done and the purposes for that use of mathematics. These purposes and contexts depend on the individuals engaged in their numeracy practices. An appropriate context and purpose for one person may not be so for another. An example of this could be the use of money in schools to teach subtraction as against the getting of change in a shop.

• *Values and beliefs*. This component is concerned with the ways individuals' beliefs, values and epistemologies affect the numeracy practices they adopt. They will make decisions on the numeracy skills and concepts they engage in depending on their beliefs and concepts about the nature of numeracy and on the values that drive their practices. The former may be performance driven (getting the task done) as against domestically driven. These are developed further in a report on research with children in a British primary school, (Baker 1996). These 'cultural' and epistemological dimensions of numeracy practices can be considered as ideological to the extent that they are concerned with social and power relations between people and ideas involved in the practice - what they see as acceptable and legitimate mathematics. The notion of 'best ways' of doing mathematics could be an example here. Arithmetic calculation of change, in school, for example, is often seen as more powerful than counting in ones to work out change. What 'counts' is very often naturalised, its conditions and claims taken for granted: this, we take as the essential feature of the ideological nature of numeracy practices.

• *Social and institutional relations*. These involve the kinds of control over content, management of context and invoking of values and ideology exercised by different institutions and roles. This is revealed in the kinds of discipline exercised, over discourse, language, turn taking associated with different roles: in schools for instance by teachers over pupils (and sometimes over parents) and at home the relations of parent, child, relative, friend etc. At a broader level, the institutions of schooling and of Education (Department of Education; Office for Standards in Education; etc) exert considerable pressure upon individuals as they enact curriculum and pedagogy.

We term this approach an ideological model of numeracy, drawing upon the notion of an ideological model of literacy (Street, 1984) in the sense that content, context, ideas and values and social and institutional relations are all infused by relations of power. A claim explored in this book is how far such an approach to literacy is applicable in the field of numeracy. Viewing all of these components as ideological can, we argue, draw attention to the contestations over mathematical meaning and legitimacy, procedures and processes, relations and interactions rather than assuming all of these to be simply neutral, incontestable and technical issues.

Such an understanding of the components of numeracy practices provides us with ways of seeking relationships between the numeracy practices we observe in homes and schools, which are a major concern of our research. An example of such practices, already mentioned, could be the ways money is taught in schools as contrasted with the ways it is used in homes (further details are provide in Section

3). Others could be the ways games are used educationally at school and ways that they are played at home, (cf. Gold and Mordecai-Phillips 2003, Baker et al, 2000).

Now we want to look more closely at the use of our notion of numeracy practices in the sites we were working in, the home and the school. We do this, firstly by classifying numeracy practices to provide a larger perspective and we will then look at the effect of analysing the numeracy practices we have observed into components to get a finer grained view.

5 CLASSIFICATION OF OTHER NUMERACY PRACTICES

There is evidence from other research of classifications of the uses and sitedness of mathematics. The variety of examples that we have selected and briefly mention below reflect the richness and value of this approach to understanding what we have called numeracy practices. We acknowledge that the authors of these studies have not made explicit use of the term numeracy practices, nevertheless their conceptual frames have a close approximation to our uses of numeracy practices.

Nunes et al (1993) and Carraher et al (1998) have studied ways that 'street' children in Brazil use 'informal' ways of calculating costs and change that are very efficient and effective in buying and selling transactions. These children operate in an environment where the calculations are essential to their lives. They operate in both old and new currencies and move seemingly effortlessly between the systems, seldom making mistakes and getting 98% of calculations correct, (Nunes, 1993, p 21). This contrasts with the formal practices of the mathematics classroom where the same children struggle to use formal schooled algorithms and procedures, getting about 37% of calculations correct.

Masingila, et al (1996) also contrast mathematics learning and mathematics practice in and out of school. In their view school practices tend to focus on mathematical problems, using algorithms for calculations (for example ratios, proportions, decimals, fractions) to arrive at a mathematical solution irrespective of the practical, real-world requirements. In some cases the schooled practices have thrown up highly unlikely and even unbelievable situations, such as fractions of eggs appearing in recipe calculations. Burkhardt (1981) labels such problem solving as dubious whatever its educational purpose. Masingila sees school practice as focusing on 'maths as object' putting most stress on what we have called the content dimension of numeracy practices. She sees out-of-school numeracy as focusing on 'maths as tool' with more stress on context. In school, learning focuses on individual learners and is often transmission oriented (the teacher aiming to transfer her knowledge to the children) with the values (such as uncontested answers) and social relations (such as authority and status) of that process inherent in it; out-of-school learning is more often collaborative, apprenticeship oriented and familiar and congruent with cultural values and social relations, (these differences in practices are developed further in Chapter 8).

Hoyles et al (2001) note the contrast between the complex numeracy practices that are used by nurses who have calculations to make about the administering of medical drugs, where failure can be life threatening, and their denial that they have these skills. In this situation the context of numeracy is foregrounded. In another study referring to the work of bank tellers, Noss (1997) notes the invisible or hidden nature of the mathematics they use. He suggests that people are often unaware of where mathematics impinges on their lives as it can be hidden in the technology they are using. This is parallel to work done by Gerdes (1986) in Africa. He gave the term 'frozen mathematics' to activities such as basket weaving or home murals where current practitioners were not explicitly aware of the mathematics that the original designers of the objects had used. The mathematics had in a sense been frozen into the practices by these earlier originators of the processes involved. In both of these cases, the values and contexts are central to the practices but are not extracted or made visible, they have been 'naturalised'.

Other authors who have taken similar positions include Saxe (1988), Scribner (1984), Lave (1992), Rogoff and Lave (1984) and Rogoff (2003). All of these studies have provided ways of understanding the different mathematics practices of the groups studied. The classifications and terminology offered have provided useful analytical and conceptual tools. Some of these were based on the site of the particular study and were then relatively easy to classify. In contrast this has proved more problematic for our research. We focussed on the practices of homes and schools and there were times when these practices overlapped. These home and school practices and their overlaps are harder to describe and classify. In the next Chapter, we attempt to distinguish between the sitedness of a practice and the domain of the practice and show how the resulting matrix provided a heuristic for ordering the numeracy events and practices that form the basis of our research data.

CHAPTER THREE: METHODOLOGY

Exploring the relationships between home and school: domains and sites,
case studies and critical incidents

1. INTRODUCTION

In Chapter 2 we laid out the theoretical and conceptual framework for the research on which this book is based. Drawing upon theory in literacy studies, we developed the concepts of numeracy events and numeracy practices, that informed both the data collection and the accounts we give here of our subjects' uses and meanings of numeracy. In applying these concepts to home and school numeracy we were drawn to developing further classifications and we developed a matrix for analysing home and school sites and domains. In this chapter we outline and justify our working methods and demonstrate how we operationalised our initial concepts and emerging classifications for research purposes. We then discuss how we moved to offering rich descriptions of the various categories identified there, through use of case studies and critical incidents. These case studies provide the main substance of Section 3 in which we provide rich detail of both the individual children and of the schools we researched, as a basis for then drawing out more analytic themes in Section 4.

2 THE CHILDREN

The researchers conducted longitudinal case studies in one class in each of three schools (see below and Introduction to the book), from Reception (1999/2000) through to Year 2 (2001/2002), focusing on about four children in each, and following them through to their homes where both observations and informal interviews were conducted. The children were chosen in consultation with the class teachers in terms of their views of the carers' willingness to participate and in the light of our concern to provide a range of rich description of children's experiences. The teachers tended to recommend this range according to levels of attainment in their class, according to such standard measures as base line assessments. as well as their own judgements as teacher. We took into account other factors, such as gender, family background and the desire to achieve some range across all of the children studied, a factor that sometimes militated against choosing a particular child who might fit well in terms of their particular classroom but might not this general

B. Street, D. Baker and A. Tomlin (eds.), Navigating Numeracies, 25-33.

requirement. In each class we began with about four children but recognised that some of these would drop out by the end of our study, whether through leaving the school (high turnover is one of the factors we discuss for Tarnside) or through parental choice (Brian moved across a number of different children at Mountford as parents indicated their unwillingness to continue in the research programme). The children chosen for the case studies in Section 3 are taken from the pool of over twelve focus children during the three years of the project. The researchers visited each child in their home across the three years of the project, in each case making 25+ visits during which we talked with the child's carers, including grandparents and other home visitors, observed parent-child interactions, especially around numeracy and interacted ourselves with the child, especially though not exclusively around school tasks brought home. Whilst these visits do not have the depth and consistency of a full 'ethnography', they represent a fuller and richer account of children's home experiences than schools usually have access to and conforms to what Green and Bloome (1997) describe as 'ethnographic-style' research.

3 THE SCHOOLS

Similarly, we chose the three schools as contrastive, 'telling' cases (Mitchell, 1984) to cover, where possible, a range of schooling and the main dimensions of suspected heterogeneity in the population e.g. class, ethnicity, urban/ suburban. We noted above that, at one level, our 'story' is simply that the children's experiences in the Case Study schools are complex and uneven and may contrast with other schools. Our aim, then, is to provide 'fine-tuned' description and analysis of such uneven and complex interactions around numeracy, in particular paying attention to the children's cultural meanings, some of which they may have brought with them from home. The schools and environments were selected according to social features that have been seen, as in the research literature we cite in Chapter 1, to affect performance, including variables such as location, ethnicity and relative affluence.

Mountford Primary is a school serving a large mainly working class white housing estate where factors such as unemployment and single parenthood have been significant. This school already had substantial existing home-school links, with home visits being made by teachers prior to a child's entry into Reception and it was felt that this would make home visits by the Focus 4 team easier to arrange. During our visits, a report on the school indicated that 51.8% of the children at the school had free school meals (Panda 2002) which is nearly 3 times the national average of 18.3%. The percentage of children identified as having special educational needs including formal statements was 68.9% which was well above the national average of 23.7%. An Ofsted report on the school in 2000 (Panda 2000) and Panda Reports (2001 and 2002) showed that the children at the school had achieved very low and well below average at Key Stage 1 and 2 compared with national averages for literacy and numeracy. The school has consistently been placed as one of the lowest two schools in the league tables for the Local Education Authority, (Panda 2000).

Rowan Primary, on the other hand, a leafy suburb white middle class school, was ranked in the top schools in its locality in all subjects and in mathematics the school's performance in the national tests at Key stage 1 (KS1), even when compared to other schools with 'similar social context', placed it high in school league tables. The percentage achieving level 3 or above put the school's results in the top 5% in the country (2000 Panda). 2.6% percentage of children were identified as having special educational needs including formal statements and 2% of the children at the school had free school meals. Rowan's children came, in the main, from comparatively privileged backgrounds and we could expect them to succeed at school.

Rowan, then, was selected as an example of a school serving a relatively middle class population, though with some mix of ethnicity and class. Tarnside was a more classically inner city school serving a very mixed ethnic population, mostly African-Caribbean and Asian and generally lower class. The school was ranked 50th of 57 schools in all subjects in its locality and 44th in maths; 42.8%of the children at the school had free school meals and 27.9% were described as having special educational needs including formal statements.

The three schools selected, then, represent case studies of a range of the social features cited in discussions of children's attainment levels in maths, across class, ethnicity and home-school links. This is in keeping with the Project aims of exploring the significance of home numeracy practices and of different home/ school relations for numeracy attainment. The research involved observation of the school and of selected classrooms and of informal situations in and out of school; interviews with teachers and with pupils; analysis of texts, including 'home text books', official curriculum documents, school policy documents, schemes of work, homework, teacher feedback etc. As in Chapter 4a,b and c on the case study children, we aim to avoid reifying the differences between home and school but rather to indicate the crossing of these boundaries and to highlight what children bring with them from one context to the other. The issues we raise in Chapter 5 on schools include: The local area and the school population; Organisation of numeracy lessons; The 'feel' of the school; home school relations; contradictory views of the school; classroom and home numeracy practices; disjunctions between teachers' and parents' perceptions and practices.

4 CASE STUDIES

Drawing upon these data regarding children and schools in relation to numeracy, and before addressing the thematic issues that arose from the research, we provide readers in Section 3 with detailed and nuanced accounts of some case studies. These involve: children as cases, following their progression over the three years of the project; schools as cases and in particular the contrasts between the three kinds of school we researched; and also 'home/school relations' as cases, focusing on particular examples of the relationships for children between their home experiences and those in school. Our notion of 'case studies' builds on Mitchell's (1984) distinction between 'enumerative induction', where the analyst attempts to generalise to a wider population from a particular 'case' and 'analytic induction' that, as in this situation, attempts to make analytic and theoretical insights from a 'telling' rather than a 'typical' case. We ask what might the examples we document be 'telling cases' of, providing sufficient empirical data on children, schools and homes to be able, then, to offer the thematic and analytic accounts in Chapters 6, 7 and 8.

5 WAYS OF WORKING

In order to maintain a common structure across the team of three researchers, (Alison Tomlin, Dave Baker and Brian Street), and over time, a number of 'framing' documents were produced. These are derived from the conceptual and theoretical issues outlined above and were continually subject to modification in the light of findings. In summary, the concepts we sought to apply and clarify in this study, therefore, were: understandings of numeracy as social; home/community/school relationships; the concepts of numeracy events and practices; the distinction between out-of-school and schooled numeracies; the notion of sites and domains and the classification of events and practices associated with each; and the notion of 'switching' between domains. These preliminary conceptual frames and hypotheses generated schedules for research observation (see Appendix A), questions and interviews that we pursued in the course of the project and which we describe in greater detail below.

Working from the most general Framework (Appendix A) - designating the features of 'numeracy practices' identified amongst different participants - we then developed interview schedules for teachers and parents, a home visit check list and a school visit check list (Appendix B, C). There is a movement to and fro between general frameworks, particular checklists and specific 'codings' of the data produced. At regular team meetings we read and commented upon field reports and reviewed the check lists and frameworks. For instance, it was agreed to take one researcher's account of a home visit and for each member of the team to attempt their own 'coding'. Whilst differences emerged in terms of style - between, for instance more general 'thematic coding' and more fine-tuned detailed coding - there was general agreement on the overall themes and questions, derived of course from the initial 'Framework'.

However, it also became apparent that some of the questions we shared remained implicit in the Framework and needed to spelled out more explicitly. The Framework had a series of headings for home visits to determine the carers/ parents' conceptions (implicit or explicit) of 'numeracy practices' and these needed to be elaborated. For example, the first heading concerned: *Understanding of maths re own uses and history*: the particular data set we were reviewing in fact had no evidence under this heading and we were reminded to put questions about this topic at a subsequent visit. Another heading, *Interpretations of/demands from current school practices* generated considerable data and we were able to group the field notes under this heading and then consider how particular statements and observations fitted. Likewise, the heading *Working with children re school requirements eg homework* provided a set of findings which were not only potentially important in terms of that child's experience, but led us to reconsider data from other children to help us refine and develop our analysis. *'Salience' and 'visibility' of different maths practices eg hidden/overt* remained an important conceptual heading, allowing the researcher to introduce interpretation at the time of data collection. Parents sometimes responded to questions about numeracy at home by denying that what we had observed eg use of calendars, video organisers, computers, 'counts' as numeracy: that is, the ordinary everyday practices in which we might identify mathematical principles were often not 'salient' for them and so their everyday numeracy practices were underplayed in contrast with the 'visibility' of schooled numeracy. This supports Coben's (1997) finding that people tend to label as maths those mathematical practices that they *cannot* do or find difficult. Collecting data under this heading contributed towards description of this phenomenon and also helped us question and analyse its relation to other features of home numeracy practices eg those located under other headings.

Whilst all of these headings, then, proved useful in these various ways, and provided 'baskets' into which subsequent data from home visits could be at least provisionally located, we also noted that a significant dimension of our questioning and evidence had not been sufficiently signalled - namely *Home/school relations as context for perceptions of numeracy practices*. This idea, of course, underpins the whole project but had remained implicit in the Framework. Much of the data indeed assumed these relations but we had not spelled them out in our check list. As we attempted to do so, in the light of the data, we generated new sub headings that reinforced the importance of earlier analytic terms eg *complement/ compensate; definite/ less definite views of school; conceptions of parenting, discipline, 'work'; 'prospects'* ,and *comparison with other parents*. All of these factors could be seen to affect the carer/ parents' model of numeracy and to therefore be significant in our consideration of how numeracy practices were conceptualised at home and how this differed from schooled models. The table was therefore revised and a second version developed as the basis for further phases of the research (See Appendix A). We were not inclined to make such changes too frequently as this would undermine the principle of consistency across visits and researchers, but with team agreement we recognised the importance of occasionally allowing the findings to wash back onto the conceptual frameworks in this way. Indeed, we saw a major aspect of the project as being the tracking of this process of iteration between concepts and data and we hope thereby to contribute to research methodology more generally, as well as offering some substantive data on home/ school numeracies.

Using these frameworks and checklists, the team came to some agreement about conventions for representing reports on classroom and home observations. Adapting Wolcott's scheme (1994), field reports were divided into columns representing 'description' (left hand side of page) and commentary/ analysis (right hand side) and also laying out headings, names, 'chunks' of time and activity (see appendix D). *Description*, in Wolcott's sense, is not so much *raw data* - as he says, there is no such thing - as the detailed accounts of what we saw and heard in the field. *interpretation* refers to the insights, claims, ideas we had (such as those derived from the framework) that were stimulated by our prior experience and perspectives and/or by the field data itself. *Analysis* lies between these two, involving the systematic trawling and collation of data under provisional headings to allow us to substantiate/ refute the claims made by Interpretation with reference to the data represented in Description. In the light of these perspectives, we then went through our field notes inter-relating Description/ Analysis/ Interpretation with respect to particular 'themes'. We variously commenced at different points but would then always take account of the others e.g. an interpretation would require a link to data and a justification through analysis and systematic coding of the claim. The team then made decisions in the light of such accounts whether to proceed with that issue. Examples of issues raised by this procedure include: starting to analyse data relevant to the theme of commercially marketed texts for home use that enabled us to check whether our Interpretations were backed up by systematic data. This told us where we needed to go back and collect more descriptions of the uses of such books in the home that would enable us to make authoritative claims. Likewise, the identification of numeracy practices helped us to hone our understandings of the application of the concept to different parties and contexts, eg the differences between carer/parents' conceptions and activities and those of their child's classroom teacher. The balance between description and analysis varied across researchers - the line between them is not clear cut. By making explicit in this way the criteria each researcher used in a particular report we hoped to be able to 'see' the data more fully.

6 CLASSIFICATION OF NUMERACY PRACTICES IN AND OUT OF SCHOOL

In the present account of this research we are particularly interested in relationships between home/community numeracy practices and schooled numeracy practices, including the participants' own perceptions of these practices. To do so we want to avoid reifying the notion of home numeracy and of schooled numeracy, since we recognise that these are constructs and that in social practice they overlap continually and are mutually constituted not separate entities. We have begun to distinguish between 'sites' - as the actual places where activities take place - and 'domains' - as areas of activity not located in specific places (cf Barton & Hamilton, 1999). School, for instance, is clearly a site where particular numeracy practices take place, but those practices may also be extended to the home. In that context, we might say that the domain of schooled numeracy practices is to be found in the site of home. An example of this would be the child doing mathematical homework set by the school and done at home where in many cases the school frames both the content and the pedagogy required (cf Chapter 5b). This is suggestive of specific research questions when we are observing at home. Likewise, numeracy practices associated with the domain of home for example playing popular games such as Snakes (Chutes) and Ladders games might be found in the site of school and used by teachers to exemplify mathematical concepts and skills. Again this is suggestive for research, leading to questions for both observation and interview. The classification based on these notions and illustrated below does not imply that the categories exist as objects or that the boundaries between them are fixed: indeed the boundaries between them may prove very rich sources of understandings and explanations. The categories of home and school in terms of domains and sites serve as a heuristic for penetrating beneath the surface features of numeracy in action.

7 TYPOLOGY OF NUMERACY PRACTICES

The classification of domains and sites at home and school provided us with a typology of four possibilities, that is school domain in a school site or in home site and home domain in a home site or school site. The potential cells for this classification are shown in table 1 below.

Table 1 Possible cells for domains and sites of numeracy practices

	Domain: Schooled Numeracy Practices	Domain: Out-of-School Numeracy Practices
School site		
Home site		

Identifying an event, locating it within each cell and then interpreting which practices it is associated with can provide a rich source for questioning of data collected at home and at school. To take the analysis further we now want to begin to place items within each of the four cells of this typology in turn and thereby add detail, exemplars and characteristics to the typology. We draw these together and summarise them in a table below.

The placement of numeracy events into the four cells of this typology is not unique, well-determined or uncontestable. The boundaries between the cells are fluid and moveable. Nevertheless a classification like this provides a way of seeking relationships, commonalities and differences between the different practices, of asking questions of the kind of data the researchers collected at home and at school, as we have seen.

From a broad social perspective what we are seeking to reveal are relationships, similarities and/or differences between schooled and out-of-school numeracy practices by labelling the numeracy practices we have seen in those terms. The labelling or placing of any numeracy event into one of the classifications, by the very fact of being debatable, forces us to question the data more closely as we attempt to link it to broader conceptual issues. For example the counting of stairs seems to represent one of the activities many parents do at home with their children. It would be interesting to find out why they do this - whether it is to help the children with their numeracy in schools or whether it is a tradition of home life or both. If the purpose of the activity is the teaching and learning of mathematical skills with someone checking whether the child was successful then it would be schooled numeracy practice in the home domain. Here the central focus is on mathematics per se and on the child learning it. Such schooled practices may become habitual in the home so that, although they are not solving a domestic problem they are part of home culture. Where the purpose is to solve a problem, (perhaps to find how far a child has jumped), and the mathematics is but a tool then this could then be seen as part of home numeracy practices. Here the central focus is the problem that needs solving rather than the mathematics.

From numeracy events we have sought to identify characteristics of the numeracy practices in the different domains to make relationships between them clearer. Drawing on the discussion above suggests that school domain numeracy practices and home domain numeracy practices have the following characteristics:

School numeracy practices tend to be:

- global in the sense that they are claimed to be useful in a wide arena;

- top down - they are concerned with an activity/concept/skill decided centrally or at least by the class teacher;

- their targets are teacher or school driven;

- talk as part of school routines involving set interactions and social relations between teachers and children;

- the motivations of the children are extrinsic.

- Teachers have authority; as part of the schooling system they frame, select and require school numeracy practices

Home practices tend to be:

- local in that they refer to local situations;

- bottom-up in that they are concerned with problems sited or chosen in a local setting;

- the purpose of doing them is about domestic situations, organising lives;

- they are solution driven with the activity and practices derived from the home's ways of doing and engaging in tasks;

- talk occurs though dialogue and negotiation between child and others

- the children are motivated intrinsically.

We provide below table 2 which summarises the classification and some of the more general qualities of the different practices that have emerged, which we describe in greater detail in the Case Study Chapters 4 and 5. Others will be drawn on in the fuller analysis of numeracy practices in different sites and domains developed in Chapter 8. The dotted vertical line stresses the permeability across the table and to show possible overlaps between schooled and home numeracy practices. The last line of the table reflects our understandings of the ways that both school and out of school numeracy practices enter different recontextualising fields (Bernstein, 1996) as they move across domains. For example the playing of Snakes and Ladders at home is recontextualised in the pedagogic domain into a number track with specific teaching objectives (cf. Baker et. al., 2003b; Gold and Mordecai-Phillips 2003).

Table 2 Classifications of Sites and Domains of Numeracy Practices: examples and qualities.

	Domain: Schooled Numeracy Practices	Domain: Out-of-School Numeracy Practices
School site	Working on number bonds, counting, calculating Numbers of children away and in class	Dates, birthdays, aspects of data and measuring, Pokemon cards, money, playground games
Home site	Homework, commercially marketed texts, counting up and down stairs, patterns on car number plates, door numbers.	Pocket money, time, laying the table, shopping, setting the video, home discipline, 'symbolic' uses of number systems ; 'finger counting' door numbers, jigsaws and calendars
Emergent Qualities	*Global* *Top down* *Targets are teacher/school driven.* *Formal educational purposes* *Talk as school routines* *Extrinsic motivation* *Learning through practice* *Teacher has authority, selects and frames practices; insider* *Child outsider*	*Local* *Bottom up* *Home purposes, problem/life organising driven* *Talk as dialogue and negotiated* *Intrinsic motivation* *Learning in practice* *Home selected activity, Child selects approach.* *Child insider*
	<---- *recontextualising fields* ---->	

It has not proved easy to find examples of out-of-school numeracy practices in the classroom, as opposed to the more general context of the school. The difficulty could add to a growing impression from research literature (de Abreu, 1995; Hannon, 1990) that classrooms do not make much use of out of school experiences or of home funds of knowledge (Moll et. al., 1992). This could contribute to low achievement in its failure to 'build' upon the knowledge and skills already familiar to children or in the demands it places on children to 'switch' between practices that are strongly divorced from one another.

We now provide, in Section 3, some detailed case studies of children and their schools based upon the procedures and concepts outlined above. We will then be in a position to move, in Section 4, to thematic and analytic renderings of the data and to thereby review our initial theoretical and conceptual framework.

SECTION THREE: INTRODUCTION TO THE CASE STUDIES

1 GENERAL ISSUES

In this section we provide fairly detailed case studies of three of the children in the research project (Chapter 4) and of the three schools they attended (Chapter 5). Our intention is to give the reader the 'feel' of the environment and experience – the habitus – that these children are socialised into and that they bring with them in some measure to their schools. This also, then, entails similarly detailed accounts of the school with particular reference to the child's experience there. We chose to start with the children in order to establish them as the central focus, building up features of their home environment that we wish to highlight, and through which to read their school experience. Having established the children and salient features of their environments in Chapters 4a,b and c, we then turn to the schools in Chapters 5a,b and c and attempt to interpret the children's numeracy practices there. We are also concerned to recognise how children cross over the boundaries between home and school, bringing features from one into the other (cf Street, ed. forthcoming). Our interpretations attempt to avoid the reification of home and of school as polarised and instead to identify the processes of crossing and mediation that are at the heart of the children's experience.

The primary criterion for selecting cases for fuller treatment of this kind was that we wished to describe in detail one child from each of the three schools. With only three children possible for such detailed case studies within the limits of this volume, we did not aim to provide any statistical or normative 'range'. A major criterion at this point was that we had sufficient rich data to allow the reader to get the 'feel' of the child's experience and to provide sufficient material from which we could then extrapolate broader points in the Themes Section 4, in conjunction with other focus children not chosen for Case Studies. The intrinsic interest and link to our themes is central to the accounts we provide in Chapter 4. We chose to focus on Seth, from Mountford School; Kim from Tarnside; and Ann from Rowan. Seth provides particularly rich insights into the ambivalence regarding 'engagement' of a white working class boy, whose father raced pigeons, mother paid into a catalogue purchase schemes and whose teachers struggled to get his attention yet recognised that when on task he could do the school mathematics set for him. In formal terms, the school saw his attainment in numeracy as below average for his class when he arrived in the school but later as just above average, which is low in national terms.

Kim, from Tarnside, was a similar boy in some ways, ranked below average in his class, but being from a Caribbean background there were cultural issues concerning his carers' ways of helping him at home (his grandmother, for instance, had run a school in Jamaica), whilst his financial background was probably more secure than Seth's. Anne, from Rowan, could seem at first sight to represent the classic middle class girl, supported at home by parents with the kind of cultural resources recognised by the school at the same time as supported individually in the school because of its more child-centred ethos. In her first term at school, Anne was seen as 'more able' in numeracy, though later on she was placed in a lower group for numeracy and it is possible that there were gender issues in both her own and her parents' approaches to her numeracy activities that provide us with an interesting contrast to the two boys chosen for this Chapter. We are careful, however, not to extrapolate too much from cases that we see as 'telling' rather than 'representative' and our aim is to provide the reader with sufficient material to take forward a complex and uneven account as we move towards the Themes Section. Any 'typicality' drawn from the apparent congruence of Anne's middle class family habitus with that of the school, for instance, has be set against the dissonance between the family's and the school's views on 'religious education' and likewise the gender dimension of her engagement in numeracy practices is too complex and varied to be seen simply as 'typical'.

We explain here briefly, why we are taking the reader through all of this data and why and how we selected this from all the things going on. From the educational perspective, in one sense our 'story' is simply that the children's experiences in the Case Study schools are complex and uneven and may contrast with other schools. Our aim, then, is to provide 'fine-tuned' description and analysis of such uneven and complex interactions around numeracy in particular paying attention to the children's cultural meanings, some of which they may have brought with them from home. We argue that such an approach can add to our understanding of the processes involved as children engage with schooled numeracy practices. It adds to that offered by policy, curriculum development, pedagogy, assessment etc in showing how we might look at what is going on through other lenses that might approximate more to the children's own perceptions. The primary contributions are methodological – shaping the lenses for such a viewing - and theoretical – refining the conceptual apparatus that helps us challenge what we otherwise take for granted – to 'make the familiar strange' (cf Agar, 1996). We are not trying to claim that we have empirical coverage, that is sufficient data to provide enumerative induction, but rather sufficient 'rich description' of Case Studies to allow for analytic induction (see Chapter 3). We are simply asking the reader to take account of these indicative sets of data and to apply it to their own context.

Whilst we therefore provide sometimes lengthy quotations from original sources, the material is, inevitably, selected and cut down to size from a much large corpus, collected over a three year period by the research team (see the Introduction to the book and Chapter 3 for fuller description of the research process). The case studies of Kim and Anne and of Tarnside and Rowan schools are taken from data originally collected by Alison Tomlin, the main researcher who was employed half time on the project; and the case studies of Seth and of Mountford school are taken from data originally collected by Dave Baker, who was employed part time on the project and who has continued to work on the writing and editing of this book along with Brian Street, the Director of the project who also conducted field work in Mountford school and in homes in the area. We have chosen to maintain the voice of the original researcher as we present the data. In keeping with contemporary concern for reflexivity and transparency in the research process, and in order to avoid the misrepresentations of the 'historic present', particular incidents and events are described in the past tense and the researcher's own participation in them is signalled. Thus Alison Tomlin, for instance, points out where a mother answered a question she raised and then indicates her own comment upon it at the time, or during her writing up of field notes. In addition, broader commentaries upon the data and analytic links to the themes of the book as a whole – such as, for instance the linking of home numeracy practices to our theme of home/ school relations or to the concept of 'cultural resources' – are presented in the collective voice of the authors of the book. Here the collective 'we' is used to indicate our meta commentary and to acknowledge our position and stance. We have attempted to select material to be not so much 'representative' of a child or school, but that best speaks to the issues raised by the book – experience of numeracy embedded in daily practices such as pigeon racing or counting door numbers in the case of the children, and issues of pedagogy and learning in the school cases, such as how far children are 'engaged' in a particular practice. Avoiding the reification of either home or school, we have tried to keep to the forefront the issue of home school relations and how far home knowledge figured in school and vice versa. We intend thereby to emphasise specific themes and arguments rather than attempting a comprehensive empirical account of all of the schools and children. As we describe individual cases, we try to keep in mind the overall cohesion and coherence of the book, referring the reader to other sections whether empirical or theoretical, where a particular point is further dealt with.

2 LINKS TO SECTION 4

The descriptions provided in Chapter 4a,b and c and Chapter 5a,b and c are intended, then, to give the reader an indicative sense of the experiences of children in numeracy classes in these schools and their experience at home as they move across both sites. We thereby hope to offer a rich ethnographic-style feel of the data from which we make more general extrapolations in the Themes Section 4. In attempting to draw out specific themes, we hope to build upon the reader's acquaintance with the environment and experience described in Section 3, plus other material drawn from our field notes in these schools and with these and other children. The implications of all of this for policy, pedagogy and curriculum might, we argue be considerable. But, before addressing these issues we feel it is important for those engaged in such decisions to understand from within the complex relationships, meanings and social practices in which pupils, carers and teachers are engaged. The combination of detailed case studies and of thematic analyses will, we hope, provide a sounder basis on which to develop such policy discussion.

CHAPTER FOUR: CHILDREN CASE STUDIES

Seth's, Kim's and Anne's Stories

4a. SETH'S STORY AT MOUNTFORD: 'cos wherever you go there's numbers'

4a.1 Setting

The actors in this account were Seth, his mother Jackie, his father Dennis, his brothers Jason and Darren and his teachers at Mountford Primary School Pamela and Zena and the researcher Dave. They lived in Mountford an area of Blatchford, a town in the south east of Great Britain.

4a.2 Seth and his family

When the researcher Dave first met Seth on the project he was just 5 years old and in the Reception class . By the end of the project he was in Year 2 at primary school and was 7 years old. He is an autumn born child and was one of the oldest in his class. He was seen as below average by the school in Reception class when he was 5 years old. By Year 2 he was seen as average or below in his class but well below average nationally. Seth was alert and lively, but large and rather over weight and was teased at school.

Seth had strong levels of concentration when doing activities he liked such as painting, drawing or writing. However, he could be distracted, particularly by his two older brothers. He was the youngest of three. Seth could be difficult to handle. When he and Dave visited a local shop during one home visit, when Seth was aged 5, the shop assistant became quite agitated and followed Seth around and became anxious when Seth began to delve into and take things off the shelves even when asked not to.

Seth lived with his mother, Jackie, in her mid-forties, who did not have a job. Dave saw Jackie as a rather anxious person with low self-esteem who seldom made eye contact, factors that he suggests help create the context for Seth's experience eof education in general and numeracy in particular. Equally significant, however, was the fact that, like most of the parents we met – and in contrast to some dominant stereotypes - she was interested in education and wanted to contribute to her children's school and schooling. Like others in our study, she appeared self-deprecating regarding schooled mathematics:

B. Street, D. Baker and A. Tomlin (eds.), Navigating Numeracies, 39-77.
© 2005 *Springer. Printed in the Netherlands.*

"I'm not that good at numbers, like maths at school and that" ... "I am afraid of numbers" (interview DB 21 Nov. 00)   "I did not get things from school. When things were too hard I could not say anything. Otherwise had the mickey taken and told you were an idiot. I missed a lot of school I just did not go.   I wasn't so good so I am encouraging my children." (DB 7 Mar 00)

Seth had two older brothers, Jason and Darren, who were close in age to him. At the start of the project Seth's father Dennis, who was in his mid-thirties, lived away from the family. By the middle of the project he seemed to have moved back in. He kept racing pigeons in the garden of the house. Dennis was a lively active engaging person who maintained clear eye contact. Like Jackie he was brought up on the estate and both of them went to Mountford School, the one that their children attend. He said that his own mathematics was OK at school. Dennis's only qualification was a driving licence and he did not have regular earnings.

Both parents, like all of the others in our research, were keen to help Seth with his schooling and saw the research project as having potential benefits for Seth. They both made time for Dave's visits and both saw education as important. Jackie said:

"Education is really important. Going for a job it is important otherwise you won't understand what you have to do" and "Oh yeh [schooling] important isn't it. Yeh, Oh, yeh, it is." (Interview DB 31 May 01).

When Dave asked why mathematics was important she said it was important for Seth because it was:

"Life. Seth will have to manage money, bills, bringing money into a home. Work needs numbers" (DB Seth 2 March 00)

Relating this to her own identity and reflecting the potentially socially oppressive nature of mathematics she said:

"It is important to me socially or in the Family Centre its embarrassing to say you can't do it". (DB Seth 23 Mar 00)

4a.3. Seth's Home

For most of the project, the family lived in a small council house on a mainly white working class estate. There were few books in the living room but there were some in the children's room upstairs together with toys. By the third year of the project they had a computer with a few games. By then Seth was able to load games and play them. At the back of the house was the shed where Dennis kept their pigeons. When Seth was aged 7 and in Year 2 the family were moved with little choice and at short notice to a larger council house. (DB Seth 19 Dec 01).

4a.4. Seth's Area

The area they lived in was seen from outside as one of the most deprived areas of the town (see Chapter 5a). Both of Seth's parents were aware of many educational and social problems in that area. There were many supportive agencies and projects involved in the area, from 'play-link' to Education Action Zones. Seth's parents were concerned about the quality of the neighbourhood in which they lived. They were concerned about the behaviours of some of the people in the area, which could be dangerous or might undermine their values. This resulted in their restricting where the children could play.

Jackie and Dennis were aware of the reputation of their area and that they could be rejected or discriminated against by people from other areas. Jackie said:

> "Say, for example, I wanted to go and get a job and it was in Hambledon. [a genteel area] – it's unheard of, you can't have anybody from Mountford area". (Interview DB 31 May 01)

And Dennis said:

> "Jackie had an occasion when she was down the bingo hall she had trouble 'cos she was from Mountford." (Interview DB 31 May 01)

The reputation of the area in which they live may not have directly affected Seth's numeracy skills but it could be seen as an aspect of the family's and the community's cultural resources, that over time and in complex not yet understood ways may affect his attainments at schooled numeracy. Dave's experience of Seth's behaviour whilst shopping (of which a brief example is given above cf also Chapter 7 where we describe Seth's mother's restrictions on his experiences of shopping.) suggests that his learning experiences of money in use and thereby his understanding of numeracy may well be affected.

4a.5. Seth and his School - Mountford

Seth went to Mountford County Primary School, the same school as his parents. Details about the school, its practices and background are given in the case study of the school, (c.f. Chapter 5a).

When in Reception class, Seth was seen to be below average in attainment for mathematics and came from a home that struggled financially. He was seen by the school as difficult and that his mother often struggled to control him. At the end of his Year 2 Seth was assessed, within national assessment procedures as level 2c for mathematics. This placed him near the middle or just into the lower half of his class in terms of this kind of assessment but he was well below average nationally. In terms of the assessment regime in schooling in England he was "not progressing well enough to achieve level 4 when he is 11", which is the expected level to be attained by average pupils. In English he achieved similar results.

The teachers wrote a formal report on Seth at the end of his Year 2, (July 02). The report in part was for school records and in part it was to communicate the school's views of Seth to his parents, The class teacher viewed Seth to be a fairly capable child who struggled with some of the practices and discourses of the classroom. He struggled with listening, sitting still, engaging and concentrating. For example, she wrote:

> "Seth can be extremely helpful and sensible boy and he responds positively to praise. However he finds it very difficult to maintain eye contact, to sit still and to concentrate. This means he sometimes has difficulty in following instructions. This is a pity as he is capable of producing lovely work. He also needs to control his tendency to 'answer back' to adults or his peers." (Report July 02)

In terms of his mathematics she said:

> "Seth shows an enjoyment of maths and sometimes joins in with the mental starter. He is beginning to use the strategies he has been taught to calculate simple addition and subtraction problems mentally. He can name some 2-D and 3-D shapes and describe them using some of their properties. He has been introduced to standard units of measurement in length, mass and capacity and can read and use simple scales. He can tell the time to the nearest hour on analogue clocks and can solve simple time problems. He has been introduced to a range of different types of graph and diagrams for data handling, pictogram, Venn, Carroll, tree and bar and is becoming increasingly confident at interpreting information from them." (Report July 02)

Her comments on mathematics could be seen as consistent with what we term an autonomous view of mathematics (see Chapter 2 and Baker and Street, 1996). There was no reference to the social in mathematics and no mention of home practices. From a social perspective, and given for instance the purpose of the document as in part a report to Seth's parents, this might seem remarkable, although it is not unusual in schools where teachers are not expected to pay attention to home practices. (see Chapter 4b, Kim, for a similar emphasis on schooled numeracy at the expense of broader conceptions).

The school's and Jackie's views of Seth at school are illustrated by the following extract from a conversation between Pamela, the Reception Class teacher and Jackie, Seth's mother, at a parents' evening when Seth was 5 years old. Dave, the researcher, attended the session and took the following notes:

> Pamela: "He is academically bright. It's the behaviour. He won't answer questions. He can't be bothered.".. "He tries it on but he comes back on line. His writing is coming on and I can have a good conversation with him."

> Jackie: "He does not use eye contact. You hold his face and he still looks down" .. "he gets the mickey taken out of him. He gets teased in the playground. Harry is picking on him".

> Pamela: "I will sort it out. Don't worry". "The Ed Psychologist says Seth is good. You should be pleased. Sitting has improved" (DB Mo 6 April 2000).

There seemed to be a real sharing of their perceptions about Seth with a mixture of educational and behavioural aspects. The teacher, Pamela, tried to suggest some things Seth and his mother could do out of school on number and tried to take responsibility for some of the bullying the mother was concerned about. Jackie raised both behavioural and academic issues.

The dialogue also revealed the teacher's view that Seth was "bright" but with behaviour problems. The mother's concern with eye contact was interesting, as Dave's experience suggests she is also reticent to use eye contact (see also the account of Kim, Chapter 4b). The Head informed us that in his view it was a feature of the people on the estate: they were perhaps justifiably wary of outside agencies that were often disrespectful so they chose not to engage (Interview with Mo Head, 10th April 2000). This, then, may reflect Seth's learning about behaviours that are appropriate in his life.

4a.6. School numeracy events and practices

The overall school's picture of Seth was of an active, alert child who challenged his mother and who concentrated at school on tasks he wanted to do. He sometimes responded well to instructions from his teachers. But given space he sometimes disengaged (cf. Chapter 6). He then would fidget, disobey instructions and disrupt others. The theme of Seth's variable engagement and disengagement was one that Dave observed over the three years. In a sense it had become part of his reactions and responses to school numeracy events and his level of participation in school numeracy practices. Data from a visit to his Year 1 class showed him engaging in some numeracy activities where the numeracy was embedded in day-to-day class management activities. In the extract below he openly disengages from a mental and oral starter in a lesson:

> Zena: We are going to do shopping as we weren't good at it yesterday. First we are going to do counting. What should we count in and what should we start at?
>
> They all counted to 100 in ones from 1 together.
>
> Seth put his fingers in his ears and fidgeted (DB Mo 22 May 01)

Seth's responses to schooled numeracy could therefore be engagement or disengagement. How he decided to participate or disengage in response to a particular event was not clear (see Chapter 6 for further discussion of these comments). But his variable reactions in class are an aspect of his school numeracy practices.

4a.7.Home numeracy events and practices

Jackie seemed to have a fairly broad view of numeracy. During the first year of the project, when Dave asked about home numeracy she said:

> "We do telephone numbers. I want them to know their own telephone number. Seth doesn't know his but does know 999. He rings that number and called them out. I had to ring and say sorry. They said he was rude to them". (DB 7 Mar 00) and "counting, adding, they share a calculator. Seth does the counting not the adding. He was not good at matching string to lengths. When I asked him for a piece that went across the road [about 10 metres] he showed me one that was less than a metre. Dates, ages, TV, phone bills, phone pad. The children can use the microwave. It has a dial to turn round." (DB 23 Mar 00) "And even Snakes and Ladders is a way of doing it, isn't it? Because you've got to go back, you've got to minus that and all that, you've got to lose your numbers, you've got to lose what you've got. And you could say to them you've got to take the number off what you just had and see how far you've got back. Because Darren, Seth's brother, likes all that." (Interview DB 21 Nov. 00).

Here Jackie showed her awareness that there are numbers in out of school numeracy events home-based activities like dates, TV, phone bills and using a microwave dial. On other occasions she spoke about the use of numbers on video recorders.

When Dave asked her views on the importance of mathematics she said:

> "But I think without numbers and that you are certainly lost. Cos wherever you go there's numbers, isn't there. I know it isn't exciting, all that, you know, maths and stuff. Or even words, well like you've got Scrabble in words, haven't you, that make words

up. Everyday words. You know. There must be some games; like you said, with dominoes but there must be other things as well that's got numbers in them. Ludo maybe – no, that ain't." (Interview DB 21 Nov. 00).

Jackie accepted the importance of numbers in day-to-day living. But then noted that mathematics was not exciting unlike words, which are used in Scrabble. Jackie did not readily accept that games involve mathematical experiences for her children. In this case she rejected the potential value for mathematics of a game like Ludo and in previous visits she was unaware of the value for mathematics of dominoes or playing cards. In an earlier study, Baker (1998) found that children from some homes in Mountford had not played Snakes and Ladders at home and that this created a problem for the children when teachers at the school assumed they had done so. Jackie's unawareness of the potential for learning schooled mathematics in less visible - and for her unexpected – contexts, such as scrabble, would mean that she would not have introduced to her family games with an educational purpose in mind like these, unlike Anne's mother Trish at Rowan, (see Chapter 4c) They would not be explicitly part of the home's cultural resources, which could contribute to schooled numeracy. That is not to say that her practices are wrong but that a lack of such experiences at home could be in conflict with schooled numeracy practices where processes and practices in games are used, as this school was attempting to do.

Like many adults (cf. Evans 2000, Coben, 2000; see also Kim's mother, Ch 4b) Jackie lacked confidence in her own numeracy skills and her ability to teach it to her children. For example, through necessity she was able to manage her supermarket shopping bill to keep to her budget. She did this through a mixture of rough calculation and by separating out essential objects from the rest; she could then remove items at the till if her bill was too high. But she did not see that as a useful or powerful numeracy practice of her own. Jackie, referring to her supermarket bill, said:

> "No. Sort of. [add them] I know, well, I've got that much, that much. I'm not that good at numbers, like maths at school and that. .. I take £20 cash .. I suppose I just know roughly. And I think to myself, you know, I've got those two items there, just in case I haven't got enough, they're put back. It's never normally over the top." (Interview DB 21 Nov. 00).

These shopping practices were effective for her domestic management. The numeracy aspects of her strategies were not always explicit and on the surface. She used estimation to limit what she put in her trolley and her strategies were effective and pragmatic. How this impacted on Seth was not clear but opportunities for him to learn about money and number through shopping were limited because his mother said she could not take him shopping with her due to his behaviour. He was likely to disrupt the stores (c.f. chapter 7). This is part of his out-of-school numeracy practices. If Seth was unable to join in his mother's shopping practices he was denied that as a learning experience. This is not only in terms of skills. It was also about the values and social relations involved in using mathematics in a shopping arena. (This is discussed further in Chapter 7 on home numeracy practices).

A home financial event that occurred during one of Dave's home visits revealed two different aspects of the family's home financial practices. The first aspect was triggered by a phone call inviting Jackie to pay money into an insurance or hospital plan to provide her with financial support to cover periods when she may become hospitalised. The invitation, according to the family, came from a shopping catalogue company, Kays. Given that Jackie was not working and therefore would not lose salary during a stay in hospital, the hospital plan was not relevant to the family's needs. The company selling the plan was requesting money and could be seen as seeking to exploit the family's potential concerns about the future. The phone call led to a conversation between Jackie and Dennis about problems they had in coping with catalogue shopping, which was the second aspect of financial practices on which Dave focused. The conversation went as follows:

> Jackie: They always try to get something off of you, don't they? Hospital Plan. Trying to get me to pay for hospital care. Like I've got a catalogue – Kays and they've obviously got me from that. And she said if you have to go into hospital, you get £35 a day, she said if you go into hospital.

> Dennis: you should fall down the steps quickly

> Jackie: Very funny. She said something about you can get £300 and something, something like that. All for £1.20 a week, she said, you know to put through Kays.

> Jackie: Kays the catalogue. How I get my boys things – because obviously I don't work and that it's easier to go through the club, isn't it and just pay so much a week. You can but I don't like to go over the top. Like, say, I need three pairs of school uniforms, like, trousers for their uniform it's much easier just to get it off the club. It's finding the cash to go in the shops. But they do put a bit of interest on the top, don't they? I'm not very good at working that out – he is.

> Dennis: Yeh. Like my sister is two grand in debt. Yours is quite higher at the moment isn't it? It must be 1% because it's £15 to cover your account.

> Jackie: Yeh, but I'm very sensible about it. I only put the limit I can put on it, that I can afford monthly. Lots of parents see it all there and it's so easy, isn't it, that they go over the top but I don't, do I? Never do. (interview DB16 June 01)

Here catalogue shopping, was seen to exploit the family's needs and create additional problems for them by charging high levels of interest. This can result in heavy costs to a family with scarce financial resources. This was a home numeracy event sited in home numeracy practice for this family that may be different from the financial practices of other perhaps wealthier families. These practices were sited in social relations, containing aspects of gender, exploitation, managing scarce home financial resources and indebtedness. All this contributed to the financial climate in which Seth was being raised.

The content of these home numeracy events and practices, had to do with shopping, cashback, money, percentages and interest charges, all of which are accepted as part of school mathematics. The problems that this family was having with compound interest charges, though not unusual, were complex. But what was particular to them was that they had to depend on this kind of scheme. They had little choice. The social relations, therefore, between the family and the catalogue/loan company were not equitable. The interests of the family were not Kays' prime concern and the company was the one with authority and power. They set the interest rates and purchasing conditions and schemes. The family on the other hand had to make these purchases if they wanted their children to have clothes or other items, to help them with their cash flows. These inequities frame the relations surrounding such events and suggest that home financial numeracy practices are ones where families may feel fairly powerless to control and run their own lives. In this event these were practices that Seth experienced as an observer. However it was an element of the background in which he lived that structured his relationships with numeracy and thence with schooled numeracy: we might say that they were part of the habitus that he took into school (cf. Chapter 7).

Another arena in which Seth and his family engaged in home numeracy practices was pigeon racing. An account of this is given in some detail in Chapter 7 on home numeracy practices. At this point it may be suffice to mention that Seth's father, engagement in breeding, caring for and racing pigeons provided a constructive, alive and 'real' context in which Seth and his brothers potentially could meet numeracy in practice. This could be about the economics of pigeon racing but it could be about money, betting, compass directions, distances, speeds, timing and ways of thinking mathematically.

4a.8. Home and School relationships: Learning at home and at school

Jackie often expressed the view that the school ought to have played a more active role in helping her with Seth's education. She needed help motivating and containing him in an educational activity, as Seth's concentration at home with his mother was fairly limited. It seemed as though there was more conflict here than in Rowan the 'leafy suburb school we also studied, (see Chapter 5c) and the family seemed not to have strategies for compensation at home, unlike Anne at Rowan and Kim at Tarnside (the 'mixed' school in the project, cf Chapter 5b).. When Dave asked what the school thought of Seth, Jackie talked about a lack of communication with teachers:

> "I don't know because I don't get no feedback really, do I? I think that they think he's coming along all right but …. But then I don't think mothers get told much." (Interview DB 30 May 01)

This links with some of the work Diane Reay (1998) has done about teachers listening to but not hearing working class mothers and the working class mothers not having the confidence to insist on being heard.

Seth's parents' views of school pedagogic practices for numeracy and the damage parents could do seemed contradictory at times. There was some evidence that they would have liked some of the 'traditional' ways of teaching tables such as learning them off by heart, (see Kim's story Chapter 4b). In some cases they saw this as successful for them, as Dennis had successfully learnt his tables. At other times they saw the need to motivate children by making mathematics more interesting. They also saw chanting as a form of motivation and then the two views meshed.

"But I think maths in children it's boring for them, really, isn't it? You're right you must make to have a fun side to it." (interview DB 16 June 01)

In terms of home pedagogic practices, Jackie discussed the ways she could encourage Seth to do schooled mathematics and her views about the effect of her teaching schooled mathematics at home. When asked whether she did school work with him when he came home from school, she said:

"Believe it or not, he doesn't want me to. .. But I don't want to make him do something that he doesn't want to do, you know. I go 'it's not minutes' and it starts into an argument and I just leave it". (Seth 21/11/00)

Here she was accepting a quite different role from that of an adult at school. She accepted that at home her son had a right to refuse to do the schooled numeracy. She also accepted that Seth might argue with her about an aspect of mathematics in a way that he would not do with adults at school, a fear perhaps arising from her own experience of schooling. These revealed quite different social relations from those in operation in schooled numeracy practices. School numeracy practices included relations with teachers that tended to be compliant and accepting with the teachers having authority, although as we have noted Seth did, on occasions, choose to disengage or answer back. At home Seth could affect what he did and could claim greater control over the activities he did.

Jackie was concerned that they could damage the children (conflict with, rather than compensate or complement the schools teaching) by using ways of doing mathematics that were different from the ways done in the school. She accepted that the school decides the way to do it and this included the current moves in schools towards mental strategies for calculating and away from written. She did not see herself as having the confidence or knowledge to challenge these approaches. She had to avoid damaging the children by not doing it the wrong way.

Jackie: Yeh, but we should do that but then if we did something like that and we don't get communication from the teachers, we don't know how far the teacher's got with them. And that, do we? The school's saying we like working with the parents, and all that but supposing I set something out with Seth and did it my way and he went to school and had to do it whatever way, you know. She might have a go at him for doing it that way because she wants him to do it her way   well it could confuse him, couldn't it? ... Because a lot these days, they don't like you writing them down, they like you to remember it up here. Whereas I do it a different way and I say if you don't know it, right, just count on your fingers but apparently that's not the way they do it now. They like them to remember it. They try to encourage them not to count – but I do it the other way, with my fingers. That's what I was told, anyway. I don't know if there's any truth in it. (interview DB 16 June 01)

4a.9. Home school relations. Access and Communication

Here Jackie was raising one of her major concerns, the lack of communication with the teacher. From Year 1 onwards her access to the class teacher at Mountford became more restricted. In Reception she had delivered Seth directly to the classroom. She was able to talk with the teacher in the classroom on a daily basis if she needed to. In the following year the school stopped this practice. This affected the immediacy of day-to-day informal contact and communication between carers and teachers. Jackie was upset and angry with this as she felt she was unaware either what Seth was doing or how well he was doing. Jackie felt that the system they had at Rowan (the middle class school in the project described to her by Dave), where parents were allowed open access to the classroom at the start of the day was the better system.

When asked about how the school could use things from homes Jackie said:

> "And they don't encourage the mothers to help them, either. These small children, I mean, you know, they should give them a rough idea of what they're doing and maybe we can help them, you know." (interview DB 21 Nov. 00)

Here she is not only responding to Dave's question about the school using things from home but also turned it around to consider how the school might use parents to help them.

Another aspect of home school relationships and communication that Jackie raised was homework. She thought that children needed homework and that the homework should relate to what they were doing at school. This way she would know more about what he was doing at school and perhaps be able to help him more. The data also suggested that the family did not do much schooled mathematics with Seth at home: in part this was because they felt that Seth would not be interested or because it was something to be left to the school, (c.f. Alexander, 2000).

Our data suggested that one numeracy area with the potential for significant sharing and one that would enable shifts to be made explicit between home and school numeracy events and practices was money. Events such as handling dinner money seemed to be a genuine crossover between home money practices and schooled numeracy. Usual home money practices involved Seth saving and counting his money and occasionally spending it when he could be taken to the shops. He also learnt that his savings were vulnerable to "stealing " by his older brothers. This gave him a sense of value in his home's money practices. In comparison, in dinner money events he was given money at home to take to school to pay for school dinner, to buy drinks and to receive change which he was expected to return home. He had no authority or control over these interactions. But these dinner money events allowed him to handle money in genuine money transactions where the exchange power of money was visible and apparent. Teachers tended to make use of these transactions at the beginning of the school day to set up some numeracy learning. In contrast tasks using money that were text book based or 'pretend', as in shop play, were more deliberate and were more contrived in the sense that they were not transactions where money changed hands. They were often about teaching specific numbers skills like subtraction. As Jackie said:

> "They need to be taken out, in school, and shown the value of money or something – what you can buy with it, you know, and change and things. Maybe even the tuck shop at school." (interview DB 16 June 01)

4a.10. Explanations for achievement in mathematics

When discussing their explanations for children's low achievement in numeracy, Seth's parents raised the effect of the image and reputation of their area on their lives and those of their children. Jackie said:

> "But they do say, though, don't they – people – if a child hasn't got a very good education it normally stems from deprived areas, doesn't it? I don't think that's always the case, because you do have brighter ones". (interview DB 31 May 01)

She could be seen as suggesting that Mountford, in the field of formal education gives children 'negative cultural capital' (cf. Chapter 7). But she was also clear that it was the families that ensured whether children developed schooled skills or life skills: on achievement she said: "I think it all comes from the parents", (interview DB 31 May 01).

4a.11 Discussion

From Seth's story how would we interpret or understand what was happening to him in schooled numeracy events in the classroom, his behaviour and his work or lack of engagement in numeracy? At one level we might question the quality of the teacher's control, her planning and organisation. For example we might question the use of a whole class oral mental starter or the teacher's ability to motivate the children. Such an analysis of the teaching in Mountford would reveal classroom processes, routines and practices that could be improved to some extent but then only at a marginal level.

Another interpretation might come from a cognitive perspective. This might suggest that Seth does not have the "ability" to learn or engage in this mathematics. Our observations suggest that he can do the mathematics set for him but often disengages from school mathematics. We do have evidence from schooling that he does engage in writing and drawing. We also have evidence that he is interested in his pocket money and therefore does engage in home numeracy practices. His disengagement from some schooled numeracy events could be because his teachers do not adequately motivate him. Such an analysis might lead teachers to seek ways of motivating him perhaps by looking at what interests him both inside and outside the classroom. Again that may work to some extent for him but may be marginal and may not work for other children. Potentially, then, Seth might appear able to handle the cognitive demands of informal mathematics, and, with appropriate pedagogy those of formal mathematics. Such an analysis might lead teachers to seek more culturally sensitive ways of motivating him, perhaps by looking at what interests him both inside and outside the classroom building on local 'funds of knowledge' (Moll et. al, 1992).

A third interpretation would be to seek ways of understanding Seth's behaviour in schooled numeracy in terms of relationships between the social practices of the classroom and his background. These relationships could contain conflicts or dissonances for Seth, (c.f. Chapter 7). There are two components of these social practices, which in schooled numeracy events seem to involve conflicting relationships for Seth. The first are the rules, discourses and practices of schooled numeracy. These schooled numeracy practices include not only the mathematical activities the children engage in, in school, but also the social relations, institutional relations, values and context in which the activities are sited. In our research we have argued that schooled numeracy practices are intricate complex interactions between these components. The practices in school may appear customary to educationalists but they may appear to Seth to be like a game (which is how Bourdieu sometimes describes different 'fields'), the purpose of which Seth is unclear about and the rules of which he is uncertain about. These rules and purposes and practices may conflict with his home practices. An example of this could be the use of money when getting change when purchasing objects out of school and in the teaching of subtraction in school (c.f. Walkerdine, 1988). The second potential conflict for Seth would be his habitus, attitude and disposition towards schooled numeracy events, (c.f. Chapter 7). To engage in them fully he would need to have accepted and internalised the value and importance of schooled numeracy practices and of the events themselves: the schooled habitus. He would, for instance, want to seek positive affirming relationships with others involved in schooled numeracy events including the teacher and his peers. This desire would have to fit with his image and his self-identity in that classroom. This is perhaps a more complex notion than the cognitive one of motivation. A resolution of such conflict would require a change of his habitus, that is something that is part of his history-in-person (Holland, 2002), his home background, his culture and whole individual make-up. A change of this magnitude at the level of habitus, though potentially possible, is much harder even if undertaken concertedly by all around them. Given that change in this direction is problematic, the alternative would seem to be a shift in the opposite direction, in schooling itself, altering schooled numeracy practices so that there are fewer dissonances and conflicts between the discourses and numeracy activities of such children and those of their school.

This last analysis provides some alternative insights and ways of understanding why Seth often did not engage fully in the schooled numeracy activities the teacher created for the class. The potential and actual dissonances and conflicts between his and the school's practices give us a model for explaining why he is less likely to succeed in attainment at mathematics than children from other backgrounds where there might be less apparent conflict.

For Seth, there may be tensions between home and school numeracy. He does not identify with schooled practices. His identity means that he may not be concerned that he is seen to be disengaged. He may not have developed ways of hiding his disengagement perhaps because he does not overly care whether anyone notices. His identity and engagement in number work are not always compatible for him. In fact his identity and disengagement are not in conflict unlike that for some middle class children. Middle class children are more likely to have strategies which hide their disengagement partly because they do not want to be seen to be disengaged.

Seth's family are keen on him doing well at mathematics, but they do not see themselves as insiders in schooled mathematics practices. His mother sees herself as very weak at both schooled and home mathematics despite being able to handle many domestic mathematics activities like shopping. His father seems to have a moderate view of his own school mathematics. He said: "I was OK at school maths" despite not getting any qualifications at the subject. He does feel more confident about his own handling of complex domestic mathematics practices despite evidence that he does not have a clear understanding of some aspects of financial mathematics such as compound interest when used in the family's catalogue and higher purchase dealings. The struggles the family has with money and the mother's disenchantment with her own mathematics are part of the environment in which Seth's understandings and mathematical identity have been fashioned.

His habitus means, then, that he does not expect to always participate in school mathematics. There are times in Seth's life when he may become passive, expecting to be outside schooled practices and yet not wanting to challenge them through disruptive behaviour. He becomes passive, maybe seeing himself as a victim and alienated from the activities around him. These schooled numeracy events are not about him or for him. Over time he will progressively become more detached from schooled mathematics. Schooling, we might say, has contributed to constructing him as disengaged, outside, a passive child in the mathematics classroom, though our research tells us that he and others like him are active at home. It may be here, that explanations for school defined low achievement amongst many such children has to be sought.

4b KIM'S STORY AT TARNSIDE: 'I am going to have to throw money after somebody to be teaching my child when I think the system's failing me'

4b.1.Introduction: Kim's school and family.

Kim attends Tarnside school; he was below average in numeracy in his year. Kim's teachers have been Marilyn in Reception Dylan in Year 1 and Thelma in Year 2. Kim lives with his grandmother Carmen, a nurse working part-time shifts, probably in her late 50s or early 60s, who has lived in the same house for 34 years, and his mother Juline, who works in a government office. Kim's father is, in Juline's words, 'not around'; she said Kim 'knows who he is but he's useless'. (He gives no practical or financial support, and Kim never mentioned him to Alison.) The house is probably Edwardian, mid-terrace, in an area which would have been largely working class housing when Kim's grandparents bought it, but is now gentrified. Kim's grandfather, with whom he was close, died during his Reception year. Carmen was Kim's main carer; she took him to/from school (usually in a minicab), and gave him tea after school. His mother would arrive home from work about 7 pm. Both Carmen and Juline went to parents' meetings at school. During Year 1, Juline took over that role, having become concerned about Kim's progress.

Juline described herself as someone who became a mother by accident; she had relied absolutely on her mother to help. She did not regard herself as knowledgeable about children of Kim's age (for example, she asked Alison, the researcher, whether Kim was 'normal' in talking to an imaginary friend). Her mother on the other hand had brought up her own children, contributed to bringing up grandchildren, and ran a home school in Jamaica.

In Juline's account her mother, Carmen, had the 'old' Jamaican culture. Carmen had gone to private school in Jamaica and therefore avoided corporal punishment, but her husband, Kim's grandfather, went to state school and suffered; Carmen and Juline talked about his having literacy difficulties resulting from his poor schooling. Carmen's experience of her own and her husband's schooling may have led her to seek to protect Kim from some aspects of schooling, and contributed to the school view of her as 'indulgent', discussed below. Juline was grateful for Carmen's help with Kim's upbringing, and saw her mother as someone who still wanted to be mothering children: 'I think I carried him [Kim] for her'.

Kim did not spend much time out of school with other children of a similar age. He spent time with his cousins, who were around ten years older; they took him with them shopping etc, but presumably didn't 'play' with him in the more usual senses. He sometimes went to the house of a boy in his class, and for a time in Year1 the daughter of people known to Carmen, whose family had recently arrived in London, stayed with Kim and went to the same school. Kim's interests (as told to Alison) revolved around TV, toys including Power Rangers, Dragonball Z and Godzilla characters, based on the TV programmes, and karate. These overlapped: he said Dragonball Z was where I learned my karate moves (AT Kim 30th Aug 01). On holiday in Jamaica he tried a karate class, and in the playground he practised karate kicks (which never make contact - it was clearly play rather than fighting) with other boys.

4b.2. Kim at home, and home perspectives

Juline's and Carmen's numeracy histories and uses of numeracy

When Alison asked Carmen whether Kim saw the adults at home using mathematics, she said he would see her, Sit on the table sometimes just writing numbers – that is, showing him how to do it. So her response to the question was in terms of showing numbers to Kim, not her own uses of numeracy. When Alison clarified the question, Carmen said

> Juline use numbers a lot … at home, because she bring work home and sometimes Kim is sitting there.

It was unlikely, since Juline's work was for the Department of Social Services in the field of benefit fraud, that Kim was at all involved in this process, though it meant that he did see his mother using mathematics (see Seth Chapter 4a for discussion of the implications of children 'seeing' those in the home using numeracy). Carmen said that although she used to keep detailed housekeeping accounts, she no longer did so at the time of the research.

> Juline told Alison that she hated maths at school, and we don't know what formal qualifications she had. Despite her professional work in benefit fraud; she professed herself, like Seth's mother, as no good at maths. Alison commented she must have pretty good at maths, and she said it was funny, she'd always done jobs with a lot of maths - a bank, then Corona soft drinks, and now social security. Alison comments that, 'since it's 'funny', the 'mathness' of the jobs was accidental, and we could speculate that she sought employment in office work which then turned out to have a big numeracy component'. As Coben (2000) comments, for many adults their everyday numeracy practices do not 'count' as maths. The maths skills of both Carmen and Juline must have been (in the researcher's terms) considerable: one was a nurse, one worked in benefit fraud. Carmen did regard herself as competent in maths, at least at the levels needed to do household budgeting, work as a nurse and educate primary age children in maths. She had brought up children who were all successful and who all used maths in their work. Juline disliked school maths and didn't see herself as 'really' using it. 'Mathematics' for both of them seemed to be the school subject, rather than what the research team term 'home numeracy practices', which simply didn't figure in their discussion. Maths was very difficult [for Juline at school] but then again they invented the calculator. But I actually do maths longhand. You know I won't use a calculator because it's kind of strange. I hate maths … I hate maths. My brothers are excellent. Especially my middle one, oh my goodness. That was his, that was his thing. but they've actually got it a lot easier than when we were taking exams, because don't forget we had to sit there and do a three, four hour paper. They've actually got projects they can do over a two year stretch and a lot of their marks go on what they've done and they've, the class the what you call it work
>
> Alison: Course work yeh.
>
> Juline: Course work and I'm thinking if I had course work I'd have come out with really flying colours because you know that's the sort of thing I'd be interested in doing. (AT Kim 30th Aug 01)

On the other hand, Juline's mother Carmen had experience of organising and running her own home school in Jamaica, for early years to secondary age, and this had led to her having confidence that she understood how to teach literacy and numeracy in a rather different way. Alison suggests that confidence was challenged by her experiences of working with Kim on his homework, starting during Year1. She initially said there was no difference in numeracy in Jamaican and London education: it's just maths. However, with Kim's homework came a realisation that what he was given at school was very different from her own experience of early years numeracy: the use of words as well as symbols; the use of relationships like more than as well as operations plus or add, for example.

Carmen and Juline's respective experiences with and perceptions of numeracy provide some, at least, of the context in which Kim began to experience numeracy for himself. That context involved also the actual numeracy practices he was exposed to at home.

4b.3. Kim's home numeracy practices

As in any other household, Kim's mother and grandmother timed events, ran their household on a fixed income, prepared food, went shopping These activities were shared by Kim, and it was seen as important (at least by Carmen) that he participate as part of his general upbringing. He did, therefore, take part in activities which (the researchers would say) involved numeracy practices.

Attention to money probably figures as the most obviously numeracy-rich topic in the family's discourse. Juline often mentioned money in Kim's hearing. Although he seemed himself (in Year1) to have little immediate idea of how much money he had, and did not recognise coins, money was important in the household's discourse. One cannot, however, simply address the numeracy dimension of money without also taking into account the values and meanings associated with it, in this case the moral frame (cf Walkerdine,).In Kim's context, the adults commented with disapproval on Juline's brothers' apparently overly money-centred way of life; similarly Carmen criticised younger nurses for working for money rather than as a commitment to their job.

In terms of practices, Juline's accounts of what she had done for Kim included the cost. Commenting on her intention to employ a private tutor for Kim, she said:

> So that means I'm going to have to throw money after somebody to be teaching my child when I think the school system's failing me.

The family had moved from comparatively poor financial circumstances in one generation, and both adults now worked in demanding and tiring jobs. There was now no question of Kim going short of toys or of educational support because of financial cost, but equally Juline was not casual about the costs of bringing up Kim. 'Throwing money' after a private tutor suggests that there are other demands for that money; Juline was conscious of conflicting needs, and resentful of spending money which should be available for other demands, and of spending money if Kim did not then value and use what she had bought for him.

In Reception, Kim already had £12 of his own money, accumulated in pocket money from his mother and an uncle. However, he didn't himself know how much he had; his grandmother told Alison about it. In Year1 she asked Kim how much money he had [AT Ta 14th Feb 01]. He said £20, but under Carmen's questioning that turned out to be a reference to a £20 note, of which he had three.   With prompting from his grandmother, he said it was £60.   He mentioned videos and a robot as what he could get with his money. However, at that time he was not sure of the names of all coins and could not himself count up his money. He had a sense of the value of money in the general way of the more you've got the more you can buy – but, the researcher felt, little more detailed than that.

Carmen said [AT Ta 14th Feb 01] when Kim went shopping with her, she might give him a pound to hand to the shopkeeper for sweets, tell him what change to expect and ask him to check it. But the meaning of 'check' here was unclear. According to Alison, he did not, for example, know the values of most coins, so 'check' may have meant that Carmen told him what he had received and whether it was right. By Year 1, Kim himself had a comparatively large amount of money (£60), but in detail still had little knowledge of how much it would buy, and did not himself spend it. Rather, he received it from adults and then it was looked after by adults. The context, as we saw with Seth, informs a child's attention to the numeracy dimension of everyday practices in ways that may tell on their school experience of numeracy but may not be immediately recognisable in the classroom.

Apart from money, Alison says that she saw almost nothing that we could identify as 'purely' home numeracy practices, though she saw numeracy pedagogy in the home, and had discussions about what numeracy went on in the home around TV and video. Kim had some videos of his own, and was allowed half an hour video time as a 'bribe' to get him to do homework (in Carmen's account: she said he did it for her without bribing).

Juline commented on Kim's noticing of numbers, and for her this seemed to be evidence of his developing numeracy - that is, it was not something she had particularly fostered as a way for him to develop number understanding, but something she was pleased to see happening. Alison asked Juline about this.

> Juline said: One time I came… [you or Carmen] said that … when [Kim] was going round the supermarket he was …noticing things like this pack of crisps that's got six in or something like that.

> Juline: Yeh he does.

> Alison : Do you think he's … generally noticing numbers like that?

> Juline: I think so, because I mean he notices door numbers. He'll walk down the road and he'll look at the door numbers and …do you know what, he doesn't just say one or two of them, he walks down this road and he calls out every single one of them. … He looks at the door numbers of every one of them. I think oh gosh! …He was coming home from school one evening and em one of my mates said hello Kim, [and he said] well I can't talk to you now I'm counting. [End of Year 1 date ref]

These accounts of home numeracy practices remain, however, tantalising few and, as we shall see below in discussing home/ school relations, Kim's carers mainly focus on home numeracy in terms of its similarity to and contribution to success in schooled numeracy. Before exploring this relationship further, however, we need firstly to attend to what counted as school numeracy for Kim.

4b.4. Kim at school, and school perspectives

Teachers, both Marilyn in Reception and Dylan in Year1, commented on the frequency of Kim's absences. He was absent for colds, for toothache, for bereavement, and for the anniversary of a bereavement. On one home visit, mid week, Kim was at home having recovered from a cold. His grandmother, Carmen, said he would not go to school for the rest of the week: there was no point, since the following week was a half term holiday. Kim's relationship with school was affected by these absences, which school staff saw as part of the 'indulgence' they ascribed to Juline and Carmen. His teachers, and the Head, all at some stage commented on his being 'indulged' and having 'two women' (his mother and grandmother) doing everything for him. Although this may mean he was used to talking with adults it didn't do much for his mathematics, according to Marilyn:

> But it just boils down to the fact that he's lazy really. He's just not motivated to numbers, letters or anything, he just doesn't care ... I mean, you just have to find very practical ways for him to do things, and just make sure he's kept on task as much as possible... Which is OK for this year, because he can do lots of physical and practical things, but as from next year he is going to have to knuckle down and he will have to put more on paper, and as they get older, the more they can put on paper, that's how they show really, their ability, there's less and less opportunity for them to show it practically and physically. [AT Marilyn interview 22 Oct 00]

Marilyn's class included the use of 'practical and physical' objects in numeracy (counting dinosaurs, for example), in which Kim was not engaged; the 'practical and physical' things she is referring to included construction and playground games. Juline later made a related observation, distinguishing between 'theory' and 'practical' activities at school (discussed below).

In Reception Kim seemed barely to respond to the overt demands of school discourse. He looked 'unfocused': when sitting on the carpet, for example, he might look in the direction of the teacher but not appear to take in what she said, or follow actions. So, in action songs involving finger counting, he would only sometimes attempt the actions, and would be behind the majority of the children in the class – a sort of delayed reaction. When working with number fans in one lesson, the Special Educational Needs (SEN) support teacher, Vera, sat behind him and held the fan for him, essentially doing everything for him. This meshes in school discourse with the view of Kim as a child who has things 'done for him', who 'doesn't have to think for himself'. In Reception it was clear, the researcher thought, that the Teaching Assistant (TA) (Cheryl) and to some extent Vera, the Special Educational Needs Co-Ordinator (SENCO), were 'doing things for him'.

This applied to all the classroom activities she observed in Reception, apart from one session when the children were asked to draw a picture of something they had done in the holiday (see Chapter 6). Kim drew a picture of his family at a recent family christening. It showed about fifteen people, and he started telling the researcher in exact detail the name and family relationship of each person. He was interrupted in this by Cheryl, who the researcher judged was embarrassed by one of the children being so boring to the researcher We infer from this that there may be topics on which Kim may be more talkative than he usually appears in school – he was usually silent, particularly when with an adult in the classroom.

The school activities Kim engaged in with enthusiasm in Reception and Year1 all involved construction toys. He made a big (about a metre long) jointed model which for some time was on display in the classroom; he told Alison the things he enjoyed at school were playing with bricks, toys and models, although she had not seen any construction toys in Kim's home. By Year 2, she reports, he had more friends (three boys) and joined them sometimes at the computer, though the others seemed to be in control both of the mouse and of the choice of programme.

In Year1 Kim seemed to Alison, on the three occasions she saw him in the classroom, to be at least for a few minutes at a time engaged in the 'carpet' sessions on numeracy. Dylan, the teacher, would ask Kim to sit at the front, near him, in order to 'help him concentrate'. Dylan's whole-class work was, according to Alison, dramatic and stylish and she suggests it may be that this influenced Kim.. In small group work Kim still tended to do nothing of the task until a teaching assistant worked directly with him. He sometimes put his head on the table and appeared to sleep.

All the teachers remarked on Kim's lack of engagement in school numeracy, though in the latter part of Year1 and in Year2 Katrina and Dylan agreed with Alison when she commented that he seemed far more engaged in whole class work than in individual work. Vera, the Special Educational Needs Co-Ordinator (SENCO), however, continued to comment on the 'poverty' of his language, and compared him unfavourably with another child getting additional SEN help, who 'tried' more.

During Year1 and Year2 Kim seemed to be more engaged in whole class teaching at the start of the numeracy lesson. By Year2 Kim was more engaged, both in whole class work on the carpet, and in the individual work set. One explanation for this might be that at the end of Year1 Juline had got a private tutor for Kim. She knew of one who lived in a satellite town (about 40 minutes away) but meanwhile had asked at the school:

> I work too hard I you know [to do much with Kim on school work], I know my shortcomings ... I can't do it. And em as it is at the moment, since I can't do it there's professionals out there who can you know....I'll pay them to do it for me. So that doesn't make me feel so bad if - You know he needs to, he needs to do it. He just needs that little bit more. His concentration span is so bad. He won't concentrate on anything. I don't know if it's his age. I've noticed the fact that sometimes he can't actually see the board because he won't wear his glasses. Or just that he's bored ... Well I spoke to 'Dylan' about it and 'Morag' [the Head Teacher]and they ... they said that a couple of teachers in the school actually do the tutoring and they'd get back to me. ... So I've got to have this all in place in the next couple of weeks. ... It's got to be done.(AT Kim Home 9 May 00)

By the end of Year2 Kim's classroom relationships had changed. In Reception, and early in Year1, he had seemed closed off from relationships, whether friendly or antagonistic, with other children as well as with teachers. By the end of Year2 Dylan saw improvements in Kim's motivation:

> What I'm noticing with Kim now is that if he's near certain children he will be, he will sit and he won't work. If he's near other children who don't disrupt him he will actually get on with his work... kid has been near him he just hasn't done any work. He loses his motivation very easily. (AT Dylan Interview 12 June.02)

Like Juline, Dylan attributed some of the increased engagement in mathematics to the private tutoring and he later regretted the fact that it had stopped.

4b.5. Home and School Relationships

As we saw in attempting to describe Kim's home numeracy practices, his carers' main concerns with numeracy were focused upon what they perceived as necessary for successful schooling. They paid particular attention to formal homework and, as we have seen, Juline eventually paid for additional private tuition at school. Street & Street (1991) suggest that, with respect to literacy, such domination of home practices by those of school is part of a broader pattern that has emerged in many western countries in the past century, which they refer to as the 'schooling of literacy'. They ask:

> Amongst all of the different literacies practiced in the community, the home and the workplace, how is it that the variety associated with schooling has come to be the defining type, not only to set the standard for other varieties but to marginalise them, to rule them off the agenda of literacy debate? Nonschool literacies have come to be seen as inferior attempts at the real thing, to be compensated for by enhanced schooling' (Street & Street, 1991, p. 143).

Their hypothesis in response to this question is:

> That the mechanism through which meanings and uses of literacy take on this role is the 'pedagogisation' of literacy. By this we mean that literacy has become associated with educational notions of Teaching and Learning and with what teachers and pupils do in schools, at the expense of the many other uses and meanings of literacy evident from the comparative ethnographic literature. We use 'pedagogy' not in the narrow sense of specific skills and tricks of the trade used by teachers but in the broader sense of institutionalised processes of teaching and learning, usually associated with school but increasingly identified in home practices associated with reading and writing. Whether we are observing parent-child interactions, the development of educational toys and software in the home, or the procedures associated with classroom learning, 'pedagogy' in this sense has taken on the character of an ideological force controlling social relations in general and conceptions of reading and writing in particular' (Street & Street, 1991, p. 144).

This volume has raised the question of whether and how the findings of literacy research and theory can be applied to the numeracy field (see Chapter 3). The arguments above about pedagogisation seem to offer one such environment for pursuing this question. Might we observe a similar process with respect to numeracy, whereby a pedagogised view of numeracy becomes the standard for judging what counts as numeracy beyond school and where home numeracy practices become subjected to the ideological force of schooled numeracy? The data we have presented from Kim has already indicated ways in which this may be so.

Kim's carers have appeared to 'count' as numeracy only those practices that are associated with schooling, despite their own evident engagement in workplace numeracy practices. And Alison's close field accounts of their attention to numeracy with respect to Kim appear to show them turning home numeracy likewise towards the purposes and styles of schooling. We provide some necessarily brief illustrations of this, but use the Kim example as a potential case study for at least raising these questions with respect to numeracy and in particular the relationship between home and school numeracy practices.

Once case from Alison's notes potentially links literacy and numeracy in the home. Carmen put up a poster with an alphabet with a picture and word for each letter (e.g. an apple, for A), and numerals written below the alphabet. She described to Alison teaching Kim to memorise the names of letters and their associated word, and said she and Juline both read to him. However, Alison comments that 'there seems to be no equivalent activity around numbers. She sang to me a children's song she has taught to Kim, which includes counting up to 3 – but she mentioned it only because I asked'.

One example shows the researcher also drawn in to schooled numeracy discourse in the home. On one of Alison's visits (AT Kim 14 Feb. 2001) Carmen asked Kim to write out numbers on a piece of paper. He had a list of numbers, from 1 to about 50, written out in a new exercise book, bought on holiday in Canada, which he was to memorise. While Carmen and Alison talked, Kim started writing out numbers. This is an extract from her notes and tape transcript (speech in italics; Alison's comments/notes in regular script):

Kim asked: Grandma what comes after 9? She says 10, you did that already. I look at his paper: he's up to 19, so I say that was 19, and tell him it's 20 next.

Carmen says: 2 and oh is 20. He writes 2 and 0, but they appear as 02 because he's reached the right hand side of the page and is now writing his next line snake-form, right to left.

Kim: And he can do it you know, come on write 20. - and write 2 and a 1.

Kim: I'm on twenty-one! (I think meaning that he shouldn't be writing 2, 1 the numbers are too small). Carmen Two in front and a 1 behind. Kim says 22. Carmen You write 2 and 2. I think she's telling Kim more than he needs, and he eventually does one by himself when I say Can you do it by yourself? I bet you can... and read out numbers so far stressing the units, 22 23, 24. I rewrite the numbers in a left to right line. He reads 20 as 22, but is then ok at reading them. He asks her [Carmen] how to do 24 and she tells him. He gets 25 by himself after I say can you do it without asking anyone? Just have a go. He gets 26, 27, 28, 29, by himself. Carmen claps and says He can do it. He suggests 21 as next number, but when I say no, says 30 without prompting. I suggest he looks at 20 to see what 30 would be, but he can't do it. I write it for him. I ask if he can make up 31, and remind him what 21 was like. Carmen tells him to take out his exercise book You can always remember what you write despite me saying to her He might be able to work it out. Kim gets out the exercise book from holiday in Canada, and keels over on the floor apparently fast asleep (AT Kim 14th Feb .01)

Likewise, disciplinary practices at home were geared to his school achievement. His mother sometimes used video and Playstation time as bribes, at least to get Kim to do homework. But it seemed also that 'book work' - the 'theory part' that Juline believed he disliked - might be threatened as a form of punishment: when Kim once interrupted a conversation she said to him

> "Kim do you know something right? You're going to get punished today. That means no tea for you, no playstation, nothing apart from book work if you continue in this vein!" ... (AT Kim 14th Feb .01)

Similarly, good things will only come to Kim after he has gone through the barrier of literacy and numeracy. He tried on Alison's motorbike helmet:

> Juline: You look like a spaceman!
>
> Kim: I want to be a biker boy!
>
> Juline: You want to be a biker boy?
>
> Kim: No I want to be a spaceman!
>
> Juline: You want to be a spaceman? But you've got to learn to read and write first and do your maths. So come on! (AT Kim 14th Feb .01)

Although as we saw above the school saw using the internet as suitable home work, Juline used computer access as part of her system of managing Kim. In the Reception year she had said she wanted a computer for Kim, before he reached the Key Stage 1 tests - that is, as a contribution to his education. At the end of Year1, when the family had a computer, she said (in Kim's hearing, so this comment itself was a contribution to disciplining him),

> "I haven't even taught him how to use [it] yet. Because he won't do things I want him to do so until he does that he won't use it. If he gets like this and then he expects me to appreciate his behaviour". (AT Kim 14th Feb .01)

On the other hand, Juline (after describing a teacher whom she criticised for shouting at the children) said she does not take the 'hard' approach to getting Kim to do homework:

> "With Kim I can't be bothered with the hard approach, it's like I don't want him to hate reading, I don't want him to hate school". (AT Kim 30th August 01)

Juline was concerned, as we have seen, for Kim to do well at school and at the end of Year1, she said

> "It is a bit hard, ... it is hard but I you know next week it's the new year and I'm going to have to be a lot stronger on him". (AT Kim 10th May 00)

Juline, then, like many mothers, was struggling with what she saw as conflicting demands: her lack of time, her wish for Kim to enjoy school and, a wariness of being too 'hard' on him but a determination that he should succeed.

Carmen showed Alison Kim's homework for one week (AT Kim 14 Feb. 2001). The single hand-written A4 sheet had some anagrams of animal names for the child to write out correctly. The instructions said the answers were 'hidden' (around the border), but Carmen had not noticed that until Alison looked at the sheet with her;

almost all the anagram answers were completed in her handwriting, not Kim's. The numeracy work was questions that took the form One more than three or Four more than three. Carmen had helped Kim rewrite them in the form $1 + 3 =$ in his exercise book, and there Kim had written the answers. Carmen was critical of the homework:

> Carmen: It a bit hard for Kim.

> Alison: Yeh, have you talked to Mr Chadwick about it being hard?

> Carmen: No, I won't tell him. Because he's a teacher, I don't have to tell him. I used to teach small kids back home, you know, used to teach before I come here. [...] This is too much for Kim. (AT Kim 14th Feb .01)

Carmen had run a 'home school' in Jamaica, taking children up to the age of 11. We take 'I don't have to tell him' to mean 'I shouldn't have to tell him'. An implication is that Carmen did not trust the school's teaching approach; but she had considerable respect for teachers and would be unlikely directly to criticise them. Carmen's own discomfort with arithmetic questions written out in words (e.g. three for 3, and more than for +) led her, in order to 'make them fit' with her own education and mathematics discourse, to represent them as traditional arithmetic. The worksheet's use of words for numbers reflects a change in British schools, and was probably unfamiliar in Carmen's own experience as a teacher.

Juline understood that Carmen's and the school's approaches were dissimilar and she wanted to be more closely involved herself. During Year1 she said she intended taking over from Carmen the main role in supporting Kim's homework and attending parents' meetings at the school; So, we turn now to Juline's relationship with Kim's schooling.

Juline offers one explanation for Kim's underachievement as lying in the distinction between theory and practice, a position we saw above also adopted by some of his teachers. She tells Alison:

> "He don't mind running around and doing practical things - like cooking. But it's the theory, he hates theory". (AT Kim 30th August 01)

In Juline's view, the way to engage Kim in literacy and numeracy would be to make it more stimulating. She compared Kim's school experience to her own responses to boring training courses:

> :No I find that when you get somebody like Kim he gets bored very easily so they've got to stimulate him. He's a bit like me in that sense because I mean training courses at work I'll be the first one to fall asleep. If I'm bored that's it, if I'm not interested that is it. So they need to stimulate him a bit more". (AT Kim Home Visit 30th August 01)

Juline believed children should start their schooling, including literacy and numeracy, as young as possible so that children learn early on what it involves and come to enjoy it:

> "You know get the basic, fundamental stuff out the way first, you know learn to read". (AT Kim Home Visit 30th August 01)

The 'basics' for Juline are the academic basics - reading, writing and arithmetic. This seemed to be an area of difference with the view of one of the teachers, Dylan who argued that some children should not be pushed too soon. Alison asked (in Year2) about the changes Dylan had seen in Kim:

> Alison: And do you think it is just kind of developmental, that he's getting older and he's changing because … kids do?

> Dylan: I think it's a lot to do with it. I think it's a lot to do with it. I mean when you think in some countries they don't start school till they're seven anyway, so I mean we do push children often before they're ready you know. And I think it's a fine line … Children do need pushing. And … there is a point at which children do need to be ready for things [untrans] on the other hand, but you know you actually have to take an active role, you can't wait around. But on the other hand I do think you have to be aware that some children just aren't ready for certain things. … There are certain children, I do tend to think Kim is one of them, who sometimes he's just not ready. But on the other hand you know, no disrespect to Kim – I hate to use the word – but he can be very lazy sometimes! … You know he just doesn't want to do things. And he needs pushing you know. So it's a question of finding the balance between the two. (AT (AT Dylan Interview 12 June.02)

Like Dylan, Juline struggled to achieve this balance. Partly, her difficulty lay in time pressures. She told Alison:

> "A lot of us [one parent families] actually work full-time. When I drop him off at school I go straight to work and I don't come home until what three hours after he's been home".

> Alison: Yeh. And he's tired by then, and you're certainly tired.

> Juline: Exactly, by the time I've come in my brain is dead. You know the amount of paperwork I do my brain is then dead. And I don't want to see figures or letters, I don't want to see it. I just want to chill out. You know sitting down an hour we talk about what's going on, have a bit of a play. He gets ready for bed. I get something to eat, he's gone to bed. I have my cigarette and a drink and I chill. By that time it's eleven o'clock. So I don't have the time. I mean I'd love to have the time but I haven't got the time. (AT Kim Home Visit 30th August 01)

For the summer holiday, Year 1, Kim had a sheet from school with a list of suggested websites, including Bob the Builder and the BBC's children's sites. But Juline had not checked Kim's bag until the end of the holiday, and he had not tried any of the sites. She commented,

> "They will call me an unfit mother because I've only just discovered certain bits of homework in the bag! I haven't had any time, I haven't had any time". (AT Kim Home Visit 30th August 01)

She had a sense of a partnership between parent and school, with the school failing to deliver its end of the partnership but her own position also at risk of criticism from the school. She sees her ambitions for her son frustrated, and feels that the school system is failing her:

> "They've got the responsibility for educating my child and I think they should be educating my child. And I think they should be doing it a bit better than they're doing it now". (AT Kim Home Visit 30th August 01)

In her desperation for Kim to succeed, Juline was concerned to compensate for the school's inadequacies but work pressures and - the school might add - different conceptions of how children learn, make this difficult. As we shall see in other cases, and develop further in Section IV, middle class parents too attempt to 'compensate' for the school. What the Kim examples shows is that such a process is not simple or obvious – Kim's carers themselves differ as to how the school can be compensated for in terms of numeracy, with Carmen invoking traditional Jamaican methods and Juline perhaps pushing harder than some of Kim's teachers saw as appropriate, whilst at the same time worrying that even when she did attend to the school's agenda she was failing him because of time constraints. To help overcome these problems, she pays for a home tutor, a strategy adopted by many middle class parents, perhaps exacerbated by the recent emphasis on testing (cf Reay and Lucey, 2000). These, then, are the kinds of pressures and contradictions that the pedagogisation of mathematics appear to lead to – as with literacy, in the account by Street and Street, there is an ideological force that so dominates home numeracy that it can almost only be seen through this lens.

4b.6. Commentary: Pedagogies and epistemologies

Many factors swirl around in this story, perhaps most importantly the facts that Kim didn't seem (in Reception and much of 1) engaged with any aspect of schooling apart from spatial and visual creative work, and that he seemed at times unhappy at school. But if we focus on numeracy, the fulcrum seems to be the meaning of mathematics itself, and hence how it should be taught and learned. Special Educational Needs Co-Ordinators and other classroom assistants struggled to help him engage and learn, as did his carers at home: like all of the parents we interviewed, Kim's mother and grandmother were committed to his education and willing to do what they could, within constraints, to facilitate this. But there were considerable differences amongst all of these parties, as well as material constraints: Kim was subjected to a variety of theories of how numeracy is learned. All, however, seemed to agree that schooled numeracy was what 'counts' and paid little attention to out of school numeracy practices. Schooled learning was brought home in a variety of ways whilst his engagement in everyday numeracy practices, whether concerning money, counting door numbers etc was more under his own control but not built upon by his carers, who saw numeracy in terms of schooling and pedagogy. Likewise, on the odd occasions when out of school engagements entered the school, as when Kim offered the researcher an account of family genealogy, he was quickly silenced.

4c ANNE'S STORY AT ROWAN : 'the cupboard had so many games
and puzzles and construction toys that they cannot find the one they want'

4c.1. Setting

The actors in this case study were Anne, her mother Trisha, her father Mick and her
sister Lisa. Anne was at Rowan school (see Chapter 5c) in a 'leafy suburb', south of
London. Anne's teachers at Rowan were Alice (Reception), Freya Andrews (Year
1), and Clemancy (Year 2). Alison was the researcher.

4c.2. Anne and her family

Anne was a child who was happy in school and doing well in school numeracy.
Initially assessed by her school as achieving above average in numeracy, she was
later assessed as average, though her teacher commented that achievement in her
class was at a particularly high level within a generally high-achieving school. Anne
was the elder of two children in a financially comfortable family, living in a large
detached house. Her mother was a child-minder so Anne often spent time with
another, younger child. Both her parents had attended schools in the locality and
gone on to get university degrees. Anne's mother, Trisha, also worked as a volunteer
in the school and, during Anne's second year she helped with reading in Anne's
class.

Trisha described herself as comparatively successful at school mathematics at a
local comprehensive school. She was not confident in mathematics and was
surprised that she had passed O-level mathematics. She described herself as
'struggling', being 'alright with figures', 'ok with algebra' but 'couldn't fathom
geometry'. Anne's father, Mick, worked for an international asset management
company, and Trisha described him as 'good at maths' but he denied that he was
much better than Trisha.

Trisha drew on her own lack of confidence in mathematics to imagine how Anne
may feel: Trisha knew "how it feels when you don't understand something" and "the
feeling of not understanding numbers". Trisha was concerned her own mathematics
may not be good enough to help Anne:

> "My maths is not going to be - my help with maths is going to be very limited... I've
> already told my husband that's his department, maths, anyway, that it isn't going to be
> mine" (AT Anne (Interview 8 Jan. 02)

Gender differences were central to Trisha's descriptions of her girls' progress
and prospects. Trisha saw men and women as thinking differently and that girls
would benefit from being educated separately, (see her views below). There was
also some suggestion that Trisha saw people falling into two broad groups: those
who were interested in, and better at, arts subjects, and those with a mathematical or

scientific bent. She described herself as an arts person. However, she identified Anne as good at both dancing and numeracy.

Trisha worked for some time for a trading company, where her role included organising shipping invoices and pricing goods. Despite this, she did not regard herself as good at 'maths'. More recently she worked as a child-minder, and had training which promoted education through play. Trisha's 'home' and 'work' lives were, for much of her day, indistinguishable; 'play' and 'learning' were similarly closely linked in her view of her own and the activities for the children she minded. She was comfortable in the popular and official discourses of early childhood education. When Anne was in Year 2 Trisha volunteered to help with reading in the class. Trisha said she tended to leave numeracy to the school, though many of the games she played with Anne at home supported schooled numeracy. But both of Anne's parents offered her what might be seen as 'extension' oral numeracy work.

They lived in an affluent area with relatively large homes and tree-lined streets a class composition that was reflected in the school intake. Family's incomes were high and the homes were materially well provided as shown in Anne's home.

4c.3. Home cultural resources, views about education and learning at home and at school

Trisha and Mick knew the area well and used their own knowledge of the local area, local contacts, debates in the public arena and information from school league tables to make their choices for Anne's education. Rowan was not Anne's parents' first choice of school; they had wanted another local school, which was even higher in the local league table of schools. So they agreed with elements of popular and official discourses regarding 'choice' in the education 'market'.

Trisha used a rich range of sources to inform herself about Anne's school life and to place her view of Anne's choices and educational development in a wider context. This contrasted with what we know of Kim's mother at Tarnside and Seth's at Mountford. In both cases the parents' sources of information were only the children, who were not communicative about schooling, and formal meetings with teachers. Trisha drew on formal and informal meetings with teachers, other parents and other local contacts. For example at a parents' meeting about numeracy (AT Ro 10 Feb, 00) she inquired into the school's policy on the use of number lines, referring to what she had heard from a school where fingers were allowed and the use of a number line was discouraged. Anne herself was a rich source of information about her classroom and on occasion this led to critiques of Rowan. Another source was Trisha's awareness of public debates. For example, she knew about homework issues. She said: "Wasn't there something in the paper this week about homework below a certain age is detrimental?"

The parents of other children in Anne's class were a resource for Trisha. For example, Trisha reported parents' discussions in the playground about the ways to help with language and the school's suggestions on reading (AT Anne 29 Sept. 00). Trisha used this as an opportunity to gather information, which might be relevant to Anne. She clearly respected other parents' views. Displays of the children's work in the Rowan classroom was another resource for Trisha enabling her to see Anne's work, and compare it to others. This gave Trisha detailed insights into her daughter's literacy.

Trisha and Mick were immersed in discourses, which informed their stance as critical friends towards the school. They had the personal contacts - other parents, the local networks, Trisha's semi-insider status in the school - and the middle class press on their side in their aim to ensure Anne had the best start.

4c.4. Anne at school

In her first term at school, Anne was seen as 'more able' in numeracy, though later on she was placed in a lower group for numeracy. The Reception class teacher, Alice, when commenting on her ability when she started school, said: "She's got the language, like 'six and four makes ten' ". This may have reflected her playgroup and home experience of numeracy.

Everything we saw of Anne at school suggested that, in general, she was comfortable and happy there and that she enjoyed learning. When puzzled about a new idea or activity in numeracy, her forehead was furrowed, she crossed her arms and sucked her thumb, and when it 'clicked' she beamed, sat up straight and asked for more.

Anne was rarely reluctant to join groups for particular activities; she seemed usually to finish all the activities set for the day, and chose for herself the full range of activities available in the classroom. She worked on activities by herself and was able to concentrate closely, looking absorbed in her chosen activity even when the classroom had many distractions. Anne was someone who had a wide range of friendships in the class and both initiated and joined activities.

4c.5. School Numeracy Events and Practices

Here we briefly describe some of the numeracy events we have seen Anne engaged in at school. Others may be found be in the case study of Rowan (Chapter 5c).

The first of these events was not directly led by a teacher. Here Anne and another girl, Zara, were playing an addition game using two dice on their own. They took turns to throw the dice, then together added up the two numbers and wrote down the two numbers and the total, sharing the same paper, with no element of competition. Anne knew all the numbers on the dice without counting dots. Both used a 'count all' strategy for adding, pointing to the dots as they did so. When Anne totalled two and three to five, and wrote down 2 3 5, Zara said *Excellent*. After Anne had totalled six and six, then counted all to get 12, she said *Six and six always makes 12*. Both girls were playing around with 'teacherly' talk, though they were not 'playing school' (AT Ro 21 Dec, 99). Here they were engaged in learning about abstract number in a somewhat informal but clear school numeracy context. The children seemed to have understood the purpose of the game. In this class, children in general made use of the play opportunities in the classroom as intended by the teacher. The children at Rowan seemed to engage fully in these non-teacher directed activities quite unlike the kinds of disengagement shown by Seth at Mountford and Kim at Tarnside. This is discussed more in chapter 6.

Next we describe in more detail an example out of many similar examples of direct numeracy instruction in Year 1, (AT Ro 19 Sept. 00). This one focused on addition using base 10 apparatus. Anne worked on this activity with the class teacher, Freya. Freya chose the 39 card and Anne put down three sticks (longs) and 10 units, correcting the units when asked to recount. Freya chose the 12 card. Anne put out the sticks and units for 12, grouped the two collections together, counted the units first and got 11. Then she counted the sticks, to 40, then counted on 41, 42 ... 51, that is, she ignored her own finding of 11 units.

Freya If I asked you to make 51, how many sticks of 10 would you expect?

Anne I've got 11 ones.

Freya Can you swap?

Anne did not reply, and looked worried - she slumped in her chair, with her forehead furrowed. Freya, without further comment, gave her a 10; Anne handed over 10 units; counted what she now had, said 51 and beamed with pleasure.

The next cards chosen by Freya were 34 and 36. Anne again looked worried. She put out 34, then 36; sorted them into 10s and units; counted in tens to 60 then in ones, exclaiming 70

Freya How many sticks would there be in 70?

Anne (who has been recounting the sticks of ten) 60! I can take them all away because I've got 10! She held up the units in one hand, above the table.

Freya But then you've only got 60.

Anne Swap them! - and beamed again.

This episode illustrated a typical direct numeracy session for Anne. It lasted about ten minutes, and Anne was able to ask to leave when she was losing interest. Two months later Anne was confidently and cheerfully doing a similar activity, (AT Ro 14 Nov. 00).

It is interesting to note in terms of the research that this was an example of schooled numeracy practice where the purpose of the activity was to teach Anne specific mathematical skills and concepts in an abstract context using dedicated educational tools for numeracy. The teacher was in direct control of the teaching situation although in Rowan unlike Tarnside and Mountford the children were given a level of choice about when and what they do.

A second teacher directed-activity was 'Comparing weights' (AT Ro 26 Sept .01). Here, in Year 2, Anne worked in a group with Perrie, a teaching assistant, comparing the weight of various items to a 1kg weight. The group was in the corridor outside the classroom. On the table in the middle of the group were large balance scales, with a bucket on the end of each arm and a 1kg weight. Each child had a sheet, in three columns, with headings *More than 1kg, Less than kg, About the same as   kg*. The children passed round in turn a book, a hole punch, and headphones. All the children guessed the items were lighter than 1kg, and as Perrie put them in the bucket and compared them to 1 kg, and found they were right, they all cheered. Perrie checked they understood by asking each a question, *Tell me something that's lighter than a kilogram.* Anne seemed to be enjoying herself. These scales were similar to those used by Anne for her weighing activity at home (see below).

So here was a girl who was enjoying her school life in general and numeracy in particular, and whose steady progress seemed set to continue. She loved it when she was successful and persisted when she was not; her play and formal lessons apparently seamlessly merge. We turn next to Anne's home life.

4c.6. Anne's home numeracy events and practices

In this section we will describe numeracy events that Alison saw in the home or that Anne's mother Trisha chose to show Alison. These included activities that had an explicit and direct link to Anne's school numeracy such as weighing whilst in others such as the playing of Junior Monopoly the link to school numeracy was more incidental. We describe both of these below together with a game, which involved money. Alison also saw events such as reading analogue clocks, and many others which we do not have space to deal with in detail in this book. However, what has emerged among other things from this home was the way that Anne's mother, Trisha, was able to recognise numeracy in activities she did with Anne. She used many of the events to exploit their potential for Anne to learn about numeracy that fitted with Anne's life in school and at home. Many of these activities would in our view contribute directly to Anne's development of numeracy in ways that were congruent with the school's practices.

The first one we have selected involved Trisha and the children showing Alison how they do weighing (AT Anne 6 May. 00).. Trisha had new but 'old fashioned' balance scales with a needle pointer and with individual 'imperial' weights. This was an unusual activity as the scales were more for show than practical use but Trisha exploited them for an activity which to the children was enjoyable and which had an educational edge. Trisha usually used spoons and cups for measurement in cooking, and the imperial weights were not useful for metric recipes. Trisha suggested that Anne and her sister weighed biscuits. Trisha started by putting a quarter ounce weight on the balance. Anne put a biscuit on the other side and said it was 'balanced'. When asked in the dialogue below how this related to weighing in school, Anne described a school numeracy event when weighing 1 kg. toy animals at school (see above). Anne seemed to have managed well at school, perhaps because of these experiences at home. It was not clear that she explicitly understood relationships between the school and the home scales but it seemed that at school Anne in some sense drew on knowledge from home:

> Alison: Have you got scales in the kitchen here? Was it similar to scales here or different ones?

Anne: Ones at school.

Alison: Right. And do the two sides go up and down?

Anne: Yeh.

Alison:So what's it like when it's balanced then?

Anne: The arrow has to be in the middle.

Trisha: A bit like mine then. She does know. […] (AT Interview Anne 14 May 01)

In school and at home the purpose of weighing was not practical in the sense of necessary. It was not, for example, related to cookery. So in both contexts the purpose was to learn about weighing. The notable difference arose from the available equipment. The big scales at school meant it was possible to compare bulky, heavier items to both a 1kg weight and to each other. Trisha was reproducing at home as closely as she could with her knowledge and equipment the activities she expected Anne to be engaged in at school.

The second was about playing games. Anne's household had many games and these were part of her home's cultural and physical resources. Anne played games with her mother and younger sister and with older cousins including matching games like monopoly, snap or a shopping game (see below). Though many of the games were not overtly educational, Trisha was conscious of their potential use in children's learning and noticed the children using new knowledge. For example, Trisha commented after Anne had been playing *Junior Monopoly*:

> She suddenly knows £8, five, a one and a two, or two threes and a two to make eight, because she had to pay you £8. She soon worked it out, three and three is six and two is eight. It's very small numbers but it's amazing how quickly - a lot of children her age can't cope with going round the board and the money. (AT Anne 26 Jan. 01)

Trisha used the game as a vehicle for asking Anne to count in twos, threes and fives, using the play money,

> Trisha: Can you make 12 with 3s, Anne?
>
> Anne: Oh yeh I can. Well these 3s go like you've got 3, and 3 makes 6, and another 3 will make 9, and another three make (.) 12. With that it makes (.) 15.
>
> Trisha; [to Alison] I didn't know she could do 3s. [to Anne] Can you count in fives?
>
> Anne: (quickly) 5 10 15 20 25
>
> Trisha: Did you do that in school?
>
> Anne: No, you taught me! (AT Anne 26 Jan. 01)

Anne seemed to be working out the threes quickly in her head as she went along, whereas the fives were a recitation from memory. When she tried counting up how much money she had in £5 notes, she went astray:

Anne :5 and 5 make ten, so I've got 10 here, and another 5 take away -

Trisha:No no no you're not taking take away you're adding up.

Anne:That makes 17.

Trisha:5, 10, remember? [5, 10 said rhythmically to remind Anne]

Anne:15. That's 20, 25, 30.

Trisha:Very good!, (AT Anne 26 Jan. 01)

School and home ways of learning numbers seemed to closely correspond. If Anne slipped up, her mother helped her by returning to ground on which Anne was familiar. This was typical of Trisha's approach, praising her children's achievements, and using their interest to extend their knowledge.

Next is an example of Trisha using a game as an opportunity for learning about money - though the exchange was extended by Alison asking a question, Anne and Trisha then engaged in it and Trisha referred to Anne's previous knowledge. The game was one in which each player was both a shopkeeper and a shopper. Players threw a die to move towards a shop, where they 'bought' goods, with plastic money, from the 'shop keeper': the winner was the one who bought the most, rather than the one with the most money at the end. Trisha said: if she hasn't won but she's got lots of money we count the money up.

Trisha asked Anne: How much money have you got, can you see how much money you've got there?

Anne: A hundred and twenty.

Trisha: What's that, two fifties and what did you have?

Anne: Two tens.

Alison: So what's that in pounds?

Trisha: What's that in pounds?

Anne: One hundred and twenty pounds.

Trisha: No it's not a hundred and twenty pounds, it's pennies isn't it.

Anne: Oh yeh.

Trisha: Fifty, two fifty pences make? Two fifty pences make?

Anne: A hundred!

Trisha: Which is how many pounds?

Anne: A hundred?

Trisha: No it's not, it's one pound isn't it. [to Alison] She knows! She knows because she's given me [when 'buying' goods in the game] like for one pound ten she's given me two fifty pees haven't you for a pound. The two fifty pees are a pound aren't they. [...] Here 'Anne' let's see if you can count mine up into how many pounds there are. One pound yeh. It's not pounds it's pennies isn't it.

Anne: I know!

Trisha: Alright then.

Anne: I've got a hundred pee.

Trisha: That's one pound there isn't it, fifty and fifty. Twenty, forty, sixty

Anne: I wanna do it on my own!

Trisha: Alright you do it then.

...

Trisha: Shall I tell you a quick way of sorting out your

Anne: Ah ee em [untrans] I'm fine.

Trisha: [Anne had picked up more coins to add to her two fifty pence pieces and two ten pence pieces.]. Yes but you've got your [untrans] there so you're going to get, give me your fifty. Because you'll get confused. Give me the fifty. Now that's a pound there isn't it.

Anne: I know!

Trisha: And you need to make up another pound there [Anne was now holding more than £1] don't you. And how would you make another pound? Fifty, sixty, what would you do to make another pound? What would you put with those two coins? ... Eighty and what else do you need next? Like that? Is that another pound? We'll leave it I think, shall we leave it?

Anne: I didn't understand what you were saying anyway.

Trisha: Didn't you? Oh it doesn't matter then, leave it then. Doesn't matter. (AT Anne Interview 8 Jan. 02)

Anne's initial answer of 120 was both physically (the coins were muddled) and metaphorically lost in this exchange. It may be that Trisha wanted me to see that Anne could indeed count money in pounds and pence (*She knows!*), or that, Anne having muddled her coins, Trisha then carried on with the coins to hand rather than the original 120p in order for Anne to have the chance to get the right answer - but Alison's and Trisha's question, *What's that in pounds?* was not answered. Anne's cries of *I know!*, said twice, and *I'm fine*, reflect her prior confidence with the toy money and perhaps her irritation at what might be felt as exposure, so *I know!* means also *Leave me alone.*

Trisha's exploitation of opportunities for learning is typical. When it was clear Anne was not going to be successful, she tried modeling the task for Anne and avoided direct instruction (*like that? Is that another pound?*). Trisha's use of questions rather than direct instruction is typical of much teacherly discourse. It may well contribute to Anne feeling comfortable in school. Trisha then abandoned it: *We'll leave it I think, shall we leave it?* and thus avoided what might develop into Anne's failing. Anne was then able to say *I didn't understand what you were saying anyway* - contradicting *I know!* but also implying that some of her difficulty was caused by Trisha not being clear. Rather than defending herself or trying again, Trisha both accepted what Anne said and left the topic.

4c.7. Home and school relationships

In this section we describe how home and school relationships impact on or were influenced by Anne's school life. We start by looking at teaching and learning issues, choice of secondary schooling, homework, access and communication and finally conflicts between home and school.

4c.7.1. Teaching and learning issues.

Rowan, as will be described in Chapter 5c, had a strong belief in encouraging children to develop as individuals and to become confident members of a community.

> Trisha said: I think [the Head] tries to foster that sense of the school as a community. … and a lot of people who are going to help, then they seem to end up working in the school anyway. (AT Anne Interview 8 Jan. 02)

Trisha in that interview seemed to value the more formal aspects of the national curriculum and testing. Yet Rowan rejected some of those values and did not follow the national literacy or numeracy strategies at key stage 1. But Trisha also valued a rounded education for children but did not see that as tied to the school's particular pedagogic strategies. She commented that the Head:

> "thinks they learn reading and writing by osmosis. She'd be surprised if she knew how many parents used reading schemes at home".

Both Anne's parents aimed to 'stretch' her and continued the work she did at school, but stopped when she became bored or frustrated. Trisha described trying to stretch Anne by saying for example *What's 40 plus 2 plus 2?*, and if Anne looked puzzled, she would ask *What's 2 plus 2?* and when Anne got 4, Trisha would go back to *What's 40 plus 4?* Trisha commented:

> I don't really do it [systematic numeracy work] with her at home now, because she's doing it at school she doesn't really want to. When she's learned something new, she's so excited, and we practise in the car [on the way home]. I tried to practise in the car [today], and unfortunately she got one wrong, and then she got very cross, and then that's the opportunity gone. I didn't actually say she was wrong, I said are you sure

that's the answer, and she said yes she was sure. So I tried to get her to go back to it a different way, and once she realised she'd got it wrong, then she just sulked. (AT Anne Interview 8 Jan. 02)

This is an example of Trisha's use of teacherly discourse: scaffolding from secure knowledge (*what's 2 plus 2?*) and avoiding direct negatives *(I didn't actually say she was wrong)* for example. Trisha here had aimed at building on Anne's school success, but the situation, the apparatus and social relations, were not the same as those at school.

Next we focus on some of the similarities between classroom and home numeracy discourses to further illustrate the seamlessness of Anne's home and school lives. Trisha observed and described Anne's numeracy techniques with an awareness of potential for formal educational development. For example, she reported that Anne was getting good at adding up to 10 using her fingers, saying she was not 'efficient' at it: 'She counts three fingers and then seven fingers, but she doesn't know you can just count on from three' (that is, Anne used a 'count all' strategy) (AT Anne 6 May. 00). This is one of the markers used by teachers for assessing children's progress. Trisha remembered a talk at Rowan from an outside speaker on numeracy, who said that if children learn that two add four is six, they will learn also that 2000 add 4000 is 6000; she commented that it was not worth trying that with Anne yet because she did not yet 'really understand big numbers'. Similarly, she judged games and comics against Anne's own knowledge, rather than accepting the advertised age suitability, for example, 'Numbers in comics only go up to 10; she's got a bit past that' (AT Anne 6 May. 00)

Trisha was, therefore, analytical both about what was involved in numeracy and about Anne's responses to her parents' efforts. Her understanding and description of Anne's learning of numeracy, and her own teaching of number, were discursively similar to those of Anne's teachers. Most of Anne's numeracy development at home, as recounted by her mother, had revolved around her parents' continuation of what Anne reported of school numeracy, and around board and other games. The specifically educational commercial resources we saw in use in the home included texts and a clock. These fell into a category somewhere between educationally designed books and informal household practices. Features of these included: overtly 'educational' design, that is, users were intended to think they would help child at school as well as 'in life'; they were not provided by the school; they required parents'/carers' presence; their use or at least purchase was led by parents/carers, not the child; and they demanded a particular time slot. It was likely that Anne had been involved in domestic numeracy practices, like Kay's (see Chapter 5a) table laying or which supported numeracy development, but educational resources in Anne's home were the type of game or text that were taken, in parents' minds, to fit dominant features of the discourse of 'school numeracy' at home. Certainly they featured in government and school discourses of appropriate home numeracy development.

Trisha was keen to spend time supporting Anne's education and intellectual development. It was part of being Anne's mother. Trisha was a working mother, which included mothering, and mothering incorporated educational practices. The borders between 'play' and 'education', and the borders between home and school, were blurred for Anne, as she 'played' and 'learnt' in both sites.

Trisha was determined that Anne should have a broad education at primary school, and was doubtful whether Rowan, which claimed an unusually wide syllabus and child-centred ethos, achieved all it claims. But we should note too that Trisha felt she knew the head's perspective on these issues; that mother-teacher relations involved compromises, and that the two were engaged in a joint project.

4c.7.2. Choice of secondary school

Despite Anne being younger than 7 years old during the project, Trisha was concerned with Anne's access to secondary school and discussed how a private tutor might help this. She felt that if Anne had the ability for an academic school, then Trisha would consider a private tutor to help her get into one of the local private schools. She said:

> and if she's academic it's a bit of a, I just think it is a bit of a waste sending her to [a comprehensive] school. [...] I think she'll do better in a more academic school. (AT Anne 8 Jan. 02)

In Trisha's view one of the advantages of a private school would be the greater element of choice of subjects. Another would be avoiding drugs problems at a local comprehensive school. She would also prefer a girl's only school arguing on the basis of her own experience, backed up by public and official education discourses:

> I think it's a shame because I think what it's been proved that girls do better if they're educated separately. And I think, and boys do better if they educated with girls. [...] And the thing is also I think because boys and girls do learn differently and think differently. But I think there are more benefits to be obtained from educating them separately because I think that [...] at University [...], men and women don't think the same way. So I think educating them separately's a good thing. (AT Anne 8 Jan. 02))

4c.7.3. Homework

Trisha did not, during the research period, want Anne to have more homework and was pleased that at Rowan they did not get as much as at other schools. In fact she had no numeracy homework but went to the French club at the school and to ballet and tap classes. Trisha said:

> "Well I think, to be honest they're so tired when they come out of school, they're really not ready to do work. (AT Anne 5 Apr. 00))

4c.7.4 Home and school relations communication and access

In this section we look at direct discussions with school staff and Trisha's work as a volunteer in the school, and then consider an educational conflict between the family and the school.

At the first parents' evening in the school, Trisha seemed to value not only the teacher's view of Anne's ability and progress, but also her view of what Anne was like as a person. The feeling that Trisha and the teacher were talking about the same child - *Yes, that's Anne!* - was as important as academic comments.

Trisha attended meetings at the school, both parents evenings and briefings for parents, whenever possible and was concerned when she could not make meetings. The formal parents' evenings were central to Trisha's confidence in the school and Anne's learning:

> I did go to the parents' evening. It was a bit strange because [...] they don't tell you very much. But Miss Andrews *[Year1 class teacher]* did say that [Anne] is [...] in the top 10 [in numeracy]. But she said the maths standard in the class was very high [...] she said probably [Anne] would be higher but she's not as quick as some of them are at maths. But she said she was good at maths. (AT Anne 5 Apr. 00)

Although Trisha believed the school was, as it claimed to be, 'accessible' to parents, she only partly succeeded in getting the quality of information she wanted.

When in Year 1, Anne repeatedly asked Trisha to do voluntary work with the school but Trisha was too busy. This suggested that Anne did not seek to separate out her school and home lives. This contrasted with Mountford where there was a distinct distance between the home and the school. Part way through Anne's Year 2, Trisha volunteered to help with reading in Anne's class. She used this to encourage Anne to read at home and in order to be able to compare Anne's achievements with other children.

4c.7.5. Conflict with the school: religious education

Despite Trisha's skills in informing herself about Anne's schooling and the school's policy of open access to parents, a gulf did develop between the home and the school which the family were unable to resolve. This focussed on religious education where the family's and the school's beliefs about relationships between humans and animals were radically different. The teacher's view that humans were animals was incredible to the family:

> Trisha: Last week Anne came home and said '[the teacher] said we are animals.' I said 'Well we are not'. 'I know we are not', she said. And she couldn't understand it. [...]. Anne's obviously got this thing when we've learnt about it in church, that we talk about animals and we talk about man being made separate. If you are going to say we are animals it puts you into the thing of saying that we've evolved from animals. Which we are not, you see [...] and she's right, Anne's right. (AT Anne Interview 14 May 01)

The school and home were presenting conflicting 'facts' to Anne, and she noticed the conflict and reported it to her mother. It seemed likely that though the Head was aware of the conflict, the class teacher was not, or chose to ignore it. It was Trisha's belief that her daughter was being taught untruths, and she tried and failed to prevent it by asking for Anne to be excluded from religious education sessions. This had been unsuccessful because of the integrated approach the school had to its teaching. The family dealt with the conflict both by reinforcing Anne's beliefs and through maintaining alternative education through the church. Though this was a fundamental split between the understandings and beliefs held by the school and by Anne's family, the conflict seemed to have been suppressed. The family decided to co-operate with the school to ensure their child's formal educational success. Their relationship with the school was rocked but not fractured by conflicts with their religious faith.

There remained some other discontinuities in the relationship between Trisha and the school. Trisha believed that some of the children's learning was due not only to the school but also to parents' educational activities with their children at home. Anne's parents were happy with many aspects of the school but compensated for those aspects they thought were insufficiently structured. There was some evidence of a gap not only between the school and home views of how literacy and numeracy skills should be learned, but also of their views of children's experiences. Trisha believed the Head did not know about children's home educational activities but in parallel Trisha did not know about Anne's structured numeracy work at school.

4c.8. Discussion

This was a family in which Anne's options were framed by their interests and abilities. Schools may be more or less appropriate to developing those options, and Anne's parents were aware of the areas in which they themselves had the resources and confidence to help her. But they did not see any insurmountable barriers to Anne's development of her full potential, whatever directions she followed. They were confident that through their knowledge of the system, gained through their own educational histories, public discourses and local contacts, and their financial resources they would be able to provide any support which may benefit her.

Data about Anne suggests that Anne's interests and abilities would be consistent with a middle-class future. She was being brought up in a family, and a school, where potential success was planned and worked for. Though the ideology was of natural development, individual character and choice, those choices were funnelled in particular directions.

We have seen that at home and at school Anne enjoyed 'playing' with numeracy and enjoyed learning. It's not just that Anne had similar numeracy practices at home and at school. It was also that those practices were supported by the ways her mother analysed Anne's numeracy, in terms very similar to the school, and how she interacted with Anne in mathematical activities, again in parallel with teachers' interactions. We have seen that both at home and at school, the discourses of 'education' and 'play' overlapped. Trisha denied offering formal 'education' at home. Yet she exploited all opportunities for numeracy development through play-like activities. School numeracy practices were comparatively formal, and certainly teacher-led - but 'play' resources chosen by Anne fitted exactly with the teacher's numeracy agenda. Trisha had a lack of confidence in mathematics herself, and poor school experience. But whatever personal factors were at play, Trisha's and Anne's relationship around numeracy dovetailed with school numeracy practices.

Discursive overlaps existed between home and school pedagogic practices. The ideology of the naturally developing child, who developed intellectually through play and the fostering of curiosity, saturated both home and school. The school emulated the ideal middle-class home; the home adopted the discourses of school, disguised as play. Anne's mother did not rest in her critical, energetic search for appropriate activities. This was not, for Trisha, 'educating' her child; it was simply bringing her up.

This did not mean that Trisha and Mick were uncritically accepting of the school. We have seen Trisha attempt and fail to change the school's organisation of religious education, and Anne's parents argue that the Head's faith in learning as 'osmosis' was misplaced. Their response was to compensate for what they saw as the school's inadequacies. They would consider organising formal compensation, through a private tutor, because they had the financial resources. They could provide other forms of compensation through personal resources. But the similarities in home and school practices - not only in numeracy, but in more widely based ideologies about the developing child and what constitutes success - overrode any differences. And Anne was thriving. Comfortable, secure, knowing when she was successful and pleased about it, she had no problems 'adjusting' from home to school; few adjustments were needed.

CHAPTER FIVE: SCHOOL CASE STUDIES

Mountford, Tarnside and Rowan

5a. MOUNTFORD: 'how much do the teachers know about the homes?' 'probably very little'

5a.1 Setting

Mountford was the school in the white working class area of Blatchford that we visited for the full three years of the project. What we give in this part of Chapter 5 is an account of the school, the area in which it is sited, home school relationships and numeracy practices at the school. During the project we focused on four children at the school. First there was Seth who we have described in our case study of him in Chapter 4a. The other children we studied were Kay, Lenny, Carla and Kerry. In this Chapter we will draw on data from all four of these children. Chris was the Head teacher and Pamela was the Reception class teacher and Zena the class teacher in Years 1 and 2.

5a.2. The School and the Local area

Mountford County Primary school was made up of the merger of an Infant School together with attached nursery classes and a Junior School in September 1999 coinciding with the start of the project. From 1999 it took children from aged 3 to 11. The school was fairly large in national terms having over 500 pupils compared with national averages of about 250. The buildings of the school were in good condition.

The school was in a mainly white working class housing estate on the edge of a large town in the south of England and is surrounded on one side by countryside and farmland. It was far enough outside the town for residents to have to use buses or their own cars to get to the town, large shops or other amenities. There was one secondary comprehensive school situated at the edge of the estate that took most of the children from Mountford primary school.

Some of the areas of the estate were built within "home for heroes" projects for returning soldiers after the First World War. These houses tended to be the larger, more comfortable houses, some owner occupied with gardens and were seen as the more affluent end of the estate. Others were built to house families from the poorer,

B. Street, D. Baker and A. Tomlin (eds.), Navigating Numeracies, 79-113.
© 2005 *Springer. Printed in the Netherlands.*

more crowded inner city areas of the town when these were demolished in the 1930s or in the 1950s from London over-spill projects. Some of this housing contained some of the poorest families in the town and these properties were largely council owned. There were local corner shops and newsagents on the estate but families tended to leave the estate to go to supermarkets.

During the last twenty years recent immigrant families had been housed in the area but the proportion of such families was very small at present, less than 2% with the school having 1.6% speaking English as an additional language (Performance and Assessment Report, [PANDA] Office for Standards in Education, 2000). This proportion was rising at the time of our research. The "percentage of pupils' mother tongue not/believed not to be English was then taken to be 8.3%" (Panda (2002). The area had high unemployment, a large number of single parent families and the population therefore had low economic capital. The estate was not entirely homogeneous but families were mainly white working class.

There is evidence that, in many cases, extended families such as the children's grandparents and their uncles, aunts and cousins did live fairly close to each other. Some of these families were proud to be living on the estate. Other families perhaps the more recent arrivals saw themselves as more transient. There were some extremes with some very positive extended families and also some very isolated, particularly those that were new to the area.

As an indicator of the school's intake it is worth noting that 51.8% of the children at the school had free school meals (Panda 2002) which was nearly 3 times the national average of 18.3%. This was not unlike Tarnside at 42.8% but strikingly different from Rowan at 2%. The percentage of children identified as having special educational needs including formal statements was 68.9% which was well above the national average of 23.7%. Tarnside was 27.9% and Rowan 2.6%.

An Ofsted report on the school in 2000 (Panda 2000) and Panda Reports (2001 and 2002) showed that the children at the school had achieved very low and well below average at Key Stage 1 and 2 compared with national averages for literacy and numeracy. League tables drawn up to compare the children's attainment at schools in the local area school regularly placed Mountford in the lowest one or two schools out of 40 primary schools in the area. Ofsted view of the school as given by the head teacher was that Mountford was a distinctive school both in terms of academic achievement and in terms of behaviour. This view tallied with the school's reputation within the local area, which was. one of a caring institution where behaviour including bullying was a major issue t being dealt with and where the children were unlikely to achieve much educationally (Interview. HT 27 Nov. 01).

Families on the estate largely used Mountford primary school and the local secondary school. Mountford seemed to be their first choice. In several cases the parents of the children went to the same schools or those that were pre-cursors of Mountford. For example Seth's and Kerry's mothers and fathers went to Mountford.

5a.3. School's views of the area and children

The school's view of the area and its intake was given by the head teacher Chris when Dave and Brian interviewed him as part of the project on 27 Nov. 01. Chris said:

> "People views of Mountford within Blatchford as a whole is going to be negative" and "they live in a very negative community".

and

> "The clientele of our school are so very different from the vast majority of schools, with a huge amount of children on free schools meals, huge amount of children on special needs. A Teaching Assistants course aimed at the average school wouldn't necessarily suit this one. This is why we always say about literacy and numeracy strategies [the National Literacy (NLS) and Numeracy Strategies (NNS)] is that they don't – well, they do not accept that our argument that we cannot put year 1 literacy to the year 1 children in our school because, for 60-70% of them it goes straight over the top of their heads – they've haven't got a clue what you're talking about."

and when we asked him for his explanations about why the children at Mountford did less well academically than those at other schools he said:

> "Well, it's a combination of things. It's sort of – the sort of parents you get at Blatcham [a middle class school] would be the sort of parents who would be taking an academic interest. I'm very wary, because people can generalise very quickly about the parents in Mountford … don't care about their children as much as, say, the parents of children at Blatcham. It's a different form of care." … "And though we deal with a much higher percentage of child abuse and so on within the school more than most schools but the vast majority of parents within the school love and care for their children as much as I do with my children but the sort of interest I may show in my child's academic work is different because, I suppose, of a different value system. So I'm a bit wary of how to word – basically you've obviously got things like parent cultures. You've got the whole genetic argument of stuff being passed down and all the rest of it. And, again, when the local education authority and government don't recognise this – when you've got children come into our school in a state of emotional upset, not on a regular basis but it maybe one day the teacher will have to spend time helping that child. You know, in Zena's class, you've got two children in there who caused such disruption within that class and it doesn't just stop Zena from teaching, I'm sure, again there's no way of proving this, that it will have an effect on the rest of the children in that class. When you've got a child kicking around, swearing and all the rest of it and of course the way a lot of children deal with this is to switch off. Within every class there are one, two, three kids who do find the restrictions of behaviour within a class difficult. That also has a knock-on effect with the amount of learning. The one thing I keep saying to teachers is, if there's a child in your class who's stopping you teaching and stopping other children learning, they shouldn't be in the class." (Interview HT Mo 27 Nov. 01)

This revealed so much about issues and problems that affected learning in the school and the ways that the cultural resources and habitus of an area can affect all the children in a school. The reputation of the area provided a backdrop for these children and their families. It affected their images of themselves and structured them as failures in formal education before they start schooling. The effect of some children's behaviour in classes in the school was disruptive to academic study, a feature that we saw also in Tarnside (Chapter 5b). The teachers at Mountford were at times distracted from their teaching by having to cope with social and behavioural problems and issues. Thus the habitus and cultural capital of classrooms, which was contributed to by the habitus and cultural capital that the children brought to school, militated against success in schooling for children in those classrooms. Certainly one of the effects of the area we saw at the school was the ways the children switched off or disengaged from the school. (We discuss issues of engagement further in chapter 6). The head teacher was aware of the negative stereotyping of the families in the area and challenged some of these by accepting the positive characteristics of the parents as caring and concerned.

He also recognised that the parents of children at Mountford may have different values (and perhaps not necessarily worse ones) from those in middle class areas: but ones that might not fit in with schooling. However, he did alert us, albeit briefly, to the notion that there were "genetic arguments" that suggested that unsuccessful parents pass their genes down to their children. The impression he left us with was one of a school battling against many odds to provide the education for the children that they were required and pressurised to do.

On the other hand, as we argue below, teachers at the school also expressed to us some negative views of homes that appeared to be based on deficit models and might have affected the teachers' relationships with the children's carers. The substance of some of these views, for example views of parents as not interested in their children's education, were not subsequently borne out by our own experience. It was as though the reputation of the area dominated and overcame direct experiences.

An example of this was seen in a discussion Dave and Brian had with Sheila, the speech therapist, at the school. The school was part of an Education Action Zone, which had been providing extra language assistance through the allocation of a speech therapist in the school, as previous evidence suggested the children were arriving at school with speech difficulties. Sheila said that her tests indicated that over 50% of these children had language problems. "The children are on average 18 months language delayed". From the perspective of contemporary sociolinguistic accounts of language variation (Labov, 1972; Gregory, 1997; Martin-Jones and Jones, 2000) these views appear to be based on a deficit model of these homes. Decades of work by sociolinguists, such as Labov's ground breaking 1972 study of New York children's actual language use, once the deficit model had been abandoned, are ignored here and the notion that the children might have had different language skills that their tests did not identify was here seen as fanciful.. Instead, the tests used by Sheila were normative to particular class/ cultural standards. The educational argument she used was clear. These children were arriving at school unprepared for the language and other demands of the classrooms. Sheila and her colleagues were designing a programme of intervention to both help the children acquire what she judged as the necessary language skills and to give the teachers training in how to offer such support.

When we asked about links from language to numeracy she said: "A lack of language affects attainment in numeracy and also affects peer group interactions in numeracy". And when asked for explanations for low achievement in numeracy she gave several including:

A low level of parental expectations and skills and parents own learning difficulties. She said: "the parents complain that their child is too quiet and yet the child is placed in front of the TV". "One parent gave solid food to a baby at 6 weeks"

Police are involved in these homes and so are drugs

Background noise in the homes which inhibits learning: "There is so much noise that the children can't distinguish between voice and background noise"

Sitting and listening, - "the children have not learnt to sit properly in a chair"

The importance of windows of development, if the children missed these then they had had it. (Sheila Interview: 11 April 00)

These explanations seemed to the researchers to place the 'blame' for low attainment firmly at the door of parents and it confirmed our image, from these interviews, from remarks by teachers in the school and more generally from discussions with education administrators, that education experts like the speech therapists here had deficit models of the homes in the Mountford area. In their view the parents did not have the history, habitus, cultural resources or skills to help their children; their domestic practices such as the use of TV, eating routines, background noise and ways of sitting, were seen as inhibiting children's formal educational development. The speech therapist also saw missed moments as un-retrievable – if the children 'missed windows of opportunity' than they 'had had it'.

This deficit model also affected the class teacher's views of the children. When we asked Pamela in the Reception class why she thought achievement of children from less affluent homes was lower she suggested:

"schools can't make up it up in 5 hours. Schools only have children for 5 hours a day; many homes lack parenting skills; unlike some homes parents don't go round counting buttons or stairs or play games as a matter of course; day to day demands, in some cases big families or lack of resources, seem to bog parents down and they don't have the time or energy to put into these activities" (Interview Pamela 16 Dec. 99)

When we said that this suggested that the school was 'compensating' for the homes, i.e. teaching and learning in school were making up for what goes on in homes, she agreed. Her rule of thumb was that her children were 18 months behind children in other schools. Her Reception children were like nursery children. The nursery in her view added a lot of value. Some children arrived there not knowing colours or counting. The National Numeracy Strategy (NNS) says that children should leave Reception able to count and to understand the adding process as putting together. Many of hers could not do that. Her children have arrived much more street-wise and less protected than middle class children. They may be more able to handle money. They do watch cartoons (which recent research by the Centre for Literacy and Media at King's College London show to involve narrative skills amongst others, Oldham et. al., 2001), and play computer games and play-station games, which Gee's recent work amongst others shows to provide considerable learning once we know how to view it (Gee, 2003) (see our accounts of children's home practices in Chapter 4). Pamela agreed she had no knowledge of these games. She felt that there was no reading matter in some homes but was heartened this year by the children's families use of the school book bags (Pamela, Interview 16 Dec. 99).

5a.4.Feel of the school

Mountford was a large school but always seemed to be organised and ordered. There were well-established routines, to do with moving around the school. The start of the day was clearly marked and, once the teachers collected the children from their parents in the playground, the parents leave. There was, then, little evidence of parents in the school. The end of the day had a similarly tight routine. Routines in the classes were clear, definite and organised with firmly set routines. Once sessions started, classes were usually calm and quiet. From our work at the other schools it was much quieter than either Rowan or Tarnside. Mountford had a feeling of concentration, earnest endeavour, with control and discipline. In some cases this was done in a very dominant manner but in others was handled more discreetly. For example Pamela, the Reception teacher, being quietly spoken, created a classroom culture of calm orderliness. The children's voices in her class were lower, and the teacher's voice was quieter than many at Tarnside, with the children talking less and not shouting as much. The calmness we observed at Mountford was not due to the children's compliance towards schooling and there was a lot of evidence that the children are not easy to control or keep calm. The head teacher talked about behaviour as a central issue in the school, where there were some children who were very difficult and even violent (Interview HT 27 Nov. 01), an issue that parents similarly saw as central to Tarnside. The teachers at Mountford accepted a role which went beyond the cognitive to the social and moral and also correct language use. For example teachers at Mountford expected the children to use words like "pardon me" when they apologised which was seen to be a correct language use but which the children did not use naturally in class and which teachers assumed was not the usual practice in homes in Mountford.

5a.5. Parent School relationships

Both parents and the school saw their relationship as vital. The school wanted to involve parents fully in order to be able to communicate its needs and to discuss various issues concerns and policies with parents. This was seldom successful. Parent returns from an Ofsted questionnaire were 8% at Mountford compared with 26% from Tarnside and 47% from Rowan The school tried a wide range of approaches to this, even ones that involved the local community in aspects such as literacy, gardening, computing, art and a community room, etc. But "they [parents] do not want to know" and "the present generation of parents are quite clearly disengaged for one reason or another" (Interview. HT 27 Nov. 01). The school wanted to engage the parents as it saw their involvement as very low. The school's view of the area was that it is "a very negative community" which had real barriers between it and the school. Parents only attended occasions at school where their own children were performing or being active, such as Christmas or summer shows, but they did not come to parents' evenings. The barriers that prevented them attending were "their expectations of life and their own experiences" (Interview. HT 27 Nov. 01).

When asked "how much do the teachers know about the homes?", the head teacher replied:

> "Probably very little, I suppose. Apart from, say, from the nursery staff I would say the rest know little. They will have their views, which will range right across from those who understand to those who just don't understand." (Interview. HT 27 Nov. 01).

Contacts between parents and teachers were maintained in different ways. In the Reception class, informal conversations occurred at the start and at the end of the day. But in later years parents were not allowed to come to the classrooms and this reduced informal contacts. This was unlike Rowan where parents and siblings of the children were allowed into the class both before and after school. More formal contacts at Mountford were maintained through discussions at parents' consultative evenings. However attendance at parent evenings was often as low as 6 out of 30 parents. Parents could also request appointments to talk about specific issues to do with their children but they seldom did this.

Nevertheless, parents saw the issue of communication and access with the school and class teachers as vital. Changes to school practices over the three years of the project resulted in less informal parental contact with teachers. This resulted in parents feeling a substantial distancing from the school and between them and their children's formal education. They did not know what the children were doing or how well they were doing. Seth's mother Jackie, for instance, felt very strongly that without such information she could not help Seth with his schooling and numeracy. (cf. Jackie's 'Seth's Story' in Chapter 4a). Other parents such as Kay's mother, felt that they could speak to the teachers but had only done so in informal situations.

Parent evenings at the school at times revealed conflicting expectations between teachers and carers/parents. The teachers wanted to discuss cognitive and learning issues and wanted to share the school's approaches and policies about learning. They wanted to raise their concerns about the parents' lack of organisation or what the parents could do at home to help the children with their schooled learning. Parents on the other hand often wanted to discuss their concerns, which in this study centred more around social than cognitive matters. They wanted to discuss their children's friendship problems or issues about bullying or teasing or the children's reluctance to go to school. (6 Apr. 00 and 1 Oct 00)

Almost all contact between parents and teachers occurred at school. The only time teachers visited homes was before the children started in nursery classes. These visits were partly to create a relationship between teachers and parents but also to enable teachers to inform parents about school routines and expectations. These were the only official and formal visits made by the school to the children's homes.

5a.6. Numeracy events and practices in the Mountford classroom

In this section we will give a brief account of the numeracy events we have seen in Mountford classrooms in order to allow comparisons with home practices and the schooled practices at Rowan and Tarnside. We will draw out from that an analysis of school numeracy practices including the pedagogical practices of the classroom.

In the Reception year the children at Mountford often met numeracy as part of an integrated day with only one group out of six groups doing maths. But after Reception the numeracy work began to fit in with the National Numeracy Strategy (DFEE 1999) and then had specific time allocated to it. It was then structured to fit the three-part lesson with a mental and oral starter, a main activity and a plenary session. This was the most common style of daily mathematics class we observed when the children were in Years 1 and 2.

We observed several kinds of numeracy events at the school. There were events both in the classroom and outside the classroom. The latter included play in the playground, which was mainly child directed games but in Reception year the teachers provided equipment that structured the children's activities. Some of these were mathematical such as three-dimensional building blocks. The classroom had a range of different types of numeracy events. Some of these were within the formal numeracy time and others were outside it. Events outside included the use of classroom management such as using the register for calculations about children's attendance. Those within the formal numeracy times mainly included 'disembedded' formal educational activities. These were mathematics-dedicated activities, where the purposes of the activities were directly linked to the mathematics curriculum. The resources used were often formal ways of representing numbers such as number lines, or counting sticks. 'Mental maths" such as strategies for pupils adding 9 in their heads was another type of formal numeracy event (this event is also discussed in chapter 4a). There were also times when the teachers used the children as a resource for numeracy such as the length of their names or classifying what they were wearing. We also saw mathematics games based on number tracks like Snakes and Ladders (c.f. Baker et al, 2000) and software on computers, songs and stories such as the three little pigs, make believe situations such as a café or a shoe shop, and chanting as in step counting.

5a.7. Discussion of numeracy events and practices

The formal events discussed above were school numeracy events in the domain of schooling (Chapter 3). They all constituted part of what we have called school numeracy practices. The content drew on the statutory curriculum for maths either from the National Curriculum or from the National Numeracy Strategy (DfEE 1999). These practices seldom drew on home experiences. There were times when the children recounted home activities in the classroom but unlike home practices, which are shared with their families these were not experiences they shared with other children or with the teacher These numeracy practices were mainly embedded in the pedagogic numeracy practices of the school (see Chapter 5b Tarnside for fuller discussion of the differences between such practices at home and at school). Increasingly over the three years of the project schooled numeracy practices were based on and conformed to those advocated in the NNS (DFEE 1999). The context of these activities was mainly disembedded seeking to develop number skills in abstract.   When the teachers attempted to embed some of them in classroom management activities, it was clear that, although the children readily participated in these activities and accepted their roles in the situation, their answers to the questions were often fairly wild and inappropriate guesses. They were not related to the context in which the teacher sited them. They lacked 'real' purposes for the children. They did not stop to think about how meaningful their answers were. They were performance driven in Lave's sense (1988) and educational problems in Burkhardt's (1981) sense. The children were not curious about such tasks, as they tended to be when faced with similar tasks at home (see Chapter 8 for comparisons), and their engagement therefore seemed only surface deep. If they had actually needed an answer for their own purposes they would probably have guessed less wildly.

In terms of social relations, there were interesting notions in these numeracy events about copying as cheating which was seen as an unacceptable strategy for children in schooled numeracy practices. This could be either a pedagogical issue (teachers believing children do not learn when copying) or as a moment to socialise the children into the dominant values of the classroom. The teacher also wanted the children to accept that it was not helpful to cheat if they wanted to learn. There were instances at home where cheating would be unacceptable, for example competitive board games, but unless mimicking schooled pedagogic practices, homes would allow children to seek answers to problems from each other (such as the sharing out of amounts of small sweets) without labelling these as 'cheating'.

Other aspects of school pedagogy within school numeracy practices that we identified in the data and which we examine briefly below (and elaborate further in the Themes Section 4), include 'uniformity and conformity', 'disembedded contexts' for school numeracy, the 'centrality of schooling' for teachers, and the 'cultural resources' of the school

In terms of 'uniformity and conformity', teachers expected the children to use approaches and resources the teachers had chosen or identified. For example in one session Zena said to the children:

> "we will play games, similar to yesterday. We will roll the dice and put a number of cubes on the table corresponding to the number on the dice"

> One child pointed out that: "we done that yesterday"

> The teacher's response was to note the child had not done it using the right resources: "Yes, but I looked at your book and you seemed not to use the cubes" (DB Mo 14 Mar 01)

The teachers and schools also conformed to the structures or directions and approaches of the NNS. An example of this is shown in these notes of a class session:

> The teacher used an approach that complied to some extent with the NNS in structure. So she had the three part lesson but missed the third part.   The warm up involved counting numbers in different steps but did not relate closely to the topic in the main section on money. The children did engage with it but needed constant encouragement.

> The teacher had her own calculation strategies and pushed the children to do this (DB Mo 22 May 01)

In the same way, following the NNS recommendations, there was a stress on conforming to approaches that used whole class teaching even when this raised substantial problems for teaching and learning. An example of this is discussed in the section on Mountford in Chapter 4a. There were children in that session such as Vinny who knew the maths concepts before the session started. Others like Kerry struggled and learnt little about those concepts, although she probably learnt more about her inability to handle school numeracy. And there some like Seth who just disengaged.

What we term the 'disembeddedness' of the pedagogical practices of schooling also led to missed opportunities to make links to home experiences or language. The numeracy event described below from year 1 at Mountford was about odds and evens. The numeracy context was clearly schooled: no attempt was made to relate it to anything beyond the children's school experiences. The numeracy content of odds and evens was not linked to house numbers (in which Seth engaged see Chapter 4a), nor to the children's language, through, for example, a discussion of the words 'odd' and 'even; and their possible meanings for the children.

> Kay drew all the odd number numicon (structural apparatus for teaching number) shapes and then the even ones.
>
> Dave: Is 4 odd or even?
>
> Kay: even.
>
> Dave: why?
>
> Kay: cos my mummy told me [perhaps evidence of parental input!!](DB Mo 27 Feb 01)

These comments are not criticisms of the teacher. They are about pedagogy, about how teachers help children relate to esoteric numeracy ideas. Odds and evens seemed to be a strong schooled numeracy concept. And although impinging on homes was not strongly in evidence this event, it raises the issue of how teachers might build on what children can do or know or what images and language metaphors they can relate to which could benefit from reference to home experiences.

Another example of the disembeddedness of school numeracy practices was the teaching of classification as an end in itself. For example on 16 May 00 Pamela asked children to identify things that were the same and different about each other. Amongst the answers were:

> Carla: both is girls
>
> Lenny: they have the same hair

These are probably not particularly interesting classifications for the children, although they were encouraged to come up with their own. The point of the activity is for them to understand the processes of classifying and matching, seeking similarities and differences and not ones that they might have focused on themselves outside of this task. At home such classifications would probably be more purposeful for the children. In terms of this project the classifying event we describe fits in to our disembedded model of schooled numeracy practices. It may be worth noting that both contexts might allow some debate about what are acceptably classified as the same and different, that is allow debate about what is right or wrong in mathematics.

The next aspect of pedagogical practice we will describe here is the ways that schooling was seen by the teachers as central, as the determining site for their work. Teaching was about learning the school curriculum and not about learning beyond the school. This centrality of schooling was shown by teachers' concerns about the children forgetting their schooled numeracy knowledge over holidays and half terms. This concern was expressed in terms of the children forgetting schooled knowledge rather than being positive about what they might learn at home.

> Pamela draws oblong on board and asks children to come up and say what it begins with - Megan says 'o'; Lenny comes up and uses stick to point to 'o' on board. Pamela asks: 'after a week's holiday will you remember them? I hope so as I will have some new ones for you to do'. Pamela later says that she fears they will have all forgotten over the half term (DB Mo15 Feb. 00).

The last aspect that we wish to mention in this discussion is the cultural resources of the school. For example during a mental and oral starter to a NNS session on 22 May 01 the following dialogue occurred:

> Zena: "We are going to do shopping as we weren't good at it yesterday. First we are going to do counting. What should we count in and what should we start at?"
>
> Carla: "Count in ones and start at 1"
>
> They all tried to count to 100 together.
>
> Kerry mouthed quietly incoherently.
>
> Seth put his fingers in his ears and fidgeted
>
> Lenny and Kay participated although Lenny was still clingy to me.
>
> Then they counted in 10s starting at 30 both up to 100 and down again. (DB Mo 22 May 01)

As a class and as a peer group for each other there were few who could do the activity easily and quickly and hence most did not provide a resource or support for others. This is part of what could be called the cultural resources of the school but only in terms of the field of schooled numeracy. In terms of this field there is a clear lack of resources compared with those at Tarnside and Rowan. At Rowan, for instance, (see Chapter 5c) children brought along cultural resources and knowledge that were consonant with schooling with both curriculum and pedagogy which was shared with others.

Overall, then, issues and themes that have emerged in this chapter include: the cultural resources of the school; school numeracy and pedagogic practices; and relationships between homes and schools.

- The cultural resources of the school include: the attitude to schooling of children from the area; the teacher's lack of detailed knowledge of home numeracy practices; the views and expectations of teachers about the homes and the children; the resources for and attitudes to numeracy that the children brought to school and their responses (e.g. disengagement) to school numeracy events; the children behaviour and attitudes to schooling;

- The school numeracy and pedagogic practices include: the teachers' focus on schooling and the resultant disembeddedness of school numeracy; the lack of use of the children's home experiences and resources; and the school's need to comply with national policies for curriculum and pedagogy. This need seemed to stem from the pressures of inspections and 'league tables' even in a school where, as the Head told us, these may not seem appropriate.. In contrast at Rowan, the 'leafy suburb school' cf Chapter 5c, the children's attainment in maths has meant that the school have been able to resist these pressures and avoid this kind of compliance.

- The relationship between school and homes includes teacher's acceptance of the centrality and primacy of school numeracy; the lack of effective communication and sharing of practices between homes and schools; and contrasts between home and school practices.

5b: TARNSIDE: 'they pushed him into lots of … very hard, formal sums'

5b.1.Introduction

Tarnside was the inner city mixed ethnicity school that we selected as a contrastive case from Mountford, the white working class school described above, and Rowan, the 'leafy suburb' middle class school, described below (Chapter 5c). This chapter includes an account of the school and the local area, home school relationships and numeracy practices at the school. At various stages during the project we focussed on five children at the school, although, as we indicate below, some left during this period. We discuss Kim in our case study of him in Chapter 4b. The other children were Darris, and her mother Ruby; Rick, and his mother Maureen; Jeffrey, and his parents; and also Aaysha and her parents. The school is the focus of this part of chapter 5 but we will draw on data from all four children. Morag was the Head teacher at Rowan, while Marilyn and Nasreen were the Reception teachers, Dylan, Thelma, and Katrina were the year 1 teachers and Cheryl was teaching assistant in Reception.

5b.2. The local area and the school population

Tarnside voluntary aided (Church of England) primary school takes children from 3 to 11. It is in a multi-ethnic urban area of London, close to a busy shopping centre. The area is rising in the property market, estate agents and coffee and wine bars are increasing in number.. The population is very mixed: housing in the area includes council estates, housing association property, a hostel for homeless people, private landlords renting out flats in big Victorian houses to both rich and poor, and, increasingly, Victorian and Edwardian houses converted back from flats to single-family accommodation for the comparatively wealthy. The LEA has vigorously supported 'choice' of school. As a result some parents whose children are not accepted at their nearest primary school, because it is oversubscribed, have had to send their children further afield to schools such as Tarnside. Thus Tarnside's children come from several wards around the school, not because it was highly sought after, but because, for some parents, it was a last resort. This was unlike Mountford where the school was the only one on the local estate and parents in many cases lacked the material and cultural resources to seek alternatives. We stress, however, that for many parents Tarnside was their first choice of school; this contradiction - first choice and last resort - reflects the complexities of life in the school itself.

The families with whom we worked in this project were mainly working class; some (for example, Kim's family) had remained in the area while house prices rose around them, and in terms of home ownership have 'done well'; others, like Darris and Rick, lived in council or housing association rented properties; whilst Aaysha's family, although living in a hostel, had been middle class professionals. Tarnside school did not reflect the full mix of the local population. Most of the children were black or Asian, with black children of Caribbean and West African heritage in the majority; there were, too, a significant number of children from refugee families This contrasts with both Rowan, which was mainly white middle class and Mountford which was mainly white working class.. A new head teacher, Morag, started at the school during the academic year immediately before our study started. The school had had a poor inspection report, which led to the change of head teacher. Those parents who could do so avoided the school, warned off by stories of fights and violence. Thus the comparatively well-off children went to neighbouring schools, and Tarnside became a largely working class school. The most recent OfSTED inspection reported that 'Staffing, resources and accommodation are all adequate' (Office for Standards in Education 2002). By contrast to Rowan, however, Tarnside had only hard surface playing areas and narrow corridors. There was no sense of anything 'spare' - every bit of space was packed: for instance, there was usually no quiet space available to which children could be taken from the classroom. The cramped conditions contributed to the general air of busy-ness at Tarnside as children moved about the school, for example, to join their numeracy set. There were queues, hold ups and the noise level rose.

Tarnside was a bigger than average school - 314 in January '02, up from 274 in 1999 and it was growing . It had a very high percentage of children speaking English as an additional language (38.4% in 2000 Panda); and the percentage of children eligible for free school meals (that is, one of the government's key markers for the social context of the school) was 42.8%, the national average being 19.7%. This was similar to Mountford but much higher than Rowan. The school had an above average percentage of children with special educational needs, at 27.9%.In the Reception class we visited three of 17 children had been referred to the education psychology service that provides statements of special educational needs. However, the service had put referrals on hold because the waiting list was too long; the school then asked the school nurse to see the children and refer them to their own family doctors, who could then support applications to the Local Education Authority (LEA).

The school's attainment in Key Stage 1 (KS1) maths tests was well below the national average (2000 Panda). Compared to other schools with similar context, the percentage of children achieving level 2 or above in the maths tests was above average; that achieving level 2B or above was average; and that achieving level 3 or above was well below average (2000 Panda).This contrasted with the school's achievement in the reading and writing tests which was close to the national average, and well above average compared to schools in a similar context (2000 Panda).

A characteristic of the school which marked it out from Rowan and Mountford was the high mobility of the school population. During the1999/2000 school year, 65 pupils left and were replaced by a similar number. High mobility affected the school's finances, as funding was clawed back (Ofsted inspection report). It also affected our own research as four of the children we began following in Reception left the school before the end of year 2.

The inspection report for 2000 noted that there appeared to be dramatic improvements in achievement in mathematics:

> Primarily, this could be attributed to the higher level of attainment on this group's entry to the school. Considering the high rates of pupil mobility, nearly 50 per cent over the seven years in the school, this may not be the only factor. The school has made significant improvements in the teaching of the subject since the last inspection and they are beginning to have a positive effect on standards.

While the Ofsted inspectors may have been referring only to changes in average academic achievement, staff credited a few children with the ability to disrupt a whole class. The Reception class we observed had a reputation as having an unusually high number of 'difficult' and 'challenging' children .The Reception class had 23 children at the start of the year, and 16 at the end. This high mobility again contrasts strongly with Rowan, where only one or two children (and none of the research project children) in a class of 30 left during the project and indeed the school as a whole increased its numbers from 274 to 314.

5b.3. Organisation and 'feel' of numeracy activities

We provide a brief account here of the organisation of numeracy lessons in the school, which inevitably can only represent part of an analysis and data on the school's numeracy practices.

Tarnside adopted the National Numeracy Strategy (NNS), and Ofsted (2000) in part attributed improvements in school mathematics to the NNS. In Reception the children had a daily numeracy lesson with their class teacher, Marilyn. In the following two years the children were in one of two mixed year 1 and 2 classes. For the first term they had numeracy lessons with their class teacher; they were then placed in three sets, the bottom set being almost all year 1, the top almost all year 2, and the middle mixed year 1 and2. The numeracy sets continued into year 2, with almost all the year 2 children being in the middle or top set. This procedure allowed smaller numbers of children in each set but, as we shall se below, placed the school's teaching resource sunder pressure.

In Reception most of the lessons Alison visited had two staff, Marilyn (the teacher) and Cheryl (the teaching assistant). This was a class which gained a school-wide reputation as 'one of the most difficult ever'; teachers called Marilyn 'a saint' for her capacity to 'cope with them' with good humour. By year 1 and 2, most of the lessons Alison visited had only one teacher, though sometimes the special needs co-ordinator (SENCO) worked with a few particular children. All of the lessons took place in fairly cramped accommodation. This contrasts with Rowan, where there were always a classroom teacher, and at least one teaching assistant Mountford also felt less cramped as there was more space and the class usually had a teaching assistant with the classroom teacher (cf chapter 5 a). Whilst at Tarnside the whole class was engaged in numeracy, and any disruption easily spread as children were distracted. At Rowan, which did not adopt the NNS, small groups met outside the classroom in the 'outside classroom' or the corridor, with an teaching assistant, thus making more physical space, and less noise, in the classroom; at Tarnside there was no opportunity for such flexibility. Thus staffing and accommodation resources impacted enormously on the feel of the classroom.

In addition, the 'feel' of the classroom was affected by the conception of numeracy held by teachers. Most of the displays we saw at Tarnside were of writing, often with children's illustrations; few were of art work, and. displays relating to numeracy were almost exclusively of learning materials - the 100 grid, number lines, posters of words to do with mathematics (e.g. plus, add, more than, with the sign +); they were designed to help children's number work, not to show off their achievements. This may have reflected the school's concentration on number work, with comparatively little on handling data (which can involve visual work on graphs and is therefore more 'suitable' for display) or on problem solving This focus on number work is also noted in the Ofsted 2000 report. The impression then was that mathematics was not seen as creative: numeracy practices were narrowly defined.

5b.4 Parent school relations: Contradictory views of the school.

Parents' access to classrooms contrasted sharply between the three project schools. Whereas at Rowan parents took children to the classroom throughout the research period, that happened at Tarnside and Mountford only in Reception year; from year1 on at both of these schools, parents left children in the playground, to be called into the classroom by teachers. At Tarnside in Reception, parents did not go more than a few feet into the room; although Marilyn greeted parents and welcomed short discussions it was clear that parents' place was to deliver children and then leave. School and home at Tarnside, as at Mountford, were quite separated. That separation contributed to some mothers' anger and alienation from both schools. Juline, Kim's mother (see Kim chapter 4 b) relied on her son's account of his day and had little trust in most teachers' accounts. Others, for example Ruby, trusted the teachers, relied on them to tell them anything they needed to know and were confident that they could speak to the teachers whenever they needed to.

Our discussions with parents and teachers further illustrate the complexity and variety of their relationship. Teachers who had good relationships with some mothers had very poor relationships with others. In part this may relate to the organisation into sets for numeracy mentioned above, which affected how often they met the child's mother both when the child was collected and at parents' evenings. Parents did not meet their child's numeracy set teacher if they were not also the class teacher. Both parents and teachers sometimes blamed 'other' children for disrupting classes, with attached blame to their parents for not bringing them up better. Parents at Mountford have expressed similar views. Whilst there were no consistent patterns, we describe two examples that provide insight into the principles underlying such variation..

We start with Ruby, the mother of Darris, a girl whom we followed from Reception. The school was Ruby's and her husband's first choice for Darris. Darris was successful in school. In a classroom practice test a few weeks before the national tests in Year 2 she was one mark short of level 3, that is, above average in her year. Ruby lived about 1.5 miles from the school but wanted a church school and although not Church of England herself, she preferred it to the closer Catholic schools. She wanted a church school not particularly for the religious input (for which the family attended church and associated activities) but 'mainly because of discipline'.

Throughout Reception Ruby was happy with the school. In Year1 she commented on the difference in pedagogy, in terms which suggest she saw herself in a partnership with the teacher:

> ... she's expected to do more [in Year 1]. Whereas nursery and reception they focus more on play, because judging by the children s age and behaviour that they learn more from play but now the teacher especially she's picking up on what Darris [can do] and she's working on that. The homework's brilliant. She does homework every week and most of the time we let her do it by herself. The reading skills they've just escalated (AT Darris 4th Dec. 00).

Ruby had come to an agreement with Marilyn that Darris did not need to be pushed but could be left to 'just carry on as we are going'.

Ruby attributed some parents' difficulties in achieving this level of agreement with the teacher to the parents' attitudes to schooling and teachers, abdicating their own responsibilities. She speaks as someone with a teacher and a student teacher in her family; although speaking as a parent, she adopted the teachers' point of view. She invoked social class as a reason for some parents' rejection of the school or poor relationship with teachers. Ruby knew of the disrupted atmosphere in Marilyn's

Reception class and attributed that to other parents' poor child-rearing practices: 'the problem is a lot of the parents … don't take their children's behaviour seriously'.

One characteristic of parents' discourse around Tarnside is that many of the parents position themselves strongly for or against the school and its individual teachers - angry or supportive, included or excluded, their child seen as 'doing well' or failing, mothers express strong views. At Tarnside and at Mountford, working class parents, whether trusting the school, like Ruby, or not, like Juline and Jackie (Seth's mother), were more trapped; they lacked the cultural resources to negotiate with the school, as middle class Rowan parents tended to do.

Maureen's son Rick was also doing well in literacy and numeracy, but her response was different. Rick was one of the children who was unsettled and in the teachers' view disrupted other children's school experience, although Maureen blamed the teacher rather than Rick. He was a 'bright' child, in the judgement of his mother and his teachers. Like Ruby, Maureen was becoming an insider in the education system. Leaving school with no qualifications, she attended adult basic education courses, including basic mathematics, and gained a place on an Access course for primary teaching. Rick went first to a state nursery, but the staff there advised Maureen to move him: he was 'playing up because he was bored'. In Chapter 4b we saw how teachers and carers likewise viewed Kim as 'bored', although Kim showed his 'boredom' in sleeping, whereas Rick expressed it through lively and sometimes disruptive behaviour and was nevertheless among the highest achievers in class.

Tarnside was Maureen's last resort school. Rick had had a place at a private school, to be paid for by Rick's (absent) father; the money didn't materialise. By then the term had started, the next three (state) schools on Maureen's list were full and Rick joined Darris's class at Tarnside. Maureen's preference for a private school was based in part on a belief it would offer better discipline and smaller class sizes, which would enable each child to achieve more at their own pace. Like Ruby, Maureen criticised some of Tarnside's parents. The first time she took Rick to Tarnside, there was a fight between parents outside the school gate. She described some of the parents as 'not friendly … loud … rough … not concerned' (about their children's education), although she was also critical of some of the parents who sent children to private schools as 'snobbish' (AT Rick 28th Feb. 00). Ruby knew Tarnside from the inside, since Darris had attended the nursery school. Maureen had to send her son to a school with a poor reputation, confirmed for her on the first day. Once Rick had started, Maureen found he was in a class that had a reputation for being 'difficult'. She described it as 'very hyper. How can Rick learn when so many of the children are disruptive?' In this she was at one with school staff who universally agreed that that class was unusually 'difficult'. When she learned that Marilyn was very experienced with older children, she was relieved, thinking Marilyn would introduce higher levels for high achieving children. She remained however convinced that Marilyn underestimated the children's ability in numeracy:

> Some of the children are more advanced than the teacher thinks … They spent too much time on 1, 2, 3, the children all knew it already.

By the end of the Reception year Rick was often in trouble. Maureen commented 'He's not innocent', knowing that he joined in the disruption led by some of the 'difficult' boys. Maureen tried to support the school's disciplinary efforts, for example sending him to bed early when Marilyn had sent him to see the Head for disciplinary reasons. But then Rick got a place in one of the (state) schools for which he had been on the waiting list, and left Tarnside. The head teacher was 'not sorry' Rick was leaving:

> His mother has the attitude that it's never her fault, she blames everyone else.

Rick's mother and school blamed each other for Rick's behaviour. They disagreed too about academic achievement: Marilyn thought Rick was doing work at home that was too advanced for him (for example, she said he did not understand the meaning of the multiplication tables on which he was working), while Maureen thought the school work was pitched at too low a level for Rick and others. Rick contributed to the high mobility statistics. When he and several others moved on from the school, behaviour among his former classmates improved.

We cannot explain, or explain away, all the contradictions in Ruby's and Maureen's views of the school. Both respect discipline; identify some mothers' child-rearing practices and personal behaviour as contributing to turbulence in the school; their children are 'bright' and academically successful; they have comparatively 'insider' relationships with teaching. Yet Ruby admires Marilyn's coping with disruptive children while Maureen thinks Marilyn lacks experience; Ruby sees the other Reception teacher, Nasreen as aggressive with children, whilst Maureen sees her as providing an orderly learning environment; Ruby's child, Darris, is happy and encouraged to work at the highest level possible, while Maureen's is developing poor behaviour and being held back. There are two general issues we can identify. Firstly, teachers and parents may start off on different footings depending on whether the school was the first choice or last resort. School staff knew that Ruby chose them and trusted them and that Maureen did not. Maureen was therefore immediately positioned as a pushy parent, and she may also have reacted defensively when the school challenged her child's behaviour or achievement. Secondly, the two children themselves were very different. Rick was physically active, vocally loud, associated with a 'disruptive' group of boys and questioned Marilyn's reasons for instructions; Darris was enthusiastic but contained, quietly spoken, associated mainly with academically successful girls and never 'talked back' with teachers.

These differences show up in teachers' responses to the children's numeracy work. From Alison's observation of Rick's numeracy work at home, working through a book with his mother helping, his work on multiplication was based on mental repeated addition, using his fingers to keep track of how many 'lots' he had added. He was not reciting the times tables. Yet his teacher thought he was learning unrelated 'facts' rather than principles, and believed Maureen overestimated his ability. In contrast, during Year1 Darris' teacher suggested Ruby should get her a Key Stage 2 (KS2) book to use at home. So Ruby was trusted to work at home with her child, and Maureen was not; Darris was pushed to greater achievement, and Rick was 'held back'. Maureen's support of her son and mistrust of the school produced her as a 'pushy mother' who had an inflated idea of her boy's ability, while Ruby's support of the school positioned her as a sensible, caring mother who could be trusted. Maureen, Ruby and the school all held some parents responsible for their children's behaviour; as the mother of a boy who became disruptive, Maureen was then to blame, trapped with her own argument. But whereas Maureen and Ruby also criticised (different) teachers for failing to work with parents and dealing poorly with children, the school held parents alone responsible and saw itself struggling against the tide of difficulties caused by disruptive (poorly brought up) children.

5b.5. Classroom and home numeracy practices: 'just everyday stuff'

Here we compare what children should learn at home (in the school's view) with what they learned at school; along the way we shall see that the school's impression of children's home numeracy lives and practices is sometimes inaccurate. The teachers whose numeracy lessons we visited, Dylan, Katrina, Marilyn and Thelma, held broadly similar views on the skills that children brought from home and what parents could do to help develop their children's numeracy.

The children's Reception teacher, Marilyn, argued like many in Mountford and Rowan, that in general the children who do well in numeracy are those who are encouraged to notice, talk about and play with anything to do with mathematics at home:

> I would imagine that on a very basic level the children who perform well in school are the ones who get any kind of extra maths practice, as it were, at home, so...... silly things like sorting or walking along the street and noticing colours and shapes and just general conversation really, at a young age. Not those who sit down quite so formally as Rick and write numbers from one to five million. But just everyday stuff that they can then bring into school and relate to what they are doing (AT Interview Marilyn 2nd Aug 99)

Like Dylan (see Kim case study, Chapter 4b) Marilyn argued it may be damaging to children's numeracy if parents give them too much formal work without sufficient underpinnings. We have seen in the discussion of the relationship between Rick, his mother Maureen and the school that Maureen's and the school's disagreement over Rick's ability was a contributing factor in his removal from the school. Marilyn believed Maureen had

> 'pushed him into lots of writing, writing the numbers. And very hard, formal sums. He's been doing division and multiplication and all that kind of stuff, it sounds like right from when he was three, when he first went to school. Because he could do it. I mean, I am sure he didn't understand what he was doing at that age, but parents like to see that sum set out on the page and that the child can get the right answer' (AT Interview Marilyn 2nd Aug 99)

Thelma (Year 1 and 2 teacher), however, noted that parents might do oral work of the kind preferred by the NNS with their children. She contrasts two of the children, Darris and Jeffrey, who are average and above average in numeracy, with others:

> Children obviously talk about things in number terms with their parents, whether it's toys or days of the week, whatever, they would talk. Perhaps, certainly somebody like

> Darris who is sparky and bright when they go out with their mum, they talk about how much things are costing at the shop. You know, adding things up and......Jeffrey as well, very quick mentally, and they obviously do talk in number terms at home and get asked to add things up .... Some children just aren't sure how to work it out, but, you know, those children put their hand up straight away, they just know exactly what the question is. You can tell they've been working it out in their minds...I think, you know, especially at this stage, at home, it is just all the time, questions, you know, if I'm buying two loaves of bread and they cost 20 p each how much money do I give? You know, just everyday situations, maths is everywhere isn't it? It's not a separate entity on it's own, it's just.... you know, there is so much at home they can talk about to do with number and I think it really shows the ones that do, compared to the ones that [don't]. (AT Interview Thelma 27 July 01)

Katrina (year 1 and 2 teacher) similarly suggests asking children number questions based on shopping and using opportunities for mathematics work as they arise:

> On some of my reports [to parents], about how to support your child and those who have trouble with maths, I say - when you go shopping, and these are year 2 children, set them problems. If something costs 30 p how much change would I have if I had fifty? And it's the sort of things that you would...... and play number games sitting in the car.... Just even reading the numbers of the buses - oh look, there's a 115, so children get to recognise numbers all around. And it's not just numbers, it's maths in general. It's just the things that you just do automatically. And the language, you know - how big is the room? We need a new sofa, that one's too big. It will never get into our room. All that sort of thing, you know, where you think some children just never are involved in that sort of conversation. (AT Interview Katrina 27 July 01)

Both Katrina and Thelma believed that some parents did have these kinds of conversation with their children, their evidence being drawn from children's classroom numeracy. This was then a belief that the language, skills and attitudes that are essential for children to develop good numeracy skills are developed in the home context as much as, or perhaps more than, at school (cf Dylan's interview in Kim case study, Chapter 4b). The teachers here reflect the dominant discourses of the relationship between the home's groundwork for education as informal and the school's delivery of the NNS. Family numeracy courses, for example, are geared to teach parents how to do numeracy-friendly play and, like the teachers, are opposed to the use of maths books at home:

> By **talking** (original emphasis) about the maths you are using as you go about your day to day routine you can help your child understand what maths is used for ... Maths is all around us not just in 'maths books'. Young children will only be able to 'do sums', later, if they know what numbers mean and what they are used for. *(Basic Skills Agency, website accessed 10 Sept.2002)*

Suggested activities include those suggested by the teachers here: going shopping, sizing goods, spotting bus numbers, and using mathematical language like *long, smaller than, how many ...?* (BSA, accessed 10. Sept.2002).

Thelma's conjecture about Darris' home life ('how much things are costing at the shop' etc.) was in part, as far as we observed, accurate. Darris and her parents certainly 'would talk': but what we observed was not 'educational' talk of the sort advocated in official texts – not setting the table, spotting bus numbers or matching socks - but talk about family relationships and attitudes to school, work and church.

The numeracy practices of home are, in this sense, different than those of school, embedded in different social relationships and fulfilling different social purposes. Darris did have numeracy-rich conversations with her parents – but about their work and do-it-yourself projects, that is, about numeracy within adult contexts. Rick too hugely enjoyed his very informal (though 'grown up') card games with Maureen, a former croupier – and as well as improving his addition skills through games like 'Vingt-et-un', he made up his own card games, with elaborate and fast-changing rules, which Maureen patiently played with him. Maureen, too, took him shopping with her and used it as an opportunity to teach him to count money. However, the school did not explicitly build on such home resources: the teachers seldom referred to everyday numeracy practices in the classroom itself. Aaysha's teacher was unaware of her number counting (cf Ch 6; Baker et. al., 2004). Similarly, in Mountford, Seth's teacher was unaware of his engagement in numeracy associated with pigeon racing (Chapter 4a). But in Rowan, the teacher not only knew that one of the children's parents was an estate agent, with the out-of-school numeracy practices this involved, but actually took the class to visit him, and to explore those practices (Chapter 5c). The relationship between home and school in terms of 'building' upon home practices, especially talk around numeracy, varies not only with individual teachers and parents but also across social class boundaries.

But there is a further complexity here – where apparent 'real life' examples are brought into the classroom, they can be fraught with cultural judgements. Here we briefly consider table-laying. With opportunities for matching, counting and multiplying, table-laying is potentially a fertile environment for the development of numeracy. It figures in the BSA's suggestions for numeracy-rich home resources; and indeed one of the mothers (Kay at Mountford) with whom we worked listed laying the table as one of the things their children did which might help develop numeracy skills. An example from Thelma's class at Tarnside shows her using table laying as a means of linking home and school for purposes of mathematics learning.

> Thelma: what do children use maths for? If your mum says lay the table and you know four people are there? and you need a knife and fork for each?

> Child: Count them.

> Thelma: So how many things altogether?

> Child: 8

> Thelma: So that's maths isn't it (AT Tarnside 7 Nov. 00).

There is a stark contrast here between school and home numeracy practices. At school it may make educational sense to work out that there are eight 'things' when you have four forks and four knives. In a sense the 4 knives and four forks have become numbers which children and school then expect to calculate on. In contrast, in a home domain, home site context, where maintaining the separation of knives and forks is domestically important, to calculate the total number of objects and get eight is not only meaningless it is unlikely to happen unless the home is seeking to mimic school practices. The reference to a pseudo home setting may well create conflicts for the children that the teacher may not be aware of. In could get in the way of learning rather than assist it.

Further some families, at Mountford and perhaps at Rowan and Tarnside, do not lay the table for children's meals, indeed may not have tables, and in both cases outsiders made cultural judgements about such practices. A Tarnside student teacher said *Families should eat together, it's awful if they don't'*. Eating together at a table has huge symbolic power – a marker, in dominant discourses, of a wholesome 'family life' in which dominant values are nurtured. None of the children in Thelma's class said, as Charlie from Rowan, might have done, that in their household they don't lay the table; had they done so, it would have been a marker for the student teacher and perhaps for others that their family life was lacking ie in 'deficit'.

Different problems also arise, however, where such 'real life' events are applied in the classroom but the 'social' dimension is 'taken out' (perhaps because of some of the cultural and judgemental problems indicated above). So teachers try to use a conception of 'everyday life' as a vehicle for the application of numeracy skills. To make this work, Thelma has to 'fill in' school numeracy-related questions for the children. As Thelma talks through some of the maths problems she identifies in 'real life', human purposes are removed and the word problems themselves become actors – the mathematics takes over the discourse, the home practices are recontextualised (Bernstein, 1996) into school practices. Thelma, for example, prefaces use of 'word problems' saying: '*We need maths in real life as well as exams and stuff so today we are doing that'. She* writes on the board:

I have 8 sweets

I eat 3 sweets

How many left?

Child: 5.

Thelma: Is it add or take away?

Child: Add

Thelma: Are you sure? You wouldn't get 5. [i.e. as the answer]

Child: Take away.

Thelma: You ate 3 so 3 are taken away [...] Look out for words. The key word is left. Something is left so they are taken away.

Thelma writes on the board: 8 - 3 = 5.

Then she writes on board:

I have 6 marbles.

I find 4 more.

How many marbles?

She focuses on the wording as clues to the operations, as the NNS suggests and reads it aloud to the class. Have a think. Is that question asking us to add up or take away?

[no response]

Thelma: Which word tells us it's an adding question? What the most important word in that sentence, I find four <u>more</u>?

Child: More [only one or two hands going up]

Thelma elicits from the children 6 add 4 equals 10 as she writes 6+4=10 on the board.

Thelma: We know the numbers because it's the only two numbers we've been given. There's no point rushing or you'll end up with the wrong answer. These are called number stories or number questions. You make the sum into a story (AT Tarnside 7 Nov. 00).

But the move to the focus on wording makes the word problems into the actor, the agent that is doing the asking, when Thelma says 'Left told us it was take away Is that question asking us to add up or take away?' The move away from the 'real world' is then completed as Thelma adds 'We know the numbers because it's the only two numbers we've been given .... You make the sum into a story'. Here we find one of the few examples in our data of a teacher endeavouring to build on 'everyday' experiences – sweets, marbles - by recontextualising them (Bernstein, 1996) into the classroom. To do that, she calls upon 'common sense' knowledge of children's homes - that is, she calls upon discourses she believes to be shared, but which turn out to be perhaps as esoteric as that of traditional textbook (cf Brown and Dowling, 1992).

So the activity has become one in which sums are turned into stories; 'real life' becomes an imposed context, rather than a source for numbers of things which can be added or taken away. Through the recontextualising of home practices into pedagogic discourse, the accounts have shifted from domestic purposes, around laying the table or sharing sweets or playing with marbles, towards a reified conception of numbers themselves asking questions and numeracy words themselves, such as 'left' in 'how many left?', providing answers eg '<u>Left</u> told us it was take away'. In this sense, whatever talk around maths may be going on at home, it is unlikely to be schooled in this sense and 'building' on home experience in this way may actually add to children's confusion.

As well as teachers invoking a notion of home life as a basis for work on numbers in school, parents sought to introduce school work on numbers into the home. At Tarnside the children were regularly, from Year 1 onwards, given worksheets for homework (one is discussed in Chapter 4b), but some parents wanted to extend homework and use commercial texts with their children. Teachers were generally resistant to this, although Thelma had talked with Darris' mother about using a Key Stage 2 (KS2) book and all parents were asked to help with homework. Alison suggests that perhaps the key here is the relationship between parents and teachers. From Darris' and Jeffrey's success in school numeracy and their teachers' relationships with their parents, the teachers assumed the parents had been conforming to dominant discourses in providing informal, play-based opportunities for language and numeracy development, where in fact they had often provided formal help at home. In contrast, Rick's teacher assumed he had more formal help than our observations suggested: this perception may have arisen because of difficulties in the relationship between the school and Rick's mother. It seems that teachers may extrapolate from children's success in school to make assumptions about their home experiences; those inferences, which sometimes are inaccurate, then confirm teachers in their agreement with the dominant discourses of how parents can best help their children's numeracy. Judging from our observations, Darris and Jeffrey did more of the 'wrong' thing and less of the 'right' at home than Rick; yet the teachers had the opposite perceptions.

5b.6 Comments: disjunctions

There are, then, disjunctions between what children do at home and how teachers recontextualise it for schooled purposes; between the teachers' ideas of what children do at home and what we have observed; between what is advocated for children at home and their experiences at school; and between what parents imagine school wants them to do- ie more schooled maths at home - and what the teachers want – ie different, informal maths that the school did not have the time or resources to provide. There are also disjunctions between the ways in which different parents address and evaluate the school and how teachers respond to them. We cannot, then, present just one picture of such a school: it is experienced differently, not only by different children and parents, but by different teachers and by the same children and teachers at different times of day, as lessons run smoothly or disintegrate. We have however tried to draw out some themes, such as the disjunctions alluded to here, that we will build on more fully in the thematic Section of the book and to make links between these specific experiences in this particular site and the more general issues that the social view of numeracy, that we are adopting in this book, raises.

5c: ROWAN:*'they'll have to go to the bank for a mortgage. Where your mummy and daddy go to get money'*

5c.1. Introduction
Rowan was the leafy suburb white middle class school that we visited for the three years of the project. This chapter includes an account of the school and the local area, home school relationships and numeracy practices at the school. During the project we focussed on four children at the school. We discuss Anne in our case study of her in Chapter 4c. The other children were Max, Charlie and Eve. In this chapter we focus on the school itself. The teachers in the school on the project were Alice in Reception, Dominic in Year 1 and Clemency in Year 2.

5c.2. The local area and the school population

Rowan Primary School lay in a suburb of London. It was about two miles from a local town centre, in an area made up largely of privately owned expensive detached and semi-detached houses. The area had a generally green feel to it, with large, well established gardens. All of the families in our study had close historical connections with the area, with at least one of the parents having themselves attended local schools. Unlike Tarnside, then, Rowan and Mountford were each at the centre of a stable community.

Rowan was a big school, with about 450 children, when the national average was 240. The percentage of children at the school speaking English as an additional language was 4.4% double that at Mountford, and higher than most English schools, but much smaller than inner city schools such as Tarnside, where it was 38.4%. The percentage of children eligible for free school meals, that is, one of the government's key indicators for the 'context' of the school, was 2%, much lower than Mountford, the national average being 19.7%. The proportion of children with special educational needs, including Special Educational Needs (SEN) statements, 2.6%, was well below the national average of 23.2%.

Rowan's children came, in the main, from comparatively privileged backgrounds and we could expect them to succeed at school. In mathematics the school's performance in the national tests at Key stage 1 (KS1), even when compared to other schools with similar social context placed it high in school league tables. The percentage achieving level 3 or above was very high, putting the school's results in the top 5% in the country (2000 Panda).

Rowan was the first choice of most the parents with whom we worked. None of the parents had the doubts and suspicions that some felt about Tarnside or Mountford. This was a school whose results in mathematics tests supported its confidence in its mathematics work.

5c.3. The 'feel' of the school

Rowan had a large school population but never felt crowded. In addition to two playgrounds, there was a playing field shared by the whole school and a smaller area outside each classroom. In Reception and Year 2, a corridor outside each classroom was wide enough to allow small groups of children to work with adults.

The school organised the curriculum through the integrated day, rather than using the National Strategies for literacy and numeracy, from which it could opt out as its inspection and league table results identified it as a high performing school. A theme, shared between all the classes in a year and lasting for a few weeks, formed the base for literacy and numeracy, and other activities, e.g. art, science, school trips and the role-play area. During the school day children were set five or six activities, which were sometimes continued the following day. At the start of the school day the teachers outlined the activities for the day. During the day, the teacher and teaching assistant called particular children to work with them on activities. The rest of the time, children themselves chose whether to play or to complete other activities, and chose their own companions. However, the distinction between 'play' and 'other activities' was often unclear. The seamless merging of play and learning was central to the school's ethos.

The classes Alison visited had about thirty children, much larger than those at Mountford and Tarnside, yet never felt crowded. This was partly because of the availability of physical space as children often went outdoors or into the corridor. But the rooms were differently laid out, too. There were fewer tables and chairs than children as they often moved about the room, whereas most of the floor area at Tarnside was taken up with tables and chairs. Thus despite the comparatively large number of children in the class at Rowan, there was unallocated space in which the children made elaborate constructions, played with a metre-square 100 grid jigsaw, used role play clothes, made long snakes of multi-link cubes and so on.

The staffing ratio also contributed to Rowan's classes feeling smaller. As a 'beacon school', it attracted additional funding. Its budget allowed for teaching assistants to work alongside class teachers. Almost all the classes Alison visited had two staff, and many had three. In Tarnside the role of the teaching assistant sometimes became that of containment assistant. In contrast, the teaching assistants at Rowan and Mountford had direct teaching roles. Many of the teaching assistants at Rowan and Mountford were or had been mothers of children at the school and therefore had similar backgrounds, including social class, to the children.

The combined effect of the physical space, the organisation of the curriculum and the level of staffing were that children seemed confidently in charge of their own space. They were 'at home' in the classroom, consistent with the school ethos that learning and play, school and home cultures should be merged. As children were at home in the classroom, so were their parents. Parents were encouraged to come into the classroom and into the school life more generally. At the start of the school day there were parents looking at the elaborate displays helping their children complete reading records, chatting to each other and to other children, and talking to the teacher. Several of the parents volunteered to work at the school, usually taking a small group for reading or numeracy; the frequent school trips, including for example a farm, a garage, an estate agent and an airport were accompanied by parent volunteers; and some became teaching assistants in the school. The school culture was strongly integrationist: the integration of the curriculum itself and of school and home life, and the formation of networks of teacher/parent collaborations.

5c.4. Parent school relationships, contacts and communication, and parents as teachers

The anchoring point of teacher-parent communication was the start of the day, when parents brought children into the classroom. This was unlike Mountford where these kind of informal contacts between parents and teachers had been restricted after the Reception class. Rowan encouraged parents to be volunteer helpers at the school. Charlie's mother Kirsten volunteered to help with reading and had close contact with the school and generally trusted the staff. Alison asked her whether she saw herself as complementing or compensating for the school's work:

I would ... definitely think of myself as a complementer rather than a compensator ... I have no criticism of the school and really to a certain extent I let them get on with it ... I know the school aren't keen on parents to sort of doing stuff at home in case it's sort of ... not quite the same sort of approach ... if opportunities for mental maths and stuff come up you know ... But I'd hate to think that he has to come home and do a certain amount of work each night. (AT Charlie March 02)

Here Kirsten drew on several of the themes running through parents' relationships with the school. The school, as in Tarnside, advised parents against direct numeracy teaching at home and instead promoted talk and games based activities. When Kirsten wanted to discuss particular issues about Charlie she arranged formal meetings with the teachers. On occasion when she had had unsuccessful communication with teachers, she showed none of the anger generated at Tarnside when the teacher-parent relationship was under threat or the rejection felt by some of the Mountford parents. She criticised the teacher, but empathised with her difficulties. Rowan's middle class parents generally had confidence that their children would succeed; that confidence informed their dealings with the school. Some, such as Eve's mother, Jo, even took positions at the school. Jo first volunteered to help at the school, and then became a teaching assistant, .Conflicts did exist between parents and the school, such as over religious education, discussed in the case study on Anne (Chapter 4c), but the general tenor of parent-school relationships was cheerful and calm..

Jo commented on the support that she had had both from Alice, the teacher with whom she worked, and from the local authority training:

We had three days of training and that {included] a maths session because how they do maths in school these days is completely different on how I learned maths. It's all done on a number line you know, they tend to work horizontally rather than vertically which is how you know we did it. ... Up till this year I think everybody was *(local)*, they either had children in the school at this moment or they had had children in this school. *(AT Interview Jo, 9 Nov. 01)*

The school drew on the cultural and material resources of the parents and community. This was shown by the way that parents contributed to the life of the school. Eve's mother Jo said:

You see we've got a very very strong PTA as well and they supply things like computers, digital cameras... the great big screens. ... Oh it's fantastic our PTA ... They completely re-did the cookery room with all new, and one of the parents is a plumber and he came in and put all the stuff in. *(AT Interview Jo, 9 Nov. 01)*

This is a description of a school working in harmony with parents who have the time, skills and commitment to support it to the hilt, including financially. It shows how the cultural resources of a community become the cultural resources and habitus of a school. Rowan was a comparatively stable school. That contrasts with Tarnside, a school where there was a history of high mobility in the school population. Rowan's beacon school status was earned in large part through the school's performance in the league tables, which led in turn to higher funding; for Tarnside, with a highly mobile school population, a child leaving the school led to a drop in its funding.

Whilst parents' communication with the school centred mainly on the daily contact with the teacher, it also extended into more formally organised work with the children. Formal discussions of children's progress took place at well-attended parents' evenings. In addition, there was a yearly 'curriculum forecast' meeting for parents outlining the curriculum for the coming year.

As an example of formal communication between home and school, we give an account of a meeting on numeracy. Eight mothers of children from one class came to the session Alison attended, compared with the eight who attended a whole school numeracy event at Mountford.

Teachers outlined the school's approaches to numeracy including that Rowan, unlike Mountford and Tarnside, had not fully adopted either the National Numeracy or Literacy Strategies. The teachers dealt with parents' negative feelings towards mathematics and explained, establishing common ground with the parents, that what children now do in mathematics had little in common with what they themselves had done. This contrasted, with a similar whole school event reviewing the numeracy curriculum and ways of teaching at Tarnside where the Head and mathematics co-ordinator maintained an edge of irony, distancing themselves from the NNS that they were introducing to the parents. That is, they sought deliberately to place themselves on the parents' side in the face of such new developments. The staff at Rowan, on the other hand, were clearly enthusiastic about the school's approaches to mathematics. They were confident that parents would follow their lead, and had no need to seek further to ally themselves with the parents against such innovations. Where staff at Tarnside called on shared knowledge that staff, parents and children are in a hard world, at Rowan there was an assumption that all face the future with confidence. Again in contrast, at Mountford teachers and parents seldom shared issues about teaching and learning in schools. This stemmed either from the problematic nature of access between them (Chapter 4a, 5a) or from assumptions that parents could not or would not help with their children's numeracy.

At the meeting a parent had brought in a newspaper cutting (Parker, 2000) on why parents must not play teacher. She had bought some children's workbooks, CDs and numeracy sticker books for her son and now wondered if she had done the wrong thing, asking the teachers what parents should do and not do. The question reflected the only issue of some tension in the discussions which was 'how much comparatively formal numeracy work should parents should offer at home?', an issue we saw was also crucial at Tarnside (Chapter 5b) where it remained a cause of disjunction rather than being opened up for discussion in this way. The teacher responded to the question by showing a classroom box of games, which could be lent to parents:

> Teacher: It's got some good challenging family maths ideas, interactive stuff, not finishing off homework.

> *Parent* A: If we go off and do our own thing, is it detrimental?

> Maths co-ordinator: Well it can be detrimental.

Teacher: If you only do the vertical layout *(illustrated with her own exercise book)* the children only think of numbers going up to 10, not bigger numbers. (Parents' numeracy meeting Ro 10 Feb. 00)

The initial focus of the meeting had been to describe school's numeracy approaches, but the parents directed it towards discussion of what they could do at home to complement the school's work. These parents were comfortable dealing with teachers and debating the detail of school approaches to numeracy. As at Tarnside and less so at Mountford, at least some parents saw no harm in supplementing the school's work with text-based books or computer work at home, although with more liaison with the school. Although Rowan had not adopted the NNS three-part lesson, many of its pedagogical approaches fitted well with the NNS: the teachers emphasised oral and mental methods and the importance of the children developing the ability to visualise a number line. As at Tarnside, the teachers feared that parents' use of commercial texts may undermine their work ("Well it can be detrimental") and sought to keep control of children's numeracy activities. However, unlike Tarnside and Mountford, the activities recommended for home, such as games (see Anne and Seth Case Studies Chapter 4a and 4c) were similar to those at school. Tarnside's advice to parents on what to offer at home contrasted sharply with what children had to do at school, whereas Rowan sought to maintain the home culture at school. We were aware, though, that the 'home culture' was that defined by Rowan and for some parents the home included, for example, commercial texts on formal mathematics which were frowned on by the school.

5c.5 Numeracy events and practices in the Rowan classroom.

Here we give a brief account of the numeracy events we have seen in the Rowan classroom. These included 10 minutes daily whole class 'mental maths' (not described here); weekly lessons in small groups where children 'do things at the edge of their capacity' with a teacher; numeracy activities as part of the 'integrated day' for children to do more independently; and children's own use of numeracy-rich activities in some of their games.

We start by looking at the small group weekly numeracy lessons. Typically these lasted 10 to 15 minutes. The children were organised according to their skills, in groups, of up to six, each group with a learning 'target', decided by the teacher but shared with the children. The example Alison describes here was in the Reception class. Three girls were working towards a target of writing subtraction sentences with an "=" sign. The children, working with the teacher, Alice, were taking handfuls of counters from a jar, counting them removing some, counting that second group, counting the remainder and writing for example $9 - 6 = 3$. Eve had reversed some numbers. All three children continued in this way. They concentrated, in good humour, on the work. Other children were milling about around them, but none interrupted.

At the end of the lesson Eve, one of our focus children, showed Alice her work, and Alice commented,

It's so good – you can do your target now. Next week I'll have to think of a new one.
(To all three children) You can do take away sentences now. (AT Ro 14 Mar. 00)

Aspects of this lesson were typical of the practices of direct numeracy teaching in small groups in Rowan. Although the numeracy event was highly controlled by the teacher, within the task children had some autonomy by picking their own quantity of counters.   The children were told their current target, which was recorded. The groups were formed so that children worked on tasks which the teacher judged were appropriate for each individual. In effect the teacher retained control and power.

Rowan's small group mathematics lessons were in sharp contrast with other numeracy activities in which children were engaged. The lessons focused on formal mathematics content, where the mathematics was not tied to particular contexts or purposes other than those of the immediate lesson. The counters could have been cubes, teddy bears or fingers. In another lesson in Year 2 which was focused on place value, the teaching assistant made use of house prices in advertisements. The link between numbers in the hundreds of thousands and local house prices was not purposeful to the children's learning but it served to illustrate a 'real' context in which such numbers appear.

So in many ways these events were detached from children's home life. On the other hand, the size of group to which children were asked to contribute, working with one adult, was closer to home life than the whole-class teaching we saw in our other schools. Teachers could record children's achievements very precisely, and thus came to 'know' children's skills and knowledge with something perhaps closer to a parent's knowledge. These specific qualities of purpose, control, organisation, values and social relations in numeracy lessons were some of the features of the school numeracy practices at Rowan.

Next we describe some of the numeracy events around a topic on the local area and housing in the first term of the Reception year. The topic included a visit to an estate agent, where the father of Judith, one of the children worked.   The topic started with the children listening to the traditional nursery story of the 'three pigs', that is a story of three pigs choosing differently constructed houses.

The language in this whole-class discussion included numeracy language and ideas such as buying, selling, tape measures, renting, 'a lot of money', which shows the potential of the topic for classroom work on numeracy. It also is an example of the cultural resources of the children in the class that are available to all of them. They all had access to the practices, in this case, of Estate Agents. This was not available to the children of Mountford or Tarnside.

The children with their teacher, the teaching assistant, and some parents first visited an empty flat with Judith's father and then walked around the town centre, the adults asking the children questions.. Some of these were number questions – for instance, counting the number of storeys of the larger buildings, and counting the number of estate agents.   At the estate agent's office, Judith's father (JF) went along with the fantasy/real mix, answering the children's questions:

JF: I believe you've got some questions for me …

JF: [Reading out from a list] 'Can the piggies buy a house?' Well, have they got any money?

Children: No.

JF: Oh. Well they'll have to go to the bank for a mortgage. Where your mummy and daddy go to get money.

The children looked at a leaflet about a house, and took turns photocopying it on the office copier. Judith's father pointed out 'this big number' (£124 000) on the leaflet as the price. He read out the number and added, 'pounds - that's what our money is'.

Next question: Do you use a tape measure?

JF: Oh no, I use a sonic tape. You know sonic, like in Star Wars?

He showed how to use it and gave a child a go. (AT Ro 9 Nov. 99)

The discussion slipped between fantasy and the real world.. The idea of buying your own home through a mortgage and the associated numeracy activities would have been more familiar to the Rowan children than the Mountford children. Photocopying of a real house advertisement was done on a real copier. Back in the classroom, Alice pinned up an advertisement for a flat, brought with others from the estate agent for the role play area. They discussed the large numbers involved in house prices. Alice said: "It cost - see all these numbers - a hundred and seventy three thousand pounds".

Thus children slipped between out of school discourses and those planned for the classroom. These included local geography, with attached numeracy issues, the fictional worlds used by the teacher to link children's imaginative worlds with classroom learning and their own real and fantasy lives. Alice was in charge of the level of planning and control of the activities, despite the school's apparently relaxed approach to the curriculum. It was also interesting, in terms of a school's or community's cultural resources for numeracy, that the children had met an unusual mathematical tool, a sonic tape measure, through one of the parents of the other children. Alice had brought into the classroom a wooden box containing a building set of bricks (each about 2 x 1 x 0.5 cm), roofing tiles, and mortar mix, all in the 'real' materials but sized down. She kept the box closed as she asked the children,

What are we working on?

Children: Estate agents ... Three little pigs ...

Alice opened box to show the bricks. They are made of real brick. She said: Could you make a real house of them?

Children; No

Child; How can it be so heavy when they are so tiny?

Child: Because there's so much of them in the box

Child: How can you make a house when they're so small?

Alice: You could make a house for playmobil people, and you can be play builders. …

Alice: … So we'll make a house. Try and make the wall strong so it doesn't fall over.
(AT Ro 16 Nov. 99)

The estate agents topic was used as an umbrella for several curriculum areas, and it included construction play, and the mathematical language of weight, density, size and number. As the children later constructed buildings with the bricks, Alice focused on shape, space and stability. The children worked hard at making their walls vertical and stable. One went outside the classroom and looked at the outside of the classroom wall, then copied the brick pattern. He said that if you pushed at the bottom of the wall, it moved but did not break. Meanwhile other children made a 'house' out of hollow wooden cuboids of different sizes (the biggest about 80 x 30 x 20 cm), big enough for them to enter.

We note, in terms of cultural resources, Alice's description of the building kit as 'precious'. Alice explained later to Alison that she wanted the children to understand that it is an especially good toy, and that since the bricks easily shatter they should look after them. However, the kit was also 'precious' in the sense of 'expensive' and, perhaps due to parental support, beyond the means of schools like Mountford and Tarnside.

The children played, but with objects such as the large cuboids and the bricks that may not be available at home. The children had a level of choice in what they did but those choices were steered by the teacher, or co-opted to her plans so that 'play' with bricks was directed to particular learning goals like making a stable wall.

Next we describe a number and data handling activity in the Reception class seen by the school as 'independent maths'. This was a small group survey of ways of doing up shoes, within a class topic on shoes. The children were expected to work comparatively independently. The children were given sheets with four columns each of 11 boxes, labelled at the bottom of the columns *Buckles, Velcro, Laces, Other.* They marked the boxes starting from the bottom, to show each occurrence of a shoe fastening method. They variously scribbled, ticked, coloured in or drew pictures. None was concerned if their sheet did not match anyone else's. Some treated it as a race, not between each other but between shoe fastenings. Most of the children did a lot of counting either to reach the top of the sheet or totting up their totals and comparing them with others'. Their language as they compared sheets included *more, most, first, least, less, top, higher, how many?*

As was usual at Rowan, they did not do it all at the same time, but when it fitted with other set activities and with their own choices, so that at any one time up to eight children were busy on the survey. It perhaps had an element of role-play. The children had clipboards and adopted the discourse of street surveys.

The shoe survey was in the 'real world' in that the children tallied real shoes worn by real children. We can compare the survey to the tallying of cars done that we saw at Tarnside. There, small groups of children tallied real cars, outside the classroom window, while others were asked to make a tally sheet of toy cars on the classroom table. Neither activity was practically purposeful for the children. At

Tarnside some of children seemed to do the activity because the teacher asked them to. Some did not engage much in it at all. At Rowan the children engaged and wanted to complete the activity in some sense for themselves. It was not clear why shoe styles generated such interest and engagement, but we can point to some contributing factors. There were opportunities for play as children did the activity with their friends; for ticking or decorating boxes on a sheet, which is easier than the formal tally marks used at Tarnside; and the activity was entirely 'real' in that the shoes, and the wearers, were present in the room. The survey itself required children to interact with each other; 'doing the survey' became the thing to do for the children that morning. Thus the activity became child, rather than teacher, led. The teachers did not intervene at all; they were meanwhile working with small groups. The survey work, then, fostered 'independent maths'. Many of the children worked together, so 'independent' did not mean isolated; indeed, it was an activity which required children to move about the room talking to, or at least looking at the feet of, others. The children's survey sheets were later displayed so contributing to the impression given by Rowan's classrooms, to parents and children, as well as researchers that numeracy was seen as a creative activity. [It is interesting to note that an interim review of the National Numeracy Strategy (Levin, 1999) recommended greater attention to 'creativity', of the kind evident from our observations at Rowan. It is also interesting that recent modifications to the NNS and NLS have resulted in a more unified Primary Strategy that explicitly encourages creativity].

So far we have described school numeracy events which were highly organised. The children typically were set about six activities for the day, the rest of the day was their own. They organised their own day, all the children spent a lot of time in 'play', with their own choice of activities and companions. Children used most of the resources of the classroom, including numeracy resources, for their games. Among the games we saw were playing with dice, making snakes out of multi-link cubes, and debating the number of cubes and length of a snake; playing teacher-and-pupil roles, including number work; playing with calculators; playing with a class-sized 100 grid jigsaw carpet and a 100-grid set of cubes; measuring shoe sizes; playing with scales; making patterns out of cubes, beads and counters; playing cards; noughts and crosses; join-the-dots pictures; making constructions; playing with sand and water; and many more. Although the focus children at Rowan had a range of games and toys at home, they had more, and different, play resources at school where more space and time was available. So for example one multi-link snake ran the length of the classroom.

5c.6. Discussion: At home at school, at school at home, and the disjunctions between home and school

We have described a picture of harmony, with children seeing numeracy lessons as part of play and teachers and parents seeing children's play as part of numeracy learning. Indeed that picture was largely accurate, and the school and homes together provided an integrated and rich environment for children's learning.

However, discussions with parents exposed some tensions and ambivalence around the school's play-as-learning ethos.

Rowan's 'integrated day' approach was unusual, at least since the near-universal nation-wide adoption of the NNS. The 'integrated' approach itself placed Anne's mother, Trisha, in conflict with the school with respect to other subject areas, as she was unable to withdraw her daughter from religious education, which was integrated throughout the day (cf. Chapter 4c). Further tensions arose from some perceptions that the school's pedagogical stance was not effective. Trisha commented that the Head thinks children learn by 'osmosis'. She believed some of their progress, claimed by the school as evidence of the success of its approaches, was due to more formally structured work at home. However, despite appearances and unknown to the parents, some of the school's small group numeracy lessons were very highly structured.

We have gathered from the parents of our focus children that some parents sought to offer additional, numeracy work of a more formal kind for their children at home, even employing private tutors. Some of the pressure for this came from parents' concerns with their children's future secondary schooling. Some looked towards private schooling, which could only be considered by families with appropriate material resources. Rowan was an area where this was possible for a proportion of families. So although Rowan, in terms of league tables, was among the highest achieving schools it may not have offered enough for some parents. For them that must include the potential for competitive entry into private secondary schools. These competitive processes were a culture quite foreign to that explicitly promoted at Rowan. They were clearly also not part of Mountford's parents' concerns.

Rowan was highly valued by parents for its cheerful atmosphere, the children's evident contentment, its success in the national tests and the school's fostering of good relationships with parents. But lingering doubts remained in many parents' minds about whether this liberal, play-centred culture prepared children for the 'real world' of competitive secondary school entry, and therefore for competition for higher education. Parents complemented the school's work in what they themselves offered at home, taking seriously the school's advice and seeking not to undermine the school culture. But as the children grew older, parents also saw the school as possibly disadvantaging their child in the race for secondary school success, and they compensated for that disadvantage through the employment of private tutors, working to a quite different agenda.

5c.7. Conclusion

In many ways Rowan offered a school environment for numeracy learning which mirrored the home experiences of its children. In this it stands in stark contrast to Tarnside and Mountford. This is not because of the particular nature of Tarnside's numeracy work (which often had parallels with the home numeracy texts used by some of the children) but because the home experiences of Tarnside's children were as diverse as its school population. The Rowan school culture was remarkably homogeneous, which was also true but in different ways for Mountford. Far more than at Tarnside and Mountford, Rowan parents and teachers had shared educational experiences, a shared language and, indeed, a lot of shared time, as parents worked in the school and parents become teaching assistants. So shared beliefs and values were strengthened by joint work. The school ethos promoted the insertion of an idea of home into school, with a focus on play and children's choice, and of school into home, as the school loaned games to children's parents and asked parents to support school topics by, for example, taking their children to see a building site.

In one respect Rowan's numeracy curriculum was organised around difference, not homogeneity: The small group numeracy lessons were highly differentiated, so that at one stage two children, Charlie (who was ahead) and Max who was seen to be falling behind, had individual lessons. This was in contrast to Mountford and Tarnside, working within the NNS. At Tarnside the children were even placed into ability sets for numeracy and the teaching was aimed at groups of about 25.

Rowan had considerable cultural and material resources. The school itself had excellent staff-pupil ratios, generous accommodation, and resources. The parents too had material resources on which the school drew. This included money, which paid for school trips, home computers, and time, which contributed to their close relationship with the school and their numeracy activities with their children. (c.f Reay, 2000 on the time available to the middle classes). Their own educational and cultural resources and habitus fitted with the teachers'. The parents may have debated with teachers why it was wrong to use text books at home, but they did so from a culture in which they shared the articles they read and the TV programmes they watched.

Rowan's teachers and parents collaborated closely in the education of a group of children who will, by and large, be successful in their schooling. This contrasts with both Mountford and Tarnside. At Mountford there was a distance between the parents and the teachers and the children were not expected to achieve academically. At Tarnside conflicting perceptions, expectations and experiences of the school led to overt disagreements and to a high mobility rate. In contrast Rowan presented a harmonious picture to the world, despite the parents supplementing the school's pedagogy and curriculum. This resulted in disguised tensions with many parents employing private tutors but without telling the school, knowing that this was part of the ground rules of schooling at Rowan.

All three schools Mountford, Tarnside and Rowan promoted similar numeracy-rich activities for children at home. At Mountford and Tarnside those activities were at times in contradiction to the children's home numeracy experiences; at Rowan they were usually a continuation. The Rowan ethos was consistent, visible and easily explained to parents and every parent knew the ground rules. In contrast at Mountford and Tarnside parents struggled to know and accept the rules of schooling and what was expected of them.

SECTION FOUR: THEMES

Having set the scene for our thematic analysis through case studies of selected children and accounts of the three schools in which we conducted research, we begin the 'Themes' Section by looking more closely at numeracy practices at school. In keeping with the general principle running throughout this book, we will keep in mind home practices as we look at school and then, in Chapter 7, keep in mind school practices as we look more closely at homes. Chapter 8 then focuses on the relationship between schools and homes. In the concluding Chapter 9 of the book we set out possible explanations for low achievement in numeracy that have emerged from the research.

In the Case Study Chapters we focussed on three children, one from each of the schools we researched: Seth from Mountford, Kim from Tarnside and Anne from Rowan. In the Themes Section we will call further upon the information we have from these children and to some extent count upon the readers' acquaintance with them. But in addition, we will bring in examples from other children in the study. From Mountford we will draw especially on evidence from Kerry, a girl from a relatively poor family, who was ranked lower in her class in both literacy and numeracy than Seth and was seen by the teachers across the three years of our visits to be not very 'engaged'; Lenny, a boy who was in a higher band according to the teacher's baseline assessments and whose family seemed to have more financial resources, providing him for instance with a computer and elaborate software on which we comment; and Kay, a middle attainment child whose family had been through a rough patch but whose desire to please her teachers and to relate well to her parents was of particular interest.. At Tarnside, in addition to Kim, the focus of the Case Study in Chapter 4b, we have already discussed Darris, who was successful in school, and her mother, Ruby, who had developed a good relationship with some of Darris' class teachers; and Rick who was one of the 'unsettled' children we noted, and whose mother Maureen's response to teachers was different than that of Ruby, but who was doing well in literacy and numeracy. We also provide a telling example from the home background of Aaysha, a young girl of Pakistani origin whose parents had recently sought asylum in England and had temporarily at least shifted from middle class relative affluence to a state of poverty and who were struggling to find appropriate work. From Rowan, we have focused on Anne in the Case Study (Chapter 4c) and here we also draw upon material from Darianne, a child listed as average in numeracy for her class and who incorporated into her play features of formal education; and Eve, a friend of Anne's and whose mother, Jo, was active in the Parent Teachers Association.

The implications of all of this for policy, pedagogy and curriculum might, we argue be considerable and we draw some of these out more explicitly in the Conclusion. But, before addressing these issues we feel it is important for those engaged in such decisions to understand from within the complex relationships, meanings and social practices in which pupils, carers and teachers are engaged. The combination of the detailed case studies in Chapter 4 and of thematic analyses building on such data in Chapter 5 will, we hope, provide a sounder basis on which to develop such policy discussion.

CHAPTER SIX: NUMERACY PRACTICES AT SCHOOL

Engagement, Coded Questions and Switching

1. INTRODUCTION

Having set the scene for our thematic analysis through case studies of selected children and accounts of the three schools in which we conducted research, we would like to begin the 'Themes' Section by looking more closely at numeracy practices at school. In keeping with the general principle running throughout this book, we will keep in mind home practices as we look at school and then, in Chapter 7, keep in mind school practices as we look more closely at homes. Chapter 8 then focuses on the relationship between schools and homes.

We will focus here on some lessons that we observed in schools, starting from the perspective of teaching and curriculum but then moving outwards towards home as we consider how these lessons may look to children from different homes. Three features of the numeracy practices of the classroom have stood out for us as we analysed these data: the notion of 'engagement'; what we term 'coded questions'; and the issue of 'switching'. The term 'engagement' was used by Lave (1992) when she referred to "things (real and imaginary) that do and do not engage learners' intentions and attention". This notion was used by some of the teachers and assistants in describing children's participation (or not) in classroom numeracy practices. We ask the questions: 'how and why do children 'engage' with the schooled numeracy practices offered them by teachers?' Part of our explanation lies in the relationship between home numeracy practices and school numeracy practices – for some children, at least, there is such a contrast between these practices that 'engagement' with the school poses serious problems. Whilst the notion of 'engagement' is, to some extent, an 'emic' term, in that participants themselves employ it to describe what they perceive as happening in the classroom, the term 'coded questions' operates at a more 'etic' level: that is, we coined the phrase to describe the ways in which the discourse of the classroom often entails relatively hidden assumptions about what is going on, what is expected of children, what kinds of answers are required for questions that, in other contexts, might legitimately be answered in other ways. The discourse pattern that is salient in these numeracy events, and that to some extent characterises what is distinctive in schooled numeracy practices, is one in which the teacher has already set up a contextual *frame* within which the deictic reference is evident (e.g. 'How many numbers?'– an

B. Street, D. Baker and A. Tomlin (eds.), Navigating Numeracies, 117-128.
© 2005 *Springer. Printed in the Netherlands.*

example we deal with in more detail below eg 'What can you tell me about the number 11?' (Marilyn cited in Ta Case Study p. 10). Similar examples were found in a literacy research project associated with this numeracy research project (Gregory et. al, 2004) eg a teacher reading a story reads out a princess's response to a dragon which had just shut a door in her face; she then asks 'What did I do then?'. One of the children knows the code and, amongst all of the things the teacher was actually doing then, picks out the one she has in mind: 'You changed your voice' (AW, Ta 15/05/02). Finally, the concept of switching, again derives from our own conceptual apparatus and, as we explained in Chapter 2, was adapted from the sociolinguistic literature on language switching. The term has helped us to describe and make sense of the considerable movement across modes of communication – oral, written, visual – and across registers – specialist and 'everyday' – as teachers attempt to engage their pupils in mathematical thinking and practice of the kind required by schooling. We weave the three concepts through the accounts of three numeracy events involving three of the children we have already described in Section 3. Rather than providing a separate section for each concept, we have attempted to maintain the integrity of the 'event' and then used the concepts to make sense of each as we go through it. However, we suggest that there is an explanatory link to be followed between them; namely that the relative engagement of these three children in these events can be explained in terms of the relationship between school and home numeracy practices and in particular the children's relationship to the particular kinds of numeracy practices that characterise schooling, namely coded questions asked by the teacher and the kinds of switching required within the classroom and between home and school practices and discourses. From the point of view of pedagogy and possible outcomes for policy, we argue that the problems we identify are especially salient where the questions and the switching remain taken for granted rather than being made explicit.

These three concepts, then, can be thought of as emergent themes, in the sense that we did not set out with them in mind at the beginning of the research, but they kept pressing themselves on us through our encounters with the schools, the children and their parents. In that sense the data generated some of the concepts although we did, of course, as we explain in Chapters 2 and 3, begin with some theoretical and conceptual apparatus that itself began to generate data. Whilst the notion of numeracy events and practices preceded the research, the particular features of these events and practices that we identify here – engagement, coded questions and switching – emerged from the data. This dialectic relationship between concepts and data represents one of the major features of ethnographic-style research and writing (cf Agar, 1996; Hammersley, 1992; Silverman, 1993) to which we are committed.

2 ENGAGEMENT AND DISENGAGEMENT

We want to focus here on the issue of how children are differentially perceived as 'engaged' or not in the schooled numeracy practices required by the institution. What do teachers and schools mean by engagement? In their case it is most likely the child being 'on task' doing what he/she is being asked to do. For the child it may be that the social relations of schooled numeracy practices means a lack of the kinds of choice and control they might have at home (see Chapter 4). Within schooled numeracy practices, the teacher has overt control. An alternative understanding of engagement would include the child choosing to do a task. for which we provide some examples. More broadly engagement also includes a child showing commitment and acceptance of a task that may have been set by someone else, whether at home or at school.

We contrast three children from our research to illustrate these themes. One child, Kim, (see Chapter 4b) comes from an African-Caribbean home in an ethnically mixed part of London and attends Tarnside school (see Chapter 5b); another, Anne (see Chapter 4c) comes from a middle class white home in a leafy suburb and attends Rowan school (see Chapter 5c); a third, Seth (see Chapter 4a) comes from a working class housing estate on the south coast and attends Mountford school (see Chapter 5a). We contrast the pathological view of Kim's engagement, where teachers and others use words like 'lazy' and shout 'listen' at him, blaming his home for 'indulging' him, with evidence of his actual engagement in things that interest him, such as family genealogy and relations, counting door numbers, construction etc. Anne is represented very differently by the Reception teacher, when commenting on her ability when she started school: *She's got the language, like 'six and four makes ten';* and in field notes the researcher summarises her classroom engagement:

> 'she is comfortable and happy there and she enjoys learning. She seems to be someone who particularly notices what she learns ... typically when she has her first correct try at the activity or problem - she beams, sits up straight and asks for more'. (AT Ta April 01)

Seth appears to be able to handle some of the mathematical concepts required and in his everyday life engages with numbers, such as in relation to his father's pigeons and to pocket money, yet appears to 'disengage' at times in lessons, occasionally surprisingly re-engaging.

How do we describe and explain such differences? What is the relative weight of individual explanations in attainment in schooled mathematics in relation to the significance of home background, class and race in these children's relative 'engagement'? From a methodological perspective, what can such 'telling cases' tell us and what are their limitations? To address these questions, we build upon the detailed accounts of our three case study children in Chapter 4.

3. 'HE'S LAZY'

We begin by recalling the account we gave of Kim at Tarnside (Chapters 4b and 5b). His teachers described him variously as 'unfocused', 'lazy' and unable to 'listen' and Alison the researcher noted how we would sometimes appear to be asleep in class. Marilyn, the class teacher in Year 1 suggested that an explanation for this lack of engagement might lie in the fact that 'he's got lots of women fussing around him' (AT Interview, Marilyn, 28 Sept. 00). On the other hand, Alison noted that he was engaged in some tasks, both at school and at home. At school, she highlighted one incident in Reception class when the children were asked to draw a picture of something they had done in the holiday (see Chapter 4b).

> Kim drew a picture of his family at a recent family christening. It showed about fifteen people, and he started telling the researcher in exact detail the name and family relationship of each person. He was interrupted in this by Cheryl, who the researcher judged was embarrassed by one of the children being so boring to the researcher We infer from this that there may be topics on which Kim may be more talkative than he usually appears in school – he was usually silent, particularly when with an adult in the classroom (AT Ta April 01).

Apart from this event, the school activities Kim engaged in with enthusiasm in Reception and Year 1 all involved construction toys. In later years, Alison did note that at times he 'surprised' the teacher by appearing to be off task and then suddenly coming up with the right answer to a question, although the teachers tended to put this down to 'luck' (AT Ta July 01). At home Kim's mother Juline commented on his noticing of numbers and one occasion, when he was going around the supermarket, 'he was … noticing things like this pack of crisps that's got six in or something like that' (AT home visits, July 01).We heard of two different Kims here. On the one hand we encountered someone who was engaged in such interests as family genealogy, counting items in supermarkets, counting door numbers, model building and some classroom numeracy tasks - we could say he was engaging in his terms. He was considered, at least by his mother, but also occasionally by teachers – as 'potentially bright'. On the other, we met someone who was disengaged, 'lazy', doesn't 'listen', falls asleep, had to 'have things done for him', 'doesn't care', is 'indulged at home and is being put on the SEN Register (We provide many of these comments in Chapters 4b and 5b). How can we explain these discrepancies? We can call upon different discourses, from individualised accounts of personality and pathologising accounts of his moral behaviour, through class and race to issues of discourse itself – such as the ways in which different parties actually converse with him, the interpersonal styles and expectations of response. Focussing on numeracy we might also note the ways in which he 'engages' with particular numeracy practices. Here, then, we would invoke the concepts associated with numeracy practices that we have been developing throughout the book (see especially Chapter 2), such as social relations, discourses, values. For instance, the social relations of this classroom practice and the discourse patterns that arise from them, are embedded in the teacher's agenda. The pupil's agenda and identity, on the other hand, could be about less compliance with teachers: on those occasions when Kim engages it is on his terms, when the social relations suit his identity, such as his account of family genealogy and his noticing of door numbers. He may deal with the conflict between teacher expectations and his own desires by disengaging, using such strategies as 'sleeping'. If the theme of the research project is the explanation of children's low achievement in schooled numeracy, then perhaps part of the explanation at least may be found in the discursive and social practices, the social relations and values, in which numeracy is embedded for Kim and other children.

Kim's family and school staff all felt there was something to be explained. They agreed that Kim did not have learning difficulties in the sense of being 'slow', but they agreed 'concentration' was difficult for Kim. One insight from his mother,

Juline, came when she compared Kim's school experience to her own responses to boring training courses:

> No I find that when you get somebody like Kim he gets bored very easily so they've got to stimulate him. He's a bit like me in that sense because I mean training courses at work I'll be the first one to fall asleep. If I'm bored that's it, if I'm not interested that is it. So they need to stimulate him a bit more. (AT Home Interview 30 August 01)

The teachers, on the other hand, invoked a discourse of pathology and deficit, as we have seen, to explain this and it came through sometimes in the way in which teachers and Special Needs staff actually spoke with Kim.

The researcher, Alison, believed 'it's not a *lack* of concentration so much as a rejection of completely contradictory and probably bewildering experiences'. In terms of our research concepts, we might identify here conflicting social relations and contexts and we might say that Kim has difficulties switching between practices or between codes. That is switching between school sited numeracy practices and home sited numeracy practices. For instance, at home his grandmother, who was a teacher in Jamaica, used traditional methods of teaching, memory and drilling, and specific pedagogic vocabulary such as 'plus' in addition tasks, whilst the school used worksheets and some exploratory principles and a different vocabulary, such as 'more' or 'add'. Faced with these contradictory discourses, Kim 'refuses engagement, by 'walking away' as his grandmother Carmen put it, or appearing to sleep, or refusing eye contact. This is despite the fact that he is an 'obedient' child, doing what he is told at home and rarely in trouble at school' (AT).

The discourses in which Kim became enmeshed may themselves, then, offer some kind of explanation for his occasional disengagement. A session involving the teacher writing on the board and asking 'how many numbers' (AT Ta April 01) illustrates this well. The session involved some off-putting interpersonal features – repeated directives 'listen to the question'; denials of attempts at an answer – 'no, just a moment' and sarcasm when some children did get what the teacher was after ' *My goodness me, I might have done something a little bit too easy!*. Where Kim appeared more engaged in this activity was where the substantive or referential features of the interaction, overrode the interpersonal dimension .The teacher wrote 2+2+6 on the board and asked: *How many numbers are you adding together there, how many __numbers__, Kim*. He said, quite confidently, 'six' and 'twenty two'. It appears that he was interpreting the text on the board as in part an addition task and in part as a place value task. That is he was seeing the numbers in "2 + 2" not as separate digits but as constituents of a single complete number, 22. This fits and is consistent with practices teachers use when they partition twenty two into two tens and two units and when they reconstruct them into a single number by addition $20 + 2 = 22$. They might talk about 2 longs and 2 units; or of two beads on the tens stick of an abacus and two on the units stick, suggesting that 2 and 2 is 22 (see Anne below). So joining them together, as Kim did, into one number did not contradict some of the teacher's practices when teaching number. His answer of twenty-two, however did not fit with what the teacher wanted at that moment, which was for the children to recognise and label the actual digits 2,2,6 and to say how many of them there were ie three.

Clues to Kim's interpretation are indeed given by the way the task is framed and set out: the kind of switching between oral, written and visual representations. The signs on the board include not only the figures themselves, 2, 2 and 6 but also + signs, which are usually seen as a requirement for pupils to do addition. Moreover, the teacher repeats orally 'how many', a phrase that may be heard as usually collocated with such addition problems as 'how many is four add six?'. The teacher eventually spells out more precisely what she wants, pointing visually in turn to the numbers on the board and counting them as figures. Kim now gets it and says 'three', that is 2,2,6 consist of three 'numbers'. However, the teacher then adds further confusion for at least some of the children by asking 'Who can tell me what those numbers are?'. This is a classic example of the kind of classroom numeracy discourse the researchers encountered many times, which we came to refer to as 'coded' questions (see above). Such known answer questions, cued by prefixes such as 'what, when, how' are familiar to children as part of the classroom routine, though outsiders – including the researchers - and also some children - often have trouble filling in the contextual cues. In the present case, the question 'Who can tell me what those numbers are?' was interpreted by one child as meaning a set of numbers to be added and, given that the numbers were written on the board as 2+2+6, responded 'ten'. The teacher said ' *Chris, have I asked you to add them together yet? No?'* The clue to what the teacher intended was given later, in another coded question, when she wrote up 9+7+4+3+3 and asks 'What are those numbers?' The researcher noted that she 'gets answer' – ie five, corresponding to the answer three she wanted from Chris earlier. Then she moved on to the task many of the children had been anticipating and instructed 'now add them all up please'. Kim, it appears, had been following and puts his hand up and said 'twenty five'. Although he then wrote 50 on the board he was able to correct this when the teacher asked 'What number did you say to me?' and he said twenty five. Both the teacher and the researcher were amazed.

The issue of children who are supposed to be not very 'bright' or good at the subject suddenly 'surprising' everyone by coming up with the 'right' answer was a not infrequent event in the classrooms we studied. As the researcher noted, it is often difficult to know exactly why they have done so on any particular occasion. But the example does indicate the discourses available to all of the parties for offering such explanations and can be seen as a 'telling case' of the discursive space within which children are struggling to make meaning and be heard. When they are told to 'listen' we might also wonder the extent to which the teachers who invoke this command are themselves 'listening' to the children and wondering what sense they can make of the complex, often contradictory and ambiguous discursive practices of the classroom. Whilst we might have predicted in this case that the discourse was of the kind likely to lead to disengagement and thus contribute to our 'explanations' for children's 'low achievement', in fact the child provides evidence that he has been engaged. So, that explanation too needs to be treated warily.

We have suggested, then, that to make sense of what is going on, and perhaps contribute to explanations for low achievement in schooled numeracy, we need to look both at the classroom itself and the discursive practices there but also at homes and the discourses with which children are brought up that might, as the researcher indicates, sometimes 'compete' with those of school. Likewise, interviews with teachers and observations of children on and off task at home and at school, can further enrich our understanding. Putting all of these together might give us a richer insight into the complexities of learning schooled numeracy than simply attending to the curriculum or to more formal features of pedagogy. A further dimension now will be to contrast this case study with that of another child, Anne, whose interaction with school, home/ school discourses, the perception of her by teachers and her 'achievement' in numeracy appear altogether different.

4. 'SHE'S GOT THE LANGUAGE'

> In her first term at school, Anne was suggested to the research team by her teacher as someone who was 'more able' in numeracy, though when numeracy groups were established she was in a lower group than the teacher expected. The Reception teacher, Alice Clark, when commenting on her ability when she started school, said *She's got the language, like 'six and four makes ten'*. This may reflect her playgroup and/or home experience of numeracy. [AT Ro April '00]

As we noted in Chapter 4c, Anne was 'comfortable and happy in school and she enjoyed learning', noticing explicitly as she found things hard or made break throughs. She was able to work by herself but also joined in with others, demonstrating both 'mathematical engagement' in the sense of engaging with the tasks themselves and 'social engagement' in the sense of working in groups. She represented a different level and kind of 'engagement' than we saw with Kim. Here we describe some of the numeracy events we have seen her engaged in at school, starting with those which are not directly led by a teacher. The classroom environment was a rich resource, (cf. The cultural resources of the classroom Chapter 5c), and the organisation of the school day meant that for much of the time Anne choose for herself what to do. Here we give only a few typical examples.

We saw in Chapter 4c how Anne engaged with a base 10 apparatus (sticks for tens, and cubes for units) and with number cards where number addition was 'modelled' with the apparatus. (AT Ro 19.Sept.00). Anne here demonstrated 'engagement' at a number of levels: in terms of her display and actual experience of enthusiasm for the tasks required, including her worried frowns when stuck and her joy when she got it right eg 'she looked worried - she slumped in her chair, with her forehead furrowed. Freya, without further comment, gave her a 10; Anne handed over 10 units; counted what she now had, said 51 and beamed with pleasure' (AT Ro 19.Sept.00 -,). She enjoyed the social relations of schooling which fitted her identity in a way that similar schooled procedures did not fit with Kim's identity. Anne's 'engagement' can also be seen in terms of internalisation of the vocabulary being modelled eg 'Anne modelled 34 (that is, selected three sticks and four cubes) and then said *Add them together*, possibly knowing that phrase from watching Eve and Annette'; and in terms of her facility with the apparatus provided, such as use of sticks for tens, and small cubes for units which entailed the kind of representation and mode switching noted also in Kim's case. For her, engagement was similar to the teacher's views of engagement: that is 'being on task', a use that does not correspond either to that quoted from Lave (1992)   above ("things (real and imaginary) that do and do not engage learners' intentions and attention") or to our use of the term in this chapter to include commitment, involvement and acceptance of the relations associated with schooled activities. Unlike Kim and Seth later, who were often seen by their teachers as not engaged., in Anne's case the social relations at school are consonant with her views of herself and perhaps her relationships with adults and with ideas of learning and thinking. There was less conflict for her over engagement than there was for Kim and Seth.

As we noted in Kim's case, teachers frequently switch between oral, visual and written representations of maths issues; in this case the 'visual' also includes the physical (cf Bruner (1960; 1990) and many mathematicians on 'enactive, iconic and symbolic'). This can be seen in the use of apparatus which students see and manipulate (physical) a practice the teacher attempts to integrate with oral and written representations. For example, 'much of the apparatus was scattered across the table, no longer in the box, and Anne, expecting to take tens and units from the box, thought there were not enough. When she realised she could re-use them, she modelled both numbers, added them, and got 44 (the correct answer)'. She was both manipulating the physical apparatus and saying the numbers and procedures whilst the teacher also introduced written formulations in the figures on cards. There was no 'surprise' here when Anne stated the correct answer, even though on occasions she appeared 'stuck'; and the word 'fluke' was not part of the vocabulary for describing her attainment.

5. 'WHAT IS THIRTY SIX ADD NINE?'

A similar surprise to that experienced at Kim's occasional 'success' in getting right answers was also evident in our data from Seth's classroom and we use this to elaborate further the notion of engagement and its possible role in children's attainment in numeracy. We give below an extract from the field notes of the researcher, Dave, surrounding a numeracy event that was observed on a school visit together with a discussion of ways of interpreting the event in the terms of these themes. We begin with some background detail from Dave's notes (cf Chapter 4a):

"to add 9 we + 10 − 1",

Seth is now 8. The class he is in contains many of the same children from the start of his schooling when they were in the Reception class. There have been several additions.. There are about 30 in the class.. There is quite a lot of number apparatus in the room including a number square on the wall. The teacher is an experienced teacher having been at the school for several years and is the mathematics co-ordinator for the school. (DB Mo 13 Nov. 02).

The children gathered on the mat in front of the teacher. Next to her was an easel with a large number square attached and facing the children. The session was the mental and oral starter part of the standard NNS "three-part" numeracy lesson.

Teacher "I am going back to what we did on Monday. You were not good at it. You need practice. What were we doing in pairs?"

After some encouragement and cajoling the children responded.

Lenny "Adding nine and ten"

Teacher "what is a quick way or rule for adding 9?"

Kay "add ten take away one"

The teacher wrote on the white board "to add 9 we + 10 – 1", using the written symbols as shown. She went through a parallel process with the children reminding them what they had done for adding eleven, that is adding ten and then one more.

In the meantime Seth, together with 3 or 4 other children, moved from in front of her towards the front wall of the class so that he could lean his back against the wall. He was also now at an oblique angle to the easel and from there he could not see the number square and the teacher could not see him directly. She was aware of him and the others and told them off for sitting against the wall. They moved away but quickly returned to it. The teacher then started to discuss the theme for the mental and oral starter. She wanted them to develop strategies for doing "add nine" and "add eleven". She wanted them to be aware that to add nine they can add ten and then take away one. In a similar manner to add eleven they could add ten and then add one. She did this by setting them examples such as thirty-six add nine to think about as a class and then to put their hands up with both their answers and their strategies. Some seemed to have the answer immediately; some tried to count up from thirty-six; others tried to add ten and take away one; others tried to use the number square; and others did not do much.

She asked the question orally and said: "What is thirty six add nine?"

Child: "forty-five. Added ten took off one"

She gave them all time to think and tried to stop those who knew the answer already from calling it out. Carla also seems to know. Kay was fully attentive and compliantly held up her hand with the answer. Lenny was looking away from the board. Kerry and Jessie were sitting next to me to the side of the mat, they seemed to have no clue what to do. Even with some quiet oral help from me they could not do what was being asked. I once gave them the answer and they then put their hands up excitedly. Seth was still sitting with his back to the wall and had a vacant look on his face. It was not clear whether he was part of the lesson or not. The look in his face suggested he was not attending to the maths at all. He found a lace on his jacket and was pulling it around his knees and shoes.

Once one child gave the answer the teacher discussed the strategy. She told them they could first add ten and then take away one. Some looked as though they understood this strategy and could add 10, others were not sure . Yet others were not attending. She then put a written representation of the strategy "+10 – 1" (add 10 take away one) on the board. She also showed them how they could use the number square. They could go down one line from 36 to 46 in order to add 10 and then move to their left to 45 to take away 1. She had therefore shown them several different ways of representing the problem and the strategy. She then moved onto another example of the same thing.

After a few minutes Seth seemed to come alive and he slid into the centre of the group in front of the teacher. When the teacher set the next problem "45 add 9", Seth put his hand up immediately and gave the correct answer "54". (DB Mo 13 Nov. 02)

How can one interpret this numeracy event? As we saw in Chapter 4a, one approach could be to question the pedagogic practices that form part of schooled numeracy practices or the effectiveness of the individual practices of this teacher. From that perspective, this kind of whole class session would seem not to work for many of the children in this class. There were some children who could handle the ideas and the problems before the session started. For them the session seemed a waste. For those who were still struggling to add two single digit numbers like Kerry it just confirmed their own notion of themselves as unable to do this. On the other hand, some pupils like Kay seemed to get a lot out of it. She felt comfortable. She was very attentive and involved and seemed affirmed by the whole process. The social aspects worked for her. She may also have learnt the mathematics and the strategies the teacher intended but we do not know this for certain, although we might begin to ask questions of unfamiliar children such as this on the basis of what we are learning from case studies and analyses of those on whom we do have considerable data, such as Seth. In this case we do know that for Seth the session was problematic. We also know that his lack of engagement for a good part of the session did not come from his lack of understanding of the mathematics the teacher was introducing: we have evidence at the end that he could cope with the mathematics involved. It seemed that his disengagement in this case was his way of coping with the social practices of the classroom around the mathematics: that is the schooled numeracy practices. Making progress in his learning of formal mathematics or being affirmed by being compliant with the teacher was not what he wanted. Nor did he show any desire to reveal his ability and knowledge to answer the question successfully. Seth's responses and behaviour are not unusual for him. It would therefore be likely that over the years he will not make as much progress in his formal schooled mathematics as other children who do engage. Understanding why he dipped out could help understand low achievements in schooled numeracy.

6 EXPLANATIONS FOR RELATIVE ENGAGEMENT

We have discussed various explanations for Seth's relative engagement in the case study about him (Chapter 4a). We looked at Seth himself and tred to understand what was happening to him. We raised the possibility of addressing the effectiveness of the teacher's approaches and strategies but noted that we had not entered the classroom as inspectors, to judge the teachers in this way, but as researchers trying to understand broader patterns. So we suggested part of the explanation might be found at the cognitive level, but again argued that the evidence here was ambivalent – as we show above, Seth might appear to be disengaged at one moment and yet would engage at another, showing that he did understand the mathematical issues required. In any case, we did not set out to address issues of cognition but instead wanted to consider what could be added to our understanding of children's relative achievement if we were to address the more social dimensions of numeracy activity. From this perspective, an explanation might lie in the dissonance between the numeracy and social practices that Seth engaged in at home and those required at school.

Navigating these dissonances would involve interpreting the coded questions and switching to which we have drawn attention in this Chapter .Such practices in school may appear customary to educationalists but they may appear to Seth and others to be like a game (cf Chapter 7), the purpose and the rules of which he is unclear about. For instance, the coded questions asked by the teacher, such as "What were we doing in pairs?" ranks, like the 'How many numbers?' in the Kim event, as setting up an assumed frame of reference that indicates what an appropriate answer will be – if a child has not recognised the coding then they might miss the meaning, even though they could in fact handle the mathematical procedures perfectly well had they been posed more explicitly. Likewise, the switching required as the teacher moves between oral, written and visual modes of representation is as demanding for Seth as it was for the children we saw in the earlier examples. In this case, the teacher, having asked orally "What is thirty six add nine?", then put a written representation of the strategy "+10 – 1" (add 10 take away one) on the board'. There is then a further switch as 'She also showed them how they could use the number square. They could go down one line from 36 to 46 in order to add 10 and then move to their left to 45 to take away 1'. As the researcher notes: 'She had therefore shown them several different ways of representing the problem and the strategy', a way of working that may ultimately derive from Dienes' theory of 'multiple embodiments' that we saw in Chapter 2. The coding and the switching, whilst embedded in classroom pedagogy, may offer us explanations for why some children at least have trouble following a lesson as the teacher asks coded questions and moves across different modes of representation that are not recognised by the children.

In these examples, we have suggested a complex relationship between classroom numeracy practices and home numeracy practices. Classroom numeracy practices may involve rules and procedures that are quite different from those of home. The coded questions and mode switching that we saw in all three events might be causes of confusion and disengagement for at least some pupils some of the time. The school and home, however, are not always dissonant. Alison, the researcher in the Tarnside event, for instance suggested that an explanation for Anne's relative achievement might lie in the congruence of her home discourse with that of the school, whilst those occasions when Kim appears more successful may be similarly explained. Likewise, for Seth it has been suggested that he 'engaged' at the point where the discourse looked more familiar and moved away from writing on the board to spoken interactions (cf Chapter 4a Seth). Whilst 'engagement' mostly takes on a different dimension for Anne, Kim and Seth, it appears that for all three 'engagement' may be contingent upon the different discursive practices of home and school, including their familiarity not only in switching between these domains but also in mode switching within one of them. These discursive practise we have located within the concept of numeracy practices, which involve such 'social' dimensions of numeracy as social relations, ideologies and values and institutions. In order to understand the role of the social factors in the relative achievement in school tasks of pupils from different backgrounds, we need now to move beyond description of numeracy practices in the classroom to some account of home numeracy practices. We will consider these, in Chapter 7, in terms of the concept of 'cultural resources'. Finally, in Chapter 8, we will look at what happens when children move between these two contexts.

CHAPTER SEVEN: NUMERACY PRACTICES AT HOME

Cultural Resources

1. INTRODUCTION

We begin this chapter by looking at some data from a home visit made during the research. This data reveals some of the complexities inherent in attempting to understand relationships between home and school numeracy practices and the possible impact of home practices on attainment in schools. So far in the book (cf. Chapter 1) we have referred to the work of Machin (1999) Feinstein (2003), Ginsberg et. al.,(1997), Walkerdine (1998), Reay (1998), and Reay and Lucey (2000) where they revealed the effect of visible social factors such as relative poverty, social class and socio-economic status on children's educational attainment in formal schooling. The event we describe below suggests that material poverty alone does not fully explain the impact of social factors on children's school educational achievements. This has led us to consider ways in which a model of cultural resources, which we have developed from Bourdieu's concept of cultural capital (see below) may help understandings of the effect of such social factors.

2 HOME DATA AND HOME NUMERACY EVENT: AAYSHA

We present extracts from the field notes of Alison during two visits to the home of Aaysha, a young girl of Pakistani origin whom we first encountered in Tarnside (Chapter4b). This School is in an ethnically and socially mixed urban area. Over 70% of the children come from minority ethnic groups and the school's attainment in Key Stage 1 (KS1) maths tests was just below the national average (2000 Panda). Compared to other schools with 'similar context', the percentage of children achieving level 2 or above in the maths tests was above average; that achieving level 2B or above was average; and that achieving level 3 or above was well below average (2000 Panda).. When we first met Aaysha in October 1999 she was 4 years old. Her teacher then saw Aaysha's achievement in numeracy as above average for her year. At the time of the home visit presented below, Aaysha was 5 years old.

B. Street, D. Baker and A. Tomlin (eds.), Navigating Numeracies, 129-143.

2.1 Field notes on Home Background

She lived with her two younger siblings and with both parents in a locally well-known very run down hostel for homeless people. The family came to the UK one and a half years ago from Pakistan and are currently living in relatively poor conditions. Their accommodation consisted of one bedroom, one reception room that served as a single bedroom, and a kitchen. The toilet and bathroom were shared with others on their corridor. There were lots of families, many with little English, crowded in an oversized "Portacabin", in a yard full of these Portacabins with gates that made it feel like a compound. ... Alison, the researcher, met Mr. and Mrs. Anwar (pseudonyms) and their three children in a room with a single bed and two hard chairs. The walls had old graffiti from previous occupants. ... The family language is Urdu; Mr. Anwar was studying English at the local college but was not yet fluent, and Mrs. Anwar was at home with the three children. Aaysha's English was by this time fluent, where at the start of her Reception year she had had very little English. Her father said with some humour, "She's the interpreter now".

Both parents had worked for an insurance company in Pakistan. Mr. Anwar was a senior manager, with responsibilities including actuarial issues, recommending changes to premium policies and levels. Mrs. Anwar was a manager but lower ranking. He had an MA in statistics and 'loves statistics'. His insurance exams were USA accredited. He was hoping they would be accepted here, and intended to look for work in insurance when his English was up to it. Mrs. Anwar said she did some things at home with Aaysha such as counting things in the flat. Aaysha helped with cooking by measuring things in terms of cups. Aaysha chose books from the library and counted how many books she had. Aaysha played teacher with her nursery-aged sister and liked 'games' on TV. According to the school neither parent saw Aaysha in school. She was quiet at home and at school. Both the father and teacher called her 'shy'. ." (AT Tarnside Aaysha, 21 Nov. 00)

2.2 Field notes on the Numeracy Event.

Alison's field-notes contain the following item:

"I said the class didn't have many children. Aaysha tried to count them by silently running through them in her mind, totting up numbers on fingers. I noticed she finger-counted in threes, three to a finger or thumb. I asked about this: Mr. Anwar says 'we' count three to a finger, so 15 to a hand, 30 in two hands. Mr. Anwar's description included folding over two fingers and saying six - I think he was saying to me that it's well internalised, you know how many several fingers represent. Implication in standard maths terms would include for example speed in multiples of 3. He said one to a finger is no good because you only get up to 10. I asked if they had taught this to Aaysha, or if she'd just picked it up from watching them. There was no clear answer to this so we don't know if it was deliberately taught or picked up from home practices. I'd expect they taught it to her, since it's unlikely (cf. English adults) her parents do it enough themselves for her to 'pick up' without prompting." (AT Tarnside Aaysha, 21Nov. 00)

On a second visit Aaysha was asked by Alison about the event above. An interpreter gave Aaysha's views:

"She can do it on hands and she can do the school like the school what they teach and she can do both ways now. And now she is using more whatever they learn in school that way. Instead of her method". Mrs. Anwar commented, through the interpreter, "She's learning much faster, you know, whatever they teach in school, instead of ... whatever she learns from home". (AT interview Aaysha 1June 01

We know that Aaysha is doing well at school, despite living in an environment, which, as we have described above, is very difficult. It is an example of poverty itself not determining success, as she comes from a home that is currently relatively poor in a financial sense. This seems to challenge some of the research on poverty and attainment as discussed in Chapter 1. But this challenge only reinforces the idea that relationships between affluence/poverty and attainment are not deterministic. There are homes such as Aaysha's where children have achieved well in formal school attainment despite poor material conditions. One explanation might be in terms of cultural resources (see below), that are helpful in some sense for her schooling. In Aaysha's particular case, her parents have participated in higher education abroad, they are highly educated, highly motivated and confident in school mathematics and languages. For example, Mr. Anwar is confident he will learn English well enough to obtain a good job of the kind he had as a senior manager in Pakistan. Aaysha's parents' background, educational experiences and attitudes can be seen as a resource that may affect the ways that Aaysha responds to her own education. We do not have enough data from Aaysha's home to pursue this in detail but what we do have is indicative of the significance of home cultural resources as factors in schooled achievement, even where objective conditions, postcode data etc suggest economic poverty.

The numeracy event itself reveals another aspect of home cultural resources. It shows a way of counting at home, using three-to-a-finger, that was different from those emphasised in schools in England where counting in ones is stressed, (Wing, 1996). These differences could have caused conflict for Aaysha. On the other hand the home practice may have affordances, be a cultural tool for thinking (Rogoff, 2003 p 261), a cultural resource that may prove helpful to her school numeracy activities and practices. For example, counting three-to-a-finger shifts attention away from closed numeracy skills towards patterns and hence towards more sophisticated calculation procedures and different ways of thinking. It could be that if the school knew about her counting practices they might be able to employ them and or extend them. On the other hand it could be the differences and distance between the home and school practices she manages and the switching she does between them provide her with the meta-cognitive skills and understandings that help raise her attainment in school numeracy: that is, it may not be the numeracy practices themselves in isolation that are significant but the contextual framing that. facilitates her recognition of different systems. This switching and meta-knowledge as well as the actual three to a finger counting system can be viewed as cultural resources and thereby contribute to her attainment (cf Chapter 6 for a fuller account of switching).

Aaysha's family, therefore, have cultural resources which may not be as different from those that support schooling as the immediate poverty of their social conditions might lead observers to expect. It may be that gross statistics on poverty and school achievement need refining with respect to qualitative accounts of cultural as well as material resources (as Reay and others, 2000, argue, cf Chapter 2). We have so far noted two aspects of Aaysha's home resources; that is her parents' educational background and her home numeracy practices. We will now develop further what we mean by the term cultural resources.

3 MEANING OF CULTURAL RESOURCES

Whilst some of the concepts and ideas developed here can in some ways be traceable to the work of the French sociologist, Pierre Bourdieu (1985, 1990), the research being reported in this book does not claim to be sited in his work. Rather we draw upon his conception of cultural capital but broaden it so that the economic basis of the metaphor is less salient. We suggest that any set of cultural resources has meaning in relation to the context/field in which they are located and no one set of such resources is intrinsically valued more than another. Every home has resources for all sorts of purposes. It would be possible to label everything in a community, a home or a school as a resource in this sense, but for purposes of this project we limit the concept to those resources that are significant to the support or development of home or school numeracy practices. This fits with the application of Bourdieu to education offered by Jenkins:

> "Pupils whose familiarisation bestows upon them the appropriate level of cultural capital - both more of it and the right kind - will necessarily achieve more academically than those whose relationship to the cultural arbitrary is more distant." (Jenkins 1992 p 112)

Some of the central concepts of interest to education are *Habitus, Field and Cultural Capital*, all three of which are posited as in dynamic relationship to each other (eg Grenfell, (1998), Jenkins (1992), Pahl (2002), Reay (1999), Bourdieu (1985, 1990). Further, the notion of 'Dispositions' links these general social processes to identity construction as itself a social rather than just an individual cognitive process. Bartlett and Holland (2002) see habitus - the active presence of the past in the present -as the 'sedimentation' of past activities in ways that help build up such identities. In Lemke's interpretation of Bourdieu, 'evaluative dispositions ... are created by our participation in the typical activities of a local social community over timescales of a decade or two', an insight which he applies to school classrooms as classic sites for identity and habitus construction,. Bourdieu, he argues, 'finds significant social class differences tied especially to education and to economic life-prospects, and comes close to proposing that social class itself be redefined in terms of the differences in 'habitus' or dispositions to action produced by different trajectories of socialisation' (Lemke, 2003, p. 2). Bourdieu' himself associates such dispositions with the notion of games -, "the feel for the game is the social game embodied and turned into a second nature" (Bourdieu 1990 p 63). This can provide us with a way of making sense of some of the relations between home and school in our own data: for instance in the ways that some children seem to find it easy to accommodate to the discourse and rules of schooling (Anne; Chapter 4c) whilst others reject it to some extent (Seth and Kerry; Chapter 4a and 5a): the ways in which the relationship between the habitus of home and that of school may be quite different for different children (compare Chapters 4 and 5); the different dispositions we observed as some children 'engaged' with schooling and with numeracy whilst others were disengaged (see above, Chapter 6). Bourdieu's approach enables us to link these specific features of dispositions and habitus with broader contexts associated with what he terms 'Field' and 'Cultural Resources'.

By Field Bourdieu refers to the context in which practice and activity occur and can be seen as a "structured system of social relations" (Grenfell, 1998, p 16). In terms of our work, Field represents the social and institutional relations in school numeracy, in homes and in relationships between homes and schools. Cultural Resources refers to the full gamut of resources appropriate and available to an individual in a particular field. The resources available to Seth's father (see Chapter 4a) from his experiences and knowledge of pigeon racing were appropriate to his recreational world but may have little or no consequence or exchange value for Seth or his father when in the field of school numeracy. In Bourdieu's terms, he may have cultural capital but not the symbolic capital to translate it into other contexts, to enter the exchange relations that give currency to such forms of capital (cf Luke, 1993; Street, 1994). We prefer to use the term cultural resources so as to avoid the implications of the metaphorical association with only monetary capital.

4 APPLICATIONS OF 'CULTURAL RESOURCES'

In the discussion about Aaysha above we referred to the *cultural resources* of the family. For some children, the cultural resources open to them at home are consonant in some sense with those required in school numeracy. In others they may be less so. In Aaysha's case it is clear that her parents had extensive experience of formal education and were confident in their approaches to mathematics and to their own learning of languages. At first the home cultural resource of finger counting appears dissonant with the explicit forms of numeracy activity valued at the school: but in the long run, the numeracy skills embedded in this local cultural practice may serve Aaysha in good stead as she progresses through school and needs to call upon some of these skills, such as recognition of patterns and more sophisticated calculation procedures, and we already saw evidence of her numeracy attainment in school that might derive from these factors. However, as we saw in Chapter 4b, Kim's mother and grandmother also provided home numeracy practices to him, without much evidence of such a positive outcome. We need to take account of further factors to distinguish between the educational outcomes described for the different children. Kim's mother was well educated in the UK and her grandmother was well educated in Jamaica and then in the UK through nursing training. A factor that might differentiate between Kim's and Aaysha's backgrounds, was that their parents' 'cultural resources' were of a different kind. Kim's (Chapter 4b) grandmother Carmen had been a primary teacher in Jamaica and came to London with what would look to contemporary teachers as a 'traditional' model of schooling; his mother Juline was experienced in numeracy at work but uncertain about its implications for Kim's schooling and did not, in any case, have time for home schooling – although as the grandmother's dissonance with the school model became apparent, Juline did join in more. Aaysha's parents' home numeracy practices and their work experience in their home country might be more consonant with her experience at school than Kim's, although the school, as we have seen, did not explicitly pick up on the affordances of the finger-counting she had learned at home. Likewise, one of the Mountford children Kerry's home involvement with jigsaws and with her father's wood cutting and floor laying, might indicate affordances on which a school could build (see below), although again this remains more apparent at the research level than in terms of curriculum or classroom practice.

We want to take account of such nuances, then, as we use the concept of cultural resources to describe, understand, contrast, and seek similarities or differences in those cultural resources that are identified in homes/communities/schools. Operationalising the concept could help the search for explanations of different achievements in numeracy. We do not expect that this will lead to an instrumental or one to one understanding and thence to predictions of what the effect of cultural resources might be. We do expect that it will lead to a way of describing relationships between home practices and school practices in terms of such resources that could shed some light on the complexities of such relationships. The notion of cultural resources, then, is a model of the richness of resources any home has to contribute to children's learning of schooled numeracy. It explicitly rejects a deficit model and instead seeks to bring to attention those home or community resources that are significant for children's achievement and that could be exploited by schools when teaching formal schooled numeracy. That does not mean that such resources are readily accessible or exchangeable but that exposing them and increasing teachers', schools' or parents' knowledge of them or about them could contribute to making schooled numeracy more accessible to more children.

In a similar way to homes, schools have cultural resources. These include the cultural resources of children as a group. Peers are a cultural resource at school that children can make use of and turn into resources for handling schooled processes and practices (cf Gregory and Williams, 2001). Such peer resources might prove to be consonant or dissonant with formal schooling or with home practices. As we discuss below, Rowan's children had resources, such as access to an estate agent's practices that Mountford's children did not. In contrast Mountford practices such as pigeon racing did not constitute a resource that was drawn upon for schooling.

In some cases the parents of many of our children, unlike those of Aaysha, have had little experience of formal education beyond compulsory schooling. Seth at Mountford (see below and Chapter 4) would be such an example. In those cases the parents engaged in experiences other than formal education, such as employment, raising a family or domestic management etc. In other cases, a carers' own experiences of pedagogy, for example Kim's grandmother (see Chapter 4b) could be seen to conflict quite drastically with the children's school pedagogy. The home cultural resources in these cases may not be as consonant with schooling as those of middle class homes (cf Anne, Chapter 5c, but we also need to recall the dissonances there too) or may not be recognised for their educational potential.

5 SETH'S, KERRY'S AND LENNY'S CULTURAL RESOURCES

This is also the case in our data from Mountford, a classic example of a school in a working class which is likely to see its catchment children as lacking in cultural resources, whilst research such as that described here has the time and the framing to indicate how many resources are actually there to be built upon. We start with the data on Seth (see Chapter 4a) which provide an opportunity to see how some cultural resources become labelled as in deficit in relation to the field of schooling. For example in this comment, Seth's mother told the researcher, Dave, that she was unable to take him shopping anymore.

> "No! I can't take him shopping; I took Seth up to the High Street with me. And I said all those pretty boxes, Seth, there's so many there and I began to count them and he got fed-up with them and kicked the boxes up in the air, so I said you've never going to come shopping with me ever again.   And letting the alarm go off in the Mall and I thought he's never going to be got out of here, so he spoilt it, you know. I can't take the boys shopping with me anyway." (DB Interview 21 Nov. 00)

This meant that, in relation to the field of schooling, his cultural resources were dissonant with those aspects of school numeracy that could draw upon shopping and he was therefore seen, in educational terms, as in 'deficit': he did not have the background on which to build the understanding surrounding money that is associated with shopping by the school, whether it is about notions of value or about transactions or formal school calculations with money. In the same neighbourhood, Kay's mother, on the other hand, took Kay shopping frequently and Kay often shared her shopping experiences with Dave when he visited her at home. In pursuing the implications of these experiences for schooled numeracy, we have been careful to specify the contextual and specific character of such so-called 'deficits' and to avoid the generalized characterization of deficit to be found in much educational literature. At the same time, we want to be able to recognize the contextualized nature of specific advantages and disadvantages that some children's experience provides with respect to the particular requirements of schooled numeracy. From a 'cultural resources' perspective rather than use the term deficit we wish to specify which resources in one context are built upon, or, in another context, which are not.

In keeping with this more anthropological stance, we need to take account of Seth's other home experiences both in their own right and in terms of their potential for building towards those specific schooled practices. Seth's father, Dennis, raced pigeons and gave one to each of his sons. When Seth was in Year 1, aged 6, he showed little interest in the pigeons but by Year 2, aged 7, he was beginning to volunteer information about how they were doing. In conversations with Dave, the family revealed some of the potential and value of keeping pigeons.

> Dave: Tell me about your pigeons. Your pigeon.
>
> …
>
> Dennis: Seth has one of the pigeons
>
> Dave: When you go racing, do you take them off and then you wait here for them? You don't go out or anything with them?
>
> Dennis: No. I spend a few hours up the garden, waiting for them to come back and praying they'll come back. What you do you start with a couple of miles up the road, we've just started training the babies now – we took them out for the first time Wednesday – we took them to the Dyke and let them out there and they took 20 minutes

to come back. They should roughly do about a mile a minute. It's only like a two/three mile race. It depends on the wind as well. Which direction the wind is in. If they've got to fight against it they'll lucky if they get 40. If it's behind them, they can go about 90 miles an hour depending on how strong it is (DB Interview 16 June 01)

There is evidence in the conversation with Seth's father that concepts of distance, directions, location, spatial relations, time and speed as well as practicalities of looking after the pigeons had numeracy aspects embedded in them. They have affordances for his education. Yet the school and the teachers, being largely unaware of the details of his home life and life outside school, did not know about his experiences with pigeons.

A further examples of home site and domain that are not much drawn upon or recognised in school, comes from a field report on a home visit by researcher Brian to Kerry, a child at Mountford school, when Kerry was in Year 1 and aged 6 . Brian comments:

'Jigsaws are a keen pastime in the home. Kerry's mother has always done them and is currently working on a 5,000 piece one called 'Titanic', which is very difficult as it is mostly dark. Kerry helps her. Kerry has her own jigsaws and brought out one of about 50 large pieces, of the Teletubbies, which she proceeded to complete efficiently and quickly. When she undid it, she carefully picked away the pieces indicating background and left the four characters – Lala etc – standing on their own on the floor. Kerry's Mother agreed she was leaning here towards the more complex ones her mother does.

Brian further commented: 'Situated learning – jigsaws in the environment, child does simpler ones with scaffolding as ZPD [Zone of Proximal development]? towards more complex ones with parent. Any sign of building on this in school? Possible maths dimensions here are: tessellation, shape, matching, sorting classifying, language, size'

On a visit to the same child on April 13th 2001, the researcher had noted: 'calendar on wall (squares with number for each day) with days crossed out: over it was a monthly calendar with a line for each day and this was Kerry's: she consulted her mother's calendar for the days crossed out and then ticked/ crossed that day on her own calendar. A clock in the form of a large wrist watch was on the wall and Kerry named the numbers that the small and large hands were pointing to. She also watches TV and knows the times of programmes. '(BS Kerry 23 March 02)

In both of these examples the numeracy dimension of the activity is embedded in home practices: they represent in our classification 'Home domain practices at home site' (cf Chapter 8), although there is evidently potential for them to be built upon for schooled numeracy purposes. For instance, as the researcher comments, Kerry's developing facility with jigsaws could be seen in numeracy terms as offering affordances for matching, classifying and sorting jigsaw shapes, whilst more generally her engagement and focus could provide a basis for her attention to task which the school often complained was lacking at school. On another visit, for instance, Brian found Kerry's father laying a laminate wood floor - sawing wood and placing pieces alongside each other in jigsaw-like connections. Seeing this as a useful source of discussion on home numeracy practices, Brian asked about Kerry's participation in this activity and seemed to stimulate a lively conversation with her father and mother. Kerry was joining in laminating the floor, counting pieces of wood, discussing where a piece went in the pattern and her parents raised the connection between this and her interest in jigsaws. Likewise, other activities seen in her home such as the use of calendars or television programming had potential for developing numeracy skills of sequencing, number recognition, adding and subtracting, matching numbers and for time both as duration and marking discrete moments. Again this potential is seldom drawn upon.

Another example from Mountford touches on a much larger theme, that would make an apt focus for further research, that of the use at home of new electronic resources such as video games (cf Gee, 2003), use of the internet and, as in the case provided below, Encyclopaedia games. This example involves Lenny, a boy seen to be in the top group in the Reception Year according to the teacher's baseline assessment, who lived with his mother and sister and whose grandfather was often present and helped out with, for example, buying a computer and. supporting Lenny in his mathematics work. On one visit (Mar 14th 2000) Brian noted the arrival of new computer software and contrasted this with the numeracy tasks in which Lenny had been involved that morning at school.

> When we got in, Lenny went immediately to the new computer which was in the back of the sitting room - he showed me the old style computing set up - the house TV plus a console - and compared it with the new fancy equipment - a Pentium with Windows 98 etc and enough power to drive encyclopaedia packages with moving images, click on information, hot spots etc. He showed me a pile of CD-Roms, including Encyclopaedia of Nature; a Maths game; History ...; and his mother's own interest 'The Human Body'. Lenny took the main seat and his mother hovered around offering advice and suggestions, occasionally insisting on moves but mostly requesting. His sister also appeared from her school and took a similar role.
>
> The maths game consisted of lots of potentially exciting environments and manipulations - fish under water, submarines that swallowed fish once you had succeeded in some task, a shop where you could buy goods with money you had earned on the tasks. Compared with all of this, the mathematics tasks themselves were fairly unexciting for Lenny. and he did not concentrate hard on them. One task involved a grid, measured out in kilometres, with NSEW at the sides; some 'treasure' appeared in one of the squares and an arrow in another and the task was to click on the NSEW in order to orient and then move the arrow towards the treasure. Once you had clicked, the arrow moved forward on its own, and Lenny soon lost interest. Once treasure had been collected, it could be retrieved by clicking on treasure chests at another level - Lenny did this occasionally to reveal jewels etc but again soon lost interest.
>
> I tried to link the maths task here to those we had engaged in during class. Both at the level of content but more obviously of environment/ context, they appeared radically different. The maths task on the computer was orienting NSEW. In class we had done some data handling (compare/ contrast children according to clothes, bodily features) and some number bonds (take five beads, hide three and show two then ask how many are hidden'; change numbers hidden/ shown and ask child to identify the numbers hidden and exposed). It was also on a different plane from classroom activities that made use of a computer: at school the equipment was an old computer with simple tasks e.g. click on numbers, get them right, a clown dances). (BS Lenny Mar 14th 2000)

Links between children's home computer activities and those of school did not seem to be explicitly addressed in either site. Lenny's mother, for instance, was keen to offer him support and had bought the computer and software with this in mind. But she had no idea what went on in school and how her home activities related. For Lenny the excitement of the high quality graphics and moving images and control were quite different from his involvement in school computing.

> But at present he just surfs about clicking and jumping images, without much structure
> or direction: meanwhile, the school activity has structure and direction but lacks the
> excitement and sheer visual and image excitement or pupil control. (BS Lenny Mar 14th
> 2000)

This remark was elaborated upon by a colleague, Shirley Heath who, in a meeting that week (Mar 12th 2000) commented on the 'frames of knowledge' that she identified urban youths deploying and bringing to school (cf Heath and Wolf, 2004). She was concerned that schools ignore these or have no developed conceptual framework for recognising them and she was in the process of preparing teacher education materials to bridge this gap. Applying this to Lenny on his computer one might identify emerging frames of knowledge regarding computer representations of knowledge (e.g. the 'scientific voice'), perhaps some maths context, certainly some serendipitous knowledge of the natural world that might hook into more structured knowledge later. One might also develop further the gender issues potentially at play here, such as Lenny's holding of the stage as his mother and sister sit back and watch him in control, whereas at school he is in the more passive role as the (usually female) teacher exercises control. And the home/school issues are considerable and will be alluded to further in the Conclusion.

For the present purpose, conversations, observations and instances such as these and the practices they were part of at home and at school were the evidence that we sought in our research project in order to explore more closely the concept of cultural resources and to avoid the negative framing carried by the notion of 'deficit' that is frequently invoked when home backgrounds are compared with school performance.

6 ANNE'S CULTURAL RESOURCES

As a further contrast we now want to draw on some data from Anne's home resources. This we draw from the account of her given in Chapter 4c. Anne attended Rowan School and was seen by her teachers as average at maths at the school. Anne's mother Trisha was comparatively successful at school but she was not confident in mathematics. In her work Trisha organised shipping invoices and pricing goods. Despite this, she did not regard herself as good at 'maths'; she saw herself as good with figures but not geometry. More recently she worked as a child-minder and had training which promoted education through play: she mentioned counting games, singing, literacy and numeracy, as planned activities. Anne's father Mick was described as 'good at maths'.

The family provided some home numeracy books for Anne before she started school but once Anne had started in Reception, they tended to leave numeracy to the school. The family did activities and games at home to support schooled numeracy. For example as shown in the next extract from (AT Ro 14 May 01) the scales Anne's mother used at home were similar to those at school as discussed in section 4c.5 in Chapter 4.):

> Anne: Weighing the same as one kilogram. How many animals weigh the same as one
> kilogram? ... Mine take twenty nine. [...] I had to put animals in the scales [...], I put
> animals in the one kilogram and when I'd put nearly all the animals in, it was the same.

And I counted out how many it was and it was twenty nine. And one of [the children] found out twelve and one of them only found out twenty-one. And one of them only found out eight. They were the same, but there was heavier and smaller ones, and we don't know what ones they used. […] I only used small animals.

Alison: And how do the scales work?

Anne: Um, they were the blue ones. The one kilogram.

Alison: Have you got scales in the kitchen here? Was it similar to scales here or different ones?

Anne: One's at school.

Alison: Right. And do the two sides go up and down?

Anne: Yeah.

Alison: So what's it like when it's balanced then?

Anne: The arrow has to be in the middle.

Trisha: A bit like mine then. She does know. […]

Anne: It was fun. Because I was the farest [furthest] person. […] No-one else had got farer than me with numbers and animals. Because no-one [.] one of them only found eight animals in. (AT Ro Anne 14 May 01)

Alison, in commenting on the activity she saw, said:

In school and at home the purpose of the weighing was not practical in the sense of necessary - the weighing was not, for example, related to cookery. So in both contexts the purpose was to learn about weighing (balance) and at school also the 'feel' of weights. The notable difference arises from the available equipment - big scales at school mean it's possible to compare bulky (often heavier) items to both a 1 kg weight and to each other. To compare the weight of much lighter items by feeling their weight in the hands would be much harder. Hence Trisha was asking girls to learn to use equipment - to look at the needle, for example - more than to directly compare weights (she didn't ask the girls to hold the weight in one hand and biscuits in other). Trisha is reproducing at home as closely as she can with her knowledge and equipment the activities she expects Anne to be engaged in at school.

The school domain is at work in the home site here (cf Chapter3 and 8). There is a sense in which the home's cultural resources, Trisha's attitudes to Anne's learning of maths and the resources she has for her, give Anne support to learn school maths. There is also evidence from Anne's home that there are so many games, rich in formal numeracy potential, in the home that they have trouble choosing one, (AT Anne 8 Jan 02). At the same time, as Alison comments, there are significant differences between home and school, for instance in the nature of the equipment which at school is dedicated to specific numeracy tasks and therefore facilitates the numeracy practices required by the curriculum – including the mastery of equipment itself - more than that of the home.

The accounts of Aaysha, Seth, Anne, and Kerry have revealed several different aspects of home cultural resources. These resources may or may not support the children's attainment in school numeracy. In Aaysha's case we have argued that her parents' educational background and home numeracy practices have supported her work in school numeracy. In Seth's case the opposite seems to be happening. His parents' educational backgrounds do not fit easily with school numeracy and school pedagogical practices. His experiences of home numeracy practices such as pigeon racing do not seem to contribute to his learning of numeracy at school. In Anne's case the home resources and practices are at times directly consonant with schooling, providing yet another context for a child to learn in. Kerry's home experiences, whilst offering potential for school use, in fact remain located in the home and are not drawn upon in school, either in terms of the numeracy practices themselves or of the broader attention and engagement that, if acknowledged in the classroom, could potentially enhance her confidence there.

7 COMPONENTS OF CULTURAL RESOURCES FOR NUMERACY

Having used our classification scheme regarding sites and domains (Chapter 2 – see also Chapter 8) and drawn upon the conceptual framework offered by the notion of cultural resources, in order to identify, compare and contrast numeracy practices at home and at school, we now consider other aspects of cultural resources that may contribute to our understandings of children's attainment in school numeracy. This is something that Diane Reay did when operationalising "Bourdieu's concept of cultural capital" in her work with primary schooling, (Reay, 1998). There she wrote:

> "I developed a list of seven main components of cultural capital within the field of home school relationships. These seven aspects of cultural capital were:
>
> Material resources;
>
> Educational qualifications;
>
> Available time;
>
> Information about the educational structure;
>
> Social confidence;
>
> Educational knowledge;
>
> The extent to which entitlement, assertiveness, aggression or timidity characterized mothers' approaches to teaching staff." (Reay 1998, page 59)

This turned out to be similar to the components we identified in the current research. Our research suggested that the cultural resources in homes that have an impact on schooling could be seen to be in categories to do with:
values and beliefs;
knowledge about schooled practices;

background and experience;
physical resources;
domestic practices;
attitudes of homes and carers to school subjects and to schooling.

We specify these in more detail below together with connections to other data in the study. We are not suggesting that this is a comprehensive or complete account of cultural resources but its value is supported by the close connection with Reay's list. We do not see cultural resources as simply a list of surface items that can be used to characterise homes or stereotype them. They represent, rather, different categories of resources. The lists themselves are exemplars. The categories are an attempt to unpack the concept of cultural resources for education. Neither are the lists additive, on some kind of linear scale – 'the more you can tick, the more chance your child has got'. Home culture or habitus, is more complex than this and our particular research lenses and standpoints can only claim to access part of the picture. However, our focus is on the possible connections between home cultural resources and those expected by the particular cultural forms developed in schooling. From this point of view, the list below indicates the kinds of features that may be consonant or dissonant between these two environments and that might help contribute to explanations for relative low achievement.

- Values and beliefs. This includes judgements and choices made by homes. For example what to do with their leisure such as playing games, doing jigsaws, visiting museums, pigeon racing etc. It can also include the purchasing or valuing of types of music, taped stories, books, video, TV, computers, Encarta, game consoles, and the classification, ordering and manipulation of such resources through such literacy and numeracy practices as keeping lists, noting times and dates, storing data in electronic form etc. (cf. Sheridan et. al., 2000). We might also include in this account choices made about noise at home, and the use and position of furniture such as tables.

Anne's mother, for instance, saw it as important for the home to support school numeracy and structured activities to do this, whilst nursery teachers at Mountford criticized homes they visited for 'lacking' tables and chairs.

- Knowledge about schooled practices. Support that is given to Schooled Numeracy Practices by siblings, parents, carers. The knowledge they have or their access to schooled knowledge and processes.

Seth's parents said they had little knowledge to help. They did not know how to help him. Kim's grandmother's knowledge of schooling conflicted with the school's pedagogy. Anne's mother had experienced child minding training and had worked in schools and made use of this knowledge at home,

- Background and experience. Parents/mothers/carers formal qualifications, histories of schooling, attitudes to schooling. Their work practices, jobs. The importance they place on kinds of music, piano, music they value or play at home.

For example Aaysha's experiences were affected by her parents' higher education compared with Seth's parents who left schooling as soon as they were legally able to. At Rowan one of the projects the class did was to look at homes. The class went on an outing to visit an estate agency where one of the children's parents worked. This cultural resource of one of the children became a cultural resource for the other children. In Seth's case the family involvement with pigeon racing was not used by the school.

- Physical resources. Whether or where parents work, type of sites or accessibility of such work. The quantity and quality of spaces in and out of the homes - garden, community, street, extended family. Support or disruption of siblings.

In Seth's case his brothers were very disruptive and he had limited space to be inside. He had to share a bedroom with two older brothers until he was seven. On the other hand, Aaysha and Rick lived in crowded homes but were more successful at school, so we would not want to cite 'physical resources' as determinate in any way, simply as factors to take into account with perhaps less weight than the 'domestic practices' we cite below.

- Domestic practices. problem solving, ways of counting, measuring, shopping, laying the table, setting the video, use of telephones, caring for pets, games, puzzles other leisure activities.

At Mountford, Kay's access to and delight in shopping practices contrasted with Seth's lack of opportunity to have experiences of shopping. Kerry's engagement with jigsaws at home contrasted with her lack of engagement at school and with absence of such home resources in the classroom. The kind of games rich in the potential for the development of numeracy skills and knowledge in Anne's home provided her with physical resources on which the school seemed able to build, whilst Lenny's home practices around the computer contrasted with his school experiences

- Attitudes of homes and carers to school subjects and to schooling; to reading; to maths; to study, to schooling; confidence when relating to teachers and schooling, helping in the classroom

Seth's and Kerry's parents had not got easy informal access to their class teacher. They felt excluded since they had to leave the children in the playground from when they were 5 years old. They felt they did not know what was happening to their children. In trying to make contact, Seth's mother was seen by the school as over demanding. Aaysha's parents did not have easy access to her teachers because of a language gap, although as their English improved they anticipated closing that gap and perhaps getting more feedback from teachers. Rowan had an open access system in the morning until at least the end of year 2 when the children were more than 7 years old and most parents seemed to feel they did have easy access to teachers.

8 CONCLUSIONS

The contrasts shown up between the cultural resources in different homes and between home and school resources and relations suggests that the model we have described in this chapter has potential to provide some explanations for children's different achievements in school numeracy. Aaysha's access to cultural resources, consonant in some sense with schooling, provided her with an environment that may help her to do well at schooled numeracy in the long run, even though her family's immediate economic resources – their economic capital – may appear to place her in an underachieving category. Anne's home cultural resources, both cultural and economic, were more directly consonant with schooling and their potential link to attainment was perhaps more direct, although there was dissonance here concerning policy on religious education that made the relationship more uneven. In Kim's home pedagogic practices seemed to be in more direct conflict with the school's pedagogic practice. Further neither Seth's nor Kerry's home resources were drawn upon at school and their peer school resources were not supportive of school numeracy.

The model of cultural resources can, then, have a role in helping us understand achievement in school numeracy. But this approach to cultural resources has led to questions that we have not yet been able to resolve on this project. These are:

- How can one decide which resources are significant for studying numeracy? If everything is cultural resources, then what counts as appropriate for schooled attainment and for home/school relationships? The list above cannot be read as equally weighted, either for each factor or for each child, although we would suggest it can be constructively read in terms of the implications of a given factor for consonance and dissonance of home and school.

- How, then, do we judge whether home cultural resources are consonant or dissonant with schooling? Our responses have been in terms of close, ethnographic-style knowledge of the practices at home and at school. Each set of practices have their value and we would want to avoid the deficit models that are predominant in education, especially when dealing with children who are outside middle class norms.

- How to change the education system (and not just the home) so that the cultural resources available to children are less unequal and allow for the full diversity of children's backgrounds?

We suggest in the Conclusion that these questions might form the basis for future research and hope that this book has made a contribution to such an enterprise.

CHAPTER EIGHT: NUMERACY PRACTICES

Relations of Home and School

1. INTRODUCTION

In seeking to understand explanations for low achievement in school numeracy we have been endeavouring to compare and contrast the experiences children have at home and at school. We have done this by analysing the numeracy practices we have found in homes and schools. This chapter seeks to look more closely at these numeracy practices to find the similarities, differences and relationships between them.

We begin with a brief review of the intentions behind our use of the idea underlying numeracy practices (see Chapter 2) and then, through looking at the characteristics of sites and domains, we attempt to arrive at a finer grained and nuanced way of describing distinctions and relationships between them.

2 REVIEW OF NUMERACY PRACTICES

If home and school contexts are different in ways that affect children's schooled achievement, as our research hypothesised, then we need ways to understand the extent to which the numeracy practices sited within them are different. In chapter 2 we outlined both the origins of and the meanings we attach to the concepts of numeracy events and practices. This drew on the concepts of literacy events and practices from the work of Heath (1983) and Street (1988; 2000). These concepts have been used in this study because they provide a different, extended (both broader and deeper) model of the social, which sees it in terms of ideology and discourse, power relations, values, beliefs, social relations and social institutions (Baker, 1999, p50). Such an approach allows for the identification, analysis, and comparisons between numeracy practices sited in different social settings and especially those in homes and schools. In Chapter 3 we then offered a way of classifying home and school numeracy practices that took account of both the sitedness of the practices as well as the domains of the practices. This led to a four way classification/typology of numeracy practices (cf. table 1 in Chapter 3) which we replicate here.

B. Street, D. Baker and A. Tomlin (eds.), Navigating Numeracies, 145-162.

Table 1 Classification of Sites and Domains of Numeracy Practices

	Domain: Schooled Numeracy Practices	Domain: Out-of-School Numeracy Practices
School site		
Home site		

We now wish to extend this analytic frame to provide a finer grained account of the salient characteristics of numeracy events and practices in the data by looking more closely at the characteristics of the practices. We began by looking at examples of events that fit into the four cells of the typology. These events serve to indicate the qualities of the practices in different domains and were summarised in table 2 in Chapter 3.

We argued there that identifying an event, locating it within each cell and then interpreting which practices it is associated with can provide a rich source for questioning of data collected at home and at school. To take the analysis further we now want to look at each of the four cells of this typology in turn and thereby add detail, exemplars and characteristics to the typology. We draw these together and summarise them in table 2 below.

2.1. School domain in school site

After a visit to the Reception class at Mountford on 7 March 00 Dave reported:

> I was asked to do number bonds to 3 and 4 with children using number apparatus. I took 3 of them and hid one under one hand leaving 2 showing. I asked how many were hidden under my hand. Repeated with other bonds to 3. Then with bonds to 4 and in some cases to 5.
>
> Kay managed 3 and 4 easily. She could not do 5.
>
> Carla also managed 3 and 4 easily but then became silly wanting to do her own thing.
>
> Jan could only do 3.
>
> Seth was not there

This activity was a mathematical activity dealing with number bonds. The children were engaged in a numeracy event that had been designed to suit the purposes and directions of schooling. We therefore placed this event in the domain of school numeracy practices, sited in a classroom. After the visit Dave analysed this event in terms of the components of numeracy practices (cf. Chapter 2) as follows:

<u>Content</u> was both number knowledge, what number pairs make 4, and understanding of ways that numbers can be broken up or joined together.

The event was sited in an abstract or pure number <u>context</u>. It was educational in purpose, using a visual mode with number apparatus and moving towards mental images but no use of written symbols. No attempt was made to relate to anything outside schooling nor to use shared experiences either inside or outside schooling. Numbers were just numbers with relationships between them to be learned.

Values included the acceptance that there was one and only one answer, which could not be debated or contested. In our research the educational contexts in number in school were largely like this.

Social relations. As the adult in the event, I was the one with authority and also the one who knew the right answers. I was the expert. But the children had to agree to do the task. One child did indeed reject the activity. It was interesting for the researcher to consider why they did the task or why they rejected it. It was fairly clear from the account that as the teacher, I spent time both encouraging and cajoling them with feedback comments such as *well done you are so clever. How did you know that?* They were learning not only about the mathematics content but also about ways of navigating through the code or rules of school numeracy practices (the nature of school mathematics), including their roles, the teacher's roles and the social relations.

We have observed and recorded many other events of this kind in our classrooms. The purposes behind these activities were school driven; the activities were selected by the teacher from the globally set school curriculum; and motivation for pupils was often external. The activity in this case was done repeatedly, an example of the very common school pedagogic practice of *learning through practice*. The teacher was the expert in this activity and the children were being inducted into it. The teacher was the insider, the children were the outsiders. They were required to do it and the extent of their mastery was used as an assessment of them. These emergent qualities are also summarised on the table 2 below (also see table 2 in Chapter 3).

2.2. Home domain practices at home

After a home visit to Kay's home, one of the focus children at Mountford, (DB Mo Kay 15 March 00) Dave reported that:

> Kay's Mother got out her project notebook of number things that she had noted since my last visit. I have listed below some of the items:
>
> "House numbers: Kay read 23 as two three; Kay counted family to 5 to get number of dinner plates when laying the table; Cakes for everyone. Kay counted how many people and then how many cakes; Counted the number of stairs going up to her bedroom; and 'when we are cross we count to three or else you go to your room.'"

Counting dinner plates when laying the table is an example of what we would classify as a home sited numeracy event in home domain numeracy practices. Its purposes were the home's domestic management, the need or desire for it having arisen within the family's day to day activities. It was about organising home life not about getting to grips with an externally specified and determined list of skills. Kay used numeracy as a tool to solve a home problem, although one might suggest that her mother is also deliberately using the home event to teach Kay counting (cf Basic Skills Agency (BSA) home numeracy guidelines, cited in Chapter 5b). The boundaries between home and school purposes and practices are often, as here, blurred and we are careful not to succumb to the tendency of the format we have adopted, using tables and cells, to reify them. In this example, the home dimension is certainly apparent in the social relations involved. Getting the right number is part of the process involved. The child did not feel an outsider in this process. Indeed she was able to choose her own way of solving it, perhaps counting the number beforehand or using previously seen patterns or by trial and error. Getting the number of plates wrong was not used to assess her skills explicitly, formatively or summatively, by others around her. The family will just adjust the number of plates and will get on with the meal. In school, errors in numeracy events can be seen as a reflection on what the child can or cannot do. The child in this activity was *learning in practice*, maybe an apprentice home dweller/maker.

As with counting plates, we were aware that counting the stairs which is listed above could be seen either as a school domain activity deriving from the school domain, the curriculum or as a home domain activity where the child was enjoying the display of her skills, to her carer or even for herself. Counting stairs was, unquestionably less 'functional' to home purposes than counting plates, although it did involve some home purposes. Again one might see aspects of school purposes entering the home even whilst the home dimension was foregrounded. These examples show that the placement of events into cells is not uniquely determined but depends on the ways the participants (including the researchers) see the events: they are not ontologically given but rather products of perception and context. The table serves a heuristic purpose in drawing attention to such home/ school constructions and boundaries.

Another example of home domain numeracy practices at home comes from a home visit to Seth (DB Mo Seth 7 March 00):

> "His mother said: ' We do telephone numbers. I want them to know their own telephone number. Seth doesn't know his but Jason (older brother) does. He does know 999. He rings that number and called them out. I had to ring and say sorry. They said he was rude to them. He also knows how to do 1234 the speaking clock".

Young children knowing their own telephone and house numbers is a central concern of families. The purpose appeared to have been home driven. It was about organising family life and personal safety. The motivation for this skill and process was local. The parent has selected this content herself. It may be linked to schooled content but is not driven by it. Phone numbers, like bus numbers, could be viewed as not primarily 'numeracy', since the numbers here could be substituted by letters without altering the function: that is, they serve as a label but do not necessarily have mathematical properties, such as being able to be added together. However, they do have other affordances for numeracy and when children recognise such number names or become aware of features of sequence in them, there are evident links with the school's numeracy curriculum. With this in mind, we would interpret Seth's use of telephone numbers as a numeracy event sited at home within home domain numeracy practices. The home pedagogy may be the family's own folk practices or may be informed by the parents' notions about school practices but the parents are in charge of it. In terms of social relations and of learning, the child is *learning in practice* perhaps as an apprentice home member: both parents and child are insiders in the activity, they do not rely on an outside expert or outside expertise. When such events enter school, the social relations and the learning will alter (be recontextiualised in Bernstein's terms (1996) but so also may their mathematical features – the numbers may then be used for further manipulations.

In these examples the numeracy dimension of the activity is embedded in home practices: they represent, in our classification, 'Home domain practices sited at home', although there is evidently potential for them to be built upon for schooled numeracy purposes.

2.3. School domain in home site

The fieldwork notes of a visit by Alison to Kim at Tarnside (AT Kim 14.02.01) when he was 5/6 years old reported on some homework he had been set by his teacher. His grandmother, Carmen, was with him.

> Carmen showed me Kim's homework for one week. The numeracy work was questions that took the form 'One more than three or Four more than two'. Carmen had helped Kim rewrite them in the form $1 + 3 =$ in his exercise book (that is, changing words to numbers and symbols), and there Kim had written the answers. Carmen was critical of the homework as too hard for him and Carmen does not trust the school's teaching approach. She is uncomfortable with arithmetic questions written out in words (e.g. *three* for *3*, and *more than* for +): in order to 'make them fit' with her own education and maths discourse, she had represented them as traditional arithmetic. The worksheet's use of words for numbers is probably unfamiliar in Carmen's own experience as a teacher. I asked Kim about his homework:

Alison: So Kim, can you tell me, these sums you've done here [in the exercise book], are these the same ones as these on here [the worksheet]?

Kim: Um yes.

Alison: Yes. So what it says on here [the homework sheet] is - one more than three. What have you written here?

Carmen: Look. Stop that and look. [Kim was playing with a toy.]

Alison: How would you say that? [1+3]

Kim: One more plus three.

Alison: One more plus three. You say plus. So how would you say this one? [4+1]

Kim:Um, um, four plus three.

Alison: Have a look at that, that's not a three. Four plus?

Kim: Eleven

Alison: No, have a look closely. Can you see it in the light?

Kim: Four plus one.

Alison: Yeah, that's it ...

Kim's wording is a mix of the worksheet's, which I had quoted ('more'), and Carmen's, using 'plus' (the school uses 'add'): that is, competing numeracy discourses became conflated, perhaps involving switching between discourses (see Chapter 6).

We see homework set by the school to do at home as events in the domain of schooled numeracy practices (SNP) but sited in the home. The actual activity of answering number questions written in words was sited within a school context. In that context, there was no attempt to relate it to the child's outside school life or any other activity. It could be seen as an abstract, formal, school arithmetic task. Although the parents/carers desire their children to succeed at this kind of numeracy, the purposes of the activity were primarily related to the school curriculum and the school's agenda for that class: they belonged to the school domain even when sited in the home. The teacher selected the activity. Here it was school that was determining numeracy activity at home although the carer had an element of control and expected the children to be given homework. It was, however, centrally about the learning of the school curriculum (see Chapter 5b). The child was being inducted into ways of navigating the codes rules and values of schooled numeracy practices, whether those of his grandmother based on Jamaican schooling or of his current teachers whose views are rather different. In both cases, the home site was dealing in school domain numeracy.

There are other related types of activities that were not homework activities. For example there is a whole genre of "Teach your child numeracy books". These contain a range of activities or exercises including sequentially "join the numbered dots" puzzles, with its content focussed on the ordinality of numbers. These activities are home sited but the purpose of this genre of books is to provide parents with ways of encouraging their children to do school domain activities at home. In a sense they try to mimic what things parents would like their children to be able to do at school. The purposes of these activities are therefore primarily about the school's agenda. The parents choose the book, the children engage in it but it is the school curriculum that drove it. There is an argument about whether parents are driving the school curriculum (cf Street & Street, 1991) or whether parents have accepted that the school curriculum is the dominant part of numeracy at school and therefore in essence it is the school that is driving the parents' actions and concepts at home. The activity, then, is centrally about the learning of the school curriculum despite schools such as Rowan rejecting this genre of books and their approaches to teaching and learning. For the purposes of this research we would label joining the numbered dots puzzle as a home sited numeracy event within the domain of schooled numeracy practices. The choice of what activities goes into these books is driven by the school curriculum – external rather than local. The child is again being inducted into the values, codes and rules of school numeracy practices.

2.4. Home domain at school site

We have found fewer examples of home domain in the school site from our classroom data than from the playground where children use Pokemon or refer to television games such as "Who wants to be a Millionaire"., We have examples from Reception classrooms where the children's birthdays were used by the teachers and where the children's clothing, heights and other qualities were drawn on for numeracy purposes. There was therefore some evidence that teachers use the children as a resource or mention some home activities. These were quite often not much more than a gesture. An example of these kinds of teacher allusion to home experiences is included below. The account is taken from a session on measurement with the children on the carpet at Tarnside where the teacher mentioned using a tape measure in different parts of the country. The children were then in year 1 and were 5 or 6 years old.

> The teacher said: You <u>can</u> use a pen to measure lengths, holding pen against book, or a paintbrush, <u>but</u> these objects are not giving you the right size. There are different sizes of pen. So the right thing is to use <u>standard</u> measurement, so you can use a tape measure in London or Scotland to measure your carpet. A tape measure is standard because they are all the same size. Cubes might be in different sizes" (AT Ta 10 Oct 00).

Here the teacher's gesture holding a pen against a book – suggests a desire of the school to turn potentially everyday objects – pens and paintbrushes – into parts of the school's numeracy inventory, where they can be used for measuring for instance. But that is not the same as using them in the home domain where the use of everyday objects for measuring length is common place. In schools they would have to lose their everyday character and be standardised in terms of formal conventions for measuring length. They would be recontextualised for schooling (cf Bernstein, 1996 pp. 66-7).

3 COMPARING AND CONTRASTING NUMERACY PRACTICES IN DOMAINS AND SITES.

Having looked at examples of events that fit into the four cells of the domains and sites classification (table 1 above), we now look more closely at how these events might be located within different practices and thereby add detail and salience to our account of the practices. Identifying an event, locating it within a domain and site, seeking its characteristics and qualities and then interpreting it in terms of numeracy practices has provided us with a rich source for comparing and contrasting data collected at home and at school. Table 2 sets out the relationship between the components of numeracy practices on the one hand and domains and sites on the other. The components consist of the content, context, values and beliefs, and social and institutional relations, discussed in Chapter 2. The content component has not been identified in the cells of table 2 because mathematics content is implicit in all numeracy practices. Table 3, sets out the relationship between pedagogical practices and the sites and domains. The features of these pedagogical practices have emerged from the data and are concerned with teaching and learning numeracy practices in the different domains and sites. They are still aspects of numeracy practices but are particularly focused on the 'pedagogical' view of the social described in Chapter 2.

They refer to a range of features including the age of the children, the organisation, the collaborative style, the learning and teaching principles, the pace, the timing, the use of language and register, and the use of resources and modes of representation (c.f. Chapter 6). We illustrate them further, following table 3, by looking at events where they occurred in our data.

The two tables are meant to be indicative of the features we observed. We selected them on the basis that they were the most salient and that they revealed the most contrasting features of numeracy and pedagogical practices. They are not meant as a complete picture of the contrasts in practices. In both cases we have omitted the fourth cell from the typology of numeracy practices, that is the school site home domain, because of the small number of observed events of this type in our data.

Table 2 Comparing and contrasting home and school site / domain and numeracy practices/events in terms of their components .

Components of Numeracy Practices	Home Site		School sited
	Home domain - domestic	School domain - School like	School Domain - School like
Content: runs throughout all of the components			
Context: This refers to the framing of those occasions when numeracy is done and the purposes for that use of mathematics. These purposes and contexts depend on the individuals engaged in their numeracy practices. An appropriate context and purpose for one person may not be so for another.	Holistic often within a conversation or activity and casual eg games or as part of domestic and other practices and therefore domestically purposeful. Day to day handling of domestic situations and management eg money to spend,	Formal set school driven homework. Less formal but still part of school agenda. School driven with homes following, mimicking schools. The discourse is more formal than usual at home. Examples are: Home tutoring books and software on computers or home selected activities eg counting going up stairs.	Curriculum externally set. Number work skills or procedures central. Taught in preset numeracy times. Some talk and activity but textbooks often used. Some contexts connected to other activities - attendance register. Home practices not used or transformed or recontextualised for school context e.g. measuring or games. Usually embedded in educational contexts with "noise" removed. Pure number i.e. abstract or esoteric
Values and beliefs. This component is concerned with the ways individuals' beliefs, values and epistemologies affect these numeracy practices they adopt. These 'cultural' and epistemological dimensions of numeracy practices can be considered as ideological to the extent that they are concerned with social and power relations between people and ideas involved in the practice - what they see as acceptable and legitimate mathematics.	Embedded in home values and interests; Such as problem solving, games, laying the table, Pokemon cards. Multiple contestable ways of solving them. Answers to problems arrived at as part of process.	Parents want their children to do well at school. Performance driven perhaps with some curiosity. Homes inclined to do it. Tending towards abstract number and towards one right answer. Hegemony of schooled maths processes and procedures	School or education system purposes. Intentions are specified as competences. School numeracy is dominant with right uncontestable answers and procedures. Homes when used are to help school numeracy. Performance driven. The children want to do it. It is serious and 'work-like'

| Social and institutional relations. These involve the kinds of control over content, management of context and invoking of values and ideology exercised by different institutions and roles. This is revealed in the kinds of discipline exercised, over discourse, language, turn taking associated with different roles. | Some negotiation of contributions and ways of living at home. Home discourses and issues, discipline, levels of care and intimacy. Parents control some contexts e.g money. Numeracy skills and solutions can vary. Maths as an institution not visible
Status varies Children struggle for status, place, turn taking in the home.
Child and home central
Local decision making about home life. Bottom up. Home based with socio/cultural inputs.
Peer groups play at doing school | Child, carer and teacher all inputs into decisions to do activity. Parents don't know maths and don't know how to help their child with school maths. Child can be pressured to engage but can reject this maths at home. | Control by teacher, e.g. rules, codes and order of oral contributions in class determined by teacher; speak when asked to.
Teacher authoritative and central. She is the knower and decides on appropriate behaviour
Discourse of the school dominant.
Child compliant expected to engage. Child rejects by disengaging. Status involves battles with peers.
Numeracy single answer, right or wrong. High status of standard maths skills and some procedures as best.
Global curriculum from Department.
Pedagogy from school or notions of best practices from Department.
Top down. |

Table 3 Comparing and contrasting home and school site and domain numeracy practices /events in terms of pedagogical practices.

Components of Pedagogical practices	Home Site		School sited
	Home domain - domestic	School domain - School like	School Domain - School like
Ages of children in events	Cross-generational, seldom same age	On own or cross-generational, with carer	Same age/peers
Nature of organisation of learning situation	Casual embedded and negotiated between child and carer eg shopping game	More formal and directive Eg homework	Time tabled.: 'ability' grouped vertically grouped
collaborative style	Imitate others, & collaborative. But competitive in games like monopoly	Individually or with carer or sibling/friend;	Some sharing but expected to do it on their own - otherwise labelled as copying or cheating
learning & teaching principles contexts motivation levels of concentration	Learning intentions are by-product of domestic activities learning through imitation & apprenticeship Inherent motivation some scaffolding with family members Eg how to 'behave' in front of adults eg copying jigsaws Learning in practice.	Learning intentions explicit to authors of home learning materials Learning directed, but family some choice what to do Scaffolding with carers or sometimes siblings. Child encouraged by carers eg reading books sent home from school	Learning intentions up front and leading. Teaching central, scaffolding, pre learner scaffolding Teacher central correcting, cajoling & motivating Children expected and required to engage and concentrate. Learning through practice
pace	Pace determined by home practices	Parents reluctant to push children.	Pace determined by teacher.

		They want it to be fun	
timing	Opportunistic, intermittent unpredictable. Child day to day participating.	Can be routine. In some cases only done when child agrees.	National Numeracy Strategy stresses importance of teaching and of pace. Time tabled. Regular. Tightly structured. Child has few choices.
Language/ register	Home discourse. Sited in context. mnemonics "20 days hath September: etc culturally linked	Mimicking schooled discourse. Can be formal and esoteric.	Specialist and technical such as sets units/tens, tables, take away odds and evens. Uniformity Mnemonics school derived
Resources Representations	Digital time, clocks watches, tape measures, real money, digital displays of equipment. If available games, and calculators, and computers	Analogue time mimicking schooling. Books, puzzle books and computer software	Analogue time, rulers scales. plastic money. Representations of abstract number on number lines, abaci, number squares, and structural apparatus. Where allowed calculators computers

We now illustrate some of these by drawing on numeracy events from our data.

We first look at a report from a home visit to Anne (a focus child at Rowan) in January 2001. Anne was then 6 years old and in year 1. Anne's mother Trisha and her 3-year-old sister Lisa were also present and involved in the home visit with the researcher Alison. During the visit Alison noted:

> Trisha Now she can read she can play games with cards.
>
> I comment on them having a lot of games [board games] in their cupboard.
>
> Trisha She's very keen on games, it's funny a lot of children her age [inaudible - I think she said a lot don't enjoy board games] ... but she's really keen. She's got older cousins and they play games with her. [I ask how much older]
>
> Trisha My two are the youngest, out of all the cousins ... Ages are 12, 10, 8. 'Even' the 12 year old will play with Anne. (AT Ro 26 Jan 01)

And then looking at a different home.

> During a visit to Seth he got out a pack of cards I had given him on a previous visit. He wanted to play a game where the largest card won. Julie and I played it with him. His recognition of the numbers and values on the cards was almost instantaneous - so developed from previous sessions. The family seem to think that these are the things I want to see when I am there. Important numeracy practices are things like reading numbers, counting, addition, and playing card games. Seth remained calm and attentive. His concentration was good. He knew what was going on etc. Once his older brother Jason appeared this changed. Seth became agitated and lost interest in the cards (DB Seth 20/2/01)

In these cases the pedagogic practices (teaching and learning) in evidence in the home domain, home sited numeracy practices have tended to be casual in the sense of unplanned, opportunistic timing and often unpredictable, cross-generational and across age, collaborative and imitative of others but genuinely competitive when playing games; this is shown on table 23 above. The learning intentions may be by-products of the activities for some carers and they might be seen as scaffolding for others (eg Trisha who is a child minder and gets these materials in her job). The purposes as revealed in the extracts above are game playing. Social relations are in turn taking in games or decisions about what to do. These are established through family negotiated and established hierarchies. The tasks are often embedded in home purposes and interests, they use home discourses and language and certainly home cultural practices. The resources available are domestic in kind with some selected educational resources such as home tutoring books and software. That is, the cells in our table are not water-tight, items may flow across the boundaries.

An example of school domain and school sited events and practices reveals different qualities and characteristics from the home domain and home sited ones, although again with some overlaps:

> Alison visited Thelma's at Tarnside (AT Ta 5.12.02). This was a class with focus children Aaysha and Darris, where the children were in year 1 but were set for maths with some year 2 children. Aaysha on time, unusually. Darris few min late. They began

with a carpet maths session. The teacher picks a number card. She shows it to the children. She selects picks one child and asks them to name that number and then count up in twos to a number she has set. Then the whole class counts back down. Sometimes she just asks the same child to do it on their own. She differentiates for the needs of the children by her choice of number. Some are given an even, small number to start from; some an odd, bigger number. Aaysha is asked to count from 64 to 80. All the children count back from 80 to 64. Aaysha's voice is quiet, apparently hesitant, but she makes it to 80 without an error. At least one year 2 child has more difficulty coming back down than Aaysha. Darris is asked to count up from 11 to 29. She hesitates, says 12 first. Teacher asks children if the start number is odd or even. Lots of hands go up, say it's odd. Darris is unusually quiet, clearly puzzled. She starts at 11. The teacher says miss out 12. Darris says 13 then has got the point and gets to 19, then long pause. Teacher says miss out 20; Darris makes it to 29. The whole class then count from zero to 30 in twos and back. The rhythm is constant, the gaps between numbers noticeable in one-syllable words like twelve and below

Thelma then says

"*we're doing problems involving length* today". She writes *6 cm + 12 cm* on the board.

Thelma "Who can tell me the whole answer, the exact answer"

Aaysha says "*18.*"

Thelma "*If we're working in centimetres then we answer in centimetres*".

There is a picture on the board of two 'rulers', labelled A and B, with lengths marked beside them ←40cm → and ← 20 cm → - using arrows.

Thelma *Who can think of a question without mentioning numbers?*

Child *Total.*

Thelma *We could say what is the total length of the rulers? So we need to add the numbers. Start at 40 and count on 20. You can all count in 10s.* Children get to 60 though at least half not confident.

Thelma *What if we want to see how much longer is one than the other? What language do I need in my question?*

One of the children says *difference.* The word is accepted by Thelma, but then not in fact used ...

Thelma writes 40 on board. *What's the next part?*

Children *Take away.*

Thelma writes - sign on board. *What's the next part?*

Children offers of 40, 60, finally 20.

They move into small groups to do planned activities. Aaysha and Darris are at the same table. They have a hand-written worksheet. That didn't seem to cause the children particular problems. They had difficulty with some words, but not because of the handwriting.

The first question has picture of two boxes, arrows and lengths underneath. *Box B is longer by _____ cm.*

Thelma says to the group: *Find out how much longer box B is. Start at 15* [Box A length] *and count up till you get to 23.*

Aaysha seems to use own finger counting method (c.f. finger counting event discussed in Chapter 7) though I can't be sure, saying 16 on first touch of fingers, then totalling the finger numbers she's got when she gets to 23. Gets 8. Aaysha is much faster at whole worksheet than rest of her table of 3. Her reading is more confident, so she starts questions while others still asking for reading help. No-one asked her for help with reading, and she didn't offer to help anyone - solitary and confident but v. quiet style.

Aaysha finishes and the other two girls say she always finishes first.

Darris: *She is a fast coach.* Neither is resentful - not competitive comment. Darris and the other use unifix cubes rather than fingers for bigger numbers.

The next part of the three part numeracy lesson is the plenary which is done at the front of the class on the board. Thelma asks one group (who've had lower level work) to 'bear with her' while she works through the worksheet Aaysha and Darris (and most of class) have just done.

One question had picture of pear and apple; heights of each marked in cm with arrows.

Thelma says one child (unnamed) had completed *The pear is taller than the apple by ____ cm* with 'apple'. Thelma *it makes no sense!* Asks what she's got to do to answer the question;

Aaysha says *add.*

Thelma says no and asks another child.

Someone else says *stick them together.* Eventually someone says *take away* and we move on.

Next question length of library and classroom. Thelma *Because it says how much longer is the classroom than the library it's a difference, isn't it, a take away.*

The pedagogic practices in evidence in the school domain, in this school sited numeracy event, were based on planing by the teacher. She worked to fit in with the centralised National Curriculum and National Numeracy Strategy (NNS). These specify the content to be done together with many of the ways the teacher will approach the session. For example the three-part lesson was specified. The teacher and the NNS determined the pace and timing of the lesson. The learning intentions were specified beforehand. The teacher knew them and she only shared this with the children in a brief statement that: *"we're doing problems involving length today*". The teaching mainly came from her although there may have been incidental learning from peers when in groups or when listening to others. In school, unlike home, the children are usually grouped in age-based contexts although, unusually for UK primary schools, this was a year 1/2 vertically grouped class. There was evidence that the children in school did not always engage collaboratively. Aaysha did not help others. On occasions sharing may occur at school but may be labelled as cheating. For example at Mountford on 17 Oct 00 the register was taken and there were four children missing. The teacher wanted to use this to develop the class numeracy skills. She said: "four not here so how many are here? No cheating. There would have been 22 and don't copy." But the teaching is clearly teacher focused. The teacher scaffolds corrects, motivates and assesses. The children do lose interest at times (c.f. 'engaging' chapter 6). The teacher is in control and she determines the order of contribution. The rules of talk and discourse are for the children to speak when asked to by the teacher. There is little or no evidence of referring to out of school experiences. Even in a lesson about the measurement of length, the teacher makes no clear link to children's earlier experiences or to cultural knowledge or experiences they may have. The resources available are particular to schooling. In the teaching of length, schools use the metric system whereas home practices in some cases still use imperial units. The rules and codes of such practices are school determined and regulated. The children have to learn to fit in with these rules and codes. The register used is technical and at times pedantic. The children have to specify the units they are working in. Thus Aaysha must not say "18" she has to say "18 centimeters" even though centimeters were explicitly part of the conversation in the classroom. We are not claiming that units are not required at home but that the register at school is often more technical and pedantic (cf Barwell et. al., 2004). The words that are linked with "how much longer than" are phrases like "take away" which can mean different things at home. There is also a moment when Thelma has two rulers on the board and wants the children to think about either totalling their lengths or finding the difference between them. This is a common request in schooling about a contrived problem and would be an unlikely event in homes. The children need to learn what the rules, codes and practices are for schooling if they are to be successful at it. This includes recognizing when the rules are 'contrived' but nevertheless significant for present purposes (a similar requirement to that entailed in responding to 'known answer' questions (cf Chapter 6).

These extracts and discussions of them provide illustrations of the similarities and differences between the four different cells of the typology laid out in the table 1 above: that is, home sited /school domain; home sited /home domain; school sited /school domain. As we have said before, the school sited/home domain cell has been omitted because of the lack of observed data of this type. .

4 SIGNIFICANT ISSUES

We have selected from this closer and finer grained analysis of the salient characteristics of numeracy practices in the four domains several features that we see as potentially having a significant impact on children's achievement in numeracy. First we list these and then discuss each of them in turn below. These are:

- significant differences between home and school numeracy practices;
- issues about communications between homes and schools;
- there are areas of substantial conflicts between homes and schools (e.g. homework)
- unexpected differences in resources and funds of knowledge in homes and schools(e.g. games)

Teaching and learning practices at home and school sites are very different in terms of their organisation, their use of language and resources, their contexts, values, social relations, roles, etc.   These differences suggest that children experience very different approaches to the teaching of numeracy at home and at school and therefore their learning.   For example at the surface level their engagement with numeracy at home often involves sharing and collaboration whereas at school such sharing may be seen detrimentally as copying. At a deeper level, numeracy practices at school provide a reinforcement for many children of the status of the teacher as the authority in mathematics in the classroom and of their relationship to mathematics itself. The latter may affect the extent to which they feel an insider or outsider to the codes and rules of mathematics.   These contrasts between the practices and how teachers and carers enable children to shift between the practices in the different domains and how they learn to navigate through them may be some of the factors that affect their achievement in school mathematics. This implies that home/school relationships have a substantial role to play here to enable all the actors in the task of learning numeracy, that is the Department of Education, the school, the teachers, and the children's carers etc. , to jointly and collaboratively examine and make explicit the shift the children need to make between these practices. By acting in this way,, we suggest, they might contribute to helping raise children's attainment in numeracy and hence overcome some children's low achievement in numeracy.

This implies a genuine sharing between homes and schools of the educational project. However, parents' perceptions that there are problems in the adequacy of home/school communication, for example at Mountford, will certainly contribute to the difficulties for children in effecting such shifts. At the very least differences between numeracy and pedagogic practices in the home and school domains shown up in this study point to the importance of genuine mutual communications between schools and homes. For this to happen there may even need to be a shift in the in balance of authority and status between the domains to encourage more effective and productive shifts between the practices in the domains.

The school domain and home sited practices such as homework created considerable difficulties and conflicts between homes and schools.   Parents themselves may also be in conflict about this, some wanting more home work, for example Kay at Mountford whilst others wanting less, for example Kim at Tarnside. In Kim's case homework created a severe conflict in pedagogical practices (teaching and learning styles and epistemological positions) between his teachers and his carer (his grandmother). Other conflicts appeared in parents reluctance to over push their children in formal numeracy at home where they thought activities ought to be fun, whilst teachers saw this reluctance as the child, Kim, being 'indulged'. There was also evidence of this conflict in what were seen to be the role of parents and schools. For instance, some parents argued that they should 'Leave number to school' (AT Anne 23/9/00). Conflict between home and school was evident, for instance, with respect to teaching time (AT Anne29/9/0 14). Anita Straker, first head of the NNS, expressed concern at a conference on the Leverhulme Numeracy Programme that parents working at home with their children using home text books might be damaging their children and Alexander's (2000) work shows that in other European countries there is less expectation that homes will contribute to school work. Other conflicts between home and school involved the use and the representations of digital time at home and analogue time at school.

We also identified some incidental links between some homes and school practices. The account of a home visit to Anne (AT Anne 23/9/00) showed her to have experienced many games at home - "lots of board games in their cupboard" - which could be related to school practices concerning number tracks which are a familiar and frequently used teaching resource. Other homes such as Seth's did not have such resources, leaving a gap between his experiences and the assumptions his teacher would make about his out of school experiences. A related issue that arose, concerned the asymmetry between these practices. Whilst there was evidence that homes made use of what the children experienced in schools, there was little evidence that schools made use of out of school experiences. The home sited activities that we identified as in the school domain were a mixture between activities with pressure from schools, such as homework, and parent selected activities, such as "Teach your child" books and software that anticipated schooled activities, not always in keeping with the school's own views. Such differences in different homes resources and funds of knowledge and teachers' awareness of these funds of knowledge may well be problematic. If teachers' awareness of homes both in terms of resources and habitus was more detailed and nuanced they might be able to build on those resources to provide a more meaningful experience in numeracy for some of the children. This may be a further argument for the provision of the study of ethnographic style approaches for initial teacher education and CPD programmes. (see Heath, S.B. and Mangiola,L 1991)

CHAPTER NINE: CONCLUSION

Explanations for Low achievement: Implications for Practice, Policy and Research

Our aim in writing this book and in the research on which it is based was to widen the range of explanatory factors in addressing children's low achievement in numeracy in primary schools. We argued that in order to do so it was necessary to extend our understanding of what counts as explanation beyond the usual emphasis in quantitative studies on statistical variables and in qualitative studies on such topics as teacher subject knowledge of mathematics, effectiveness, school management, and educational structures, which have tended to dominate research and policy in recent years. We have tried to provide a complementary set of research principles and a conceptual apparatus that we believe offers new insights and a different set of lenses to view problems in teaching and learning numeracy that have troubled educators in recent years.

1 A SOCIAL MODEL OF NUMERACY

That apparatus and the research methods associated with it derive from a theoretical understanding of numeracy as a social practice. This led us to develop what we term an 'ideological' model of numeracy (Baker and Street, 1996), with an associated set of terms for identifying the object of enquiry, including the notions of 'numeracy events' and 'numeracy practices', the components of which comprised content, context, values and social and institutional relations; and the distinction between site and domain. The research question these concepts and distinctions allowed us to ask: was 'what are the relationships between events and practices on the one hand and different sites and domains on the other?' We argue that the complex answers that arise from asking this question can provide new ways of explaining low achievement in schooled numeracy and that they require an ethnographic-style approach. For instance, the terms and the question led us to distinguish between 'schooled numeracy practices' and home numeracy practices, as a possible source for such explanation. We were not making value judgements as between these different sets of practices but rather, by identifying the varied practices that children engage in, suggesting that the switch between one set and another may itself be a source of difficulty for some children.

An ethnographic-style approach enabled us to explore more deeply the context, values and beliefs and social and institutional practices that underpinned such

B. Street, D. Baker and A. Tomlin (eds.), Navigating Numeracies, 163-169.
© 2005 *Springer. Printed in the Netherlands.*

variation and that might help explain some children's difficulties with the practices required by formal schooling. This required data that could not be found in schools alone, hence a major aspect of the project involved research on numeracy practices in children's homes as well as in their classrooms. Our aim was not to judge the different domains but rather to try to understand their relationship. We neither wanted to romanticise the 'home' nor privilege the school. Rather, home/ school relations became the object of study. Although we began with some concepts that we had taken from the field of New Literacy Studies, where the notions of an ideological model of literacy, of literacy as a social practice and of literacy events and practices have been salient for two decades now (cf Street, 1984), we remained provisional as to how far they might be applicable to the field of numeracy. Indeed, one of the questions we wished to address was 'how far might the new conceptual apparatus developed in the field of literacy studies be applicable or adaptable to the field of numeracy?' It is for the reader to judge how far such a question can help those working in numeracy and whether our responses to it have provided any new insights into the questions posed by mathematics educators, regarding children's low achievement in schooled numeracy. We would argue that there are indeed gains to be made by making such associations between these fields, even whilst acknowledging significant difference.

In fact we were engaged, during the period of this project, in a parallel project, also supported by the Leverhulme Trust, precisely looking at home/ school literacy practices in the same schools, along with literacy research colleagues Eve Gregory and Anne Williams (cf Williams et. al., 2004). One parallel question we asked was 'do children have very different experiences as they step into literacy in different classrooms?' We argued there that: 'Apart from the results of official tests, we still have little knowledge of what actually takes place between teachers and children in early years classrooms in Britain' so we chose to focus 'precisely upon such classroom microcultures' and to ask:

> 'how different they might be in three reception classrooms; how the rules and routines of these are constructed by the teachers within the wider framework of the school in its community and finally, how children situate themselves within each of these microcultures (Williams et. al., 2004, p. 1).

A major finding was that very different learning took place in the three schools we were also researching for the numeracy project and that these patterns related to the different language interactions in the different classrooms. In this sense the findings of the two projects complemented each other. In answer to the question: 'Is children's low achievement in schooled numeracy a generalised problem associated with schools' difficulties in building on or relating to out-of-school practices, or is it particular for numeracy?' our findings suggested a general pattern. We argue, then, that what we have found stands as a home/school numeracy case study of schooling more generally. Numeracy teaching/learning, then, implicates 'other' factors, such as in this case literacy, language, and other forms of communication and more broadly the values, beliefs and institutional relations that we signalled above. The specifics of how children experience schooled literacy as also different from home experience will be different from their numeracy experience, but some underlying principles may be the same. In the present case we take numeracy to represent an extreme case of the autonomous model in that claims for neutrality and lack of a cultural dimension appear stronger here even than in some traditional literacy perspectives and therefore can illustrate the general case .

2 THEMES

In the 'Themes' section (section 4) of the book we have elicited from our data three sets of patterns and of terms for describing and analysing children's relative achievement in numeracy that could also be applied to the field of literacy – and to other areas of the curriculum – but which in the first instance are distinctive to the field of numeracy on which our studies focused. The different ways in which children 'engaged' in schooled numeracy practices and the ways they 'switched' between home and school discourses (Chapter 6); the relative use of home cultural resources in school, whether by children themselves or by their teachers (Chapter 7); and the differences and interacting of numeracy practices as children moved between home and school (Chapter 8); were all issues that arose from the data we collected on numeracy practices at home and at school. For instance, one of the themes that runs through the book is the various disjunctions between home and school that may help account for some of the 'disengagement' from schooled numeracy evident amongst some children. Teachers often attempted to overcome these disjunctions, for instance calling upon the principles suggested by the Basic Skills Agency (see Chapter 5b) to incorporate reference to home numeracy experiences in the classroom. Although we did not find much evidence of this in our data, where we did, as we describe in Chapter 5b.6, teachers tended to recontextualise home for schooled purposes. There were, moreover, disparities between the teachers' ideas of what children did at home - laying the table, counting sweets etc - and what we observed. But there were also disparities between what parents imagined school wanted them to do - that is more formal schooled mathematics at home - and what the teachers wanted - that is different, informal mathematics that the school did not have the time or resources to provide. These different images of each other's expectations and practices held by the parties are strangely contrary, homes imagining the school wants them to be more school like and the school imagining they are being home like when they are actually recontextualising home into schooled discourse. At the same time, some parents resisted what they saw as the school's desire to get them to do schooled mathematics at home – as Alexander (1996) notes for other European countries, such parents argue that this is the school's job not theirs, so they did not, for instance, encourage their children to do homework. But others were buying 'Smith's books' (commercial books on numeracy) to give children practice with school work at home, a practice not all teachers encouraged. Such complexities were manifold throughout our data and made us wary of generalisation, certainly of making empirical generalisations from data that was anyway collected as 'case studies' but also of making any claims to what 'parents' or 'teachers' as a whole do or think. We cannot, then, present just one picture of school or home: mathematics is experienced differently, not only by different children and parents, but by different teachers and by the same children and teachers at different times of day, as lessons run smoothly or disintegrate.

We have instead tried to draw out some themes, such as the disjunctions alluded to here, that we build on more fully in the thematic Section 4 of the book and we do attempt to make links between specific experiences in a particular site and the more general issues that the social view of numeracy raises. We are asking the reader, then, not so much to assume they will replicate our findings in their own contexts as to take our questions and concepts and our data into their own sites and to ask whether they help to illuminate what is going on there. From a theoretical perspective, this might involve modifying or adapting our concepts and themes to the local site and thereby throwing back at us a refined version of the social model of numeracy. To assist in such a task we try to draw out here what we have found that is specific to numeracy in this study, in terms of both our conceptualisation of the field and of the data our conceptual framework generated.

3 NUMERACY IN THEORY AND PRACTICE

The first aspect that has emerged from our study concerned epistemology, the nature of representation of mathematics and the mathematics curriculum. On the one hand there was a view of mathematics, as often seen from those outside the discipline, as a narrow and closed set of skills, procedures and processes. On the other there was a more open and broad vision, as seen by some from inside mathematics education. We would argue that this more open vision can be extended further to represent mathematics as a contestable theory of reality, which would encourage discussion and debates and could make the subject more relevant and provide a more active role for learners. Our extension of the 'Social Turn'(see Chapter 2) to a conceptualisation of mathematics as social practice leads to understandings of multiple mathematics practices and therefore that formal abstract schooled mathematics practices may be only one of many possible practices. The removal from mathematics education of what the narrow view takes to be the 'social' dimension as though it were 'noise' evident in making mathematics practices more abstract and the privileging of this formal practice may lead to tensions within and amongst people trying to learn mathematics in such academic settings.   These academic approaches can result in conflicts, for instance, with students' sense of their identities and of how they could engage with that particular mathematics practice and thereby lead to the lack of engagement we have seen. Mathematics through this lens is seen as more complex than has often been portrayed. This theoretical shift is timely, as debates about mathematics in terms of society's and individual needs and interests and developments in technology (ICT) lead to more flexible, contested and changing views of the school mathematics curriculum from inside and outside of the school itself. The privileging of abstract formal mathematics practices e.g. proof, correctness, minimalism, elegance, rationality, and a lack or suppression of emotion are being challenged so that, for instance, problems of 'transfer' across contexts, (using and applying abstract mathematical ideas to problem solving) will have to take account of the varied needs and interests of learners. In this new scenario, schooled mathematics too will have to become more openly contested and alive with students actively engaging in these debates.

4 IMPLICATIONS FOR PRACTICE, POLICY AND RESEARCH IN NUMERACY

The research, based on a representation of mathematics as social, has revealed the importance of teachers building on students interests, experience, knowledge of mathematics and drawing on home based funds of knowledge of mathematics. As teachers themselves come to appreciate that mathematics can be more than a formal body of knowledge they can help it become an active, alive experience for their students. This involves awareness of the kinds of conflicts students experience with their own identities when being asked to engage with formal mathematics practices in an academic setting. To do this effectively involves teachers knowing as much as possible about their students and that means knowing more than the kind of information that can be gleaned from formal tests of schooled mathematics knowledge. The latter can tell a great deal about what skills and procedures someone can do under test conditions but is unlikely to reveal anything deeper about their interests and needs and the kinds of experiences and funds of knowledge they may have acquired during their lives. To take account of such knowledge and experience requires teachers to be culturally sensitive, to value and valorise these experiences and seek ways of exploiting them, in order to develop the kinds of numeracy skills and understandings necessary for navigating the world pupils are entering. A way to approach the implementation of this could be encouraging and enabling teachers to think of themselves as ethnographers, of both their own mathematics practices and those of their pupils, in both programmes for initial teacher education and in continuing professional development. Adopting an 'ethnographic perspective', in the sense described by Green, and Bloome, (1997) (see Chapter 3) involves learning to be critically reflexive of one's own beliefs and intuitions and engaging in close observation of and participation in the cultural practices of different groups from a social theory perspective. This is too important to be left to the university researchers alone. As Cochran-Smith & Lytle (1993) have shown, classroom teachers as ethnographers can generate new kinds of knowledge and can offer new insights into pedagogy and learning. In the field of literacy the link between research and practice is being developed in exactly this way, as the insights of new literacy studies and of literacy as a social practice are followed through in imaginative learning projects in many different countries (Street, 2004; Pahl & Rowsell, 2005). The present book can be seen as a step along a similar path in the field of numeracy. We would like to call for programmes and projects in the learning of mathematics that take forward –and amend – in practical and imaginative ways, the insights developed here regarding mathematics as a social practice.

The notion of changing practice towards a more social approach to mathematics could be interpreted as suggesting that mathematics be made more 'functional' and 'everyday' both in terms of pedagogy and curriculum. However, we are going beyond that by suggesting that there is scope for different classroom practices that include a pedagogy that seeks to mediate between the formal school curriculum and home practices. This approach also provides scope for the development of curricula that go beyond the privileged formal school curriculum and functional notions of mathematics towards more culturally sensitive and flexible mathematics

Such approaches, of course, raise issues to do with power and social relations and the gate-keeping role of mathematics. Teachers, parents and children need to be aware of the formal schooled mathematics game. They need to know the code and navigate the system. That is in order to navigate through the system of school mathematics and to engage effectively with school numeracy practices they need to know both why the ideas they are meeting are seen as important and powerful and in what ways they are relevant and important to them and their lives. This might go some way to countering the 'boredom' with formal mathematics and its 'irrelevance', to which Smith (2004) refers as a factor in children's low attainment in mathematics in the UK. This means that where appropriate aspects of the social relations in schooled numeracy practices have to be unpacked and made explicit to teachers, parents and children.

Our research has suggested, then, that policies should be changed with respect to: teacher education and continuing professional development of teachers; social relations in educational institutions; and the representation of mathematics in classroom pedagogy and curriculum development. With regard to teacher education more stress could be placed on teachers as ethnographers, as we have outlined above, rejecting deficit models of homes and instead seeing homes and their practices as cultural resources and funds of knowledge. With regard to educational institutions, we envisage changes in terms of image, purposes, social relations, and the mathematics curriculum. Educational institutions might then become more sensitive to problems that parents and carers experience in the social relations associated with schooled mathematics and encourage more open access, communication and sharing of information between schools and homes. The problems of conflicting identities, that is being insiders or outsiders in mathematics and numeracy, could be faced by being more aware of the social relations involved in school numeracy practices and through that being able to respond differently to the varied positions children, parents and teachers take in relation to formal school mathematics.

Lastly representing mathematics as social practice has proved a useful model for our research into problems of low attainment in school numeracy. It has enabled us to reveal often un-stated and implicit values, beliefs, social, institutional and power relations in particular mathematics practices that might help explain the recurring problem of low attainment. Example of these are the privileging of schooled numeracy practices over home ones, the deficit models some teachers have of homes and the disjunctions we found between homes and schools, for instance over recontextualising home practices in schools. We therefore encourage others, where appropriate, to use these approaches in their research in other educational contexts and thereby to broaden the mathematics education community's understandings of mathematics itself, of the response to it by many pupils and of issues in the teaching and learning of mathematics. We see the research described here as an initial step towards fuller and more extensive inquiries of this kind and look forward to others engaging in such an enterprise, looking more closely at questions that we have only been able to touch on here, such as those listed at the end of Chapter 7. If this book has contributed to the development of such understandings and enterprises then we will have fulfilled our purpose.

APPENDIX A

Numeracy Practices: 'Framework 2'

Numeracy Practices: criteria for identification (somewhere between 'maths as everything' and maths as schooled cognitive)	
Source of VIEWS /visions (perceptions) of NP Evidence/examples of views /understandings/ perceptions	**RELATIONS** Analysis, interpretations
Research-based: *conceptions of numeracy based on research theory and methodology*	**BETWEEN VIEWS OF PARTIES**
eg'Funds of Knowledge' (Moll)	**(contrast within and**
eg Adult learners/ Parent Learners (Civil)	**between homes,**
eg Home/ school Discourses (Freebody)	**schools - MATRIX?)**
eg Home measurement, approximation (Massingila)	
eg Cultural systems of representation (Abreu)	**eg content/ pedagogy**
eg Material values, money, poverty (Walkerdine)	**different pedagogies**
eg Home socialisation/ school learning programmes (Cairney)	**eg salience/ visible**
eg Literacy research - events and practices (Heath, Street, Barton)	**eg mobilise/ demobilise**
eg 'Variables' literature (mother's education; reading to children;	**eg switching (mode; h/s)**
books at home, WPPSI etc)	
descriptions of Numeracy practices & social Baker Street Johnson	**DIRECTION/ STRENGTH OF**
pedagogical practices constructivist situated	**LINKS**
cultural resources Bourdieu Pollard	
	eg determination
Mathematicians: essentialist, fallibilist, social linear hierarchical,	**eg authority**
ordered well defined, subject knowledge, pedagogical subject	
knowledge etc. Importance values and social relations.	**EXPLANATORY**

Correctness minimalist, compliance Explanations for achievement in maths	**POWER**

Carer-based:
 	
Home/school relations as context for perceptions of numeracy practices: eg definite/ less definite views of school eg conceptions of parenting, discipline, 'work', 'prospects', eg comparison with other parents.
   Understanding of maths re own uses and history
   Interpretations of /demands from current school practices
eg working with children re school requirements eg homework eg Teaching and learning numeracy practices at home.
   What numeracy practices are described at home: what is valued, selected eg 'Salience' and visibility of different maths practices eg hidden/ overt eg may count only what is 'difficult'
   Explanations for achievement in maths
	similarities /
	differences between
	parties 'explain'
	children's
	underachievement?
	  cultural resources

Child-based: What they bring from home to school;
       their view of relationships; what they see as school demands
       their roles in numeracy practices
       what children do or could do in numeracy terms
 	
   Policy: a) National
   National Curriculum; Agencies eg Ofsted; TTA
   Maths Education and Teacher Education
   Public Discourses
 	
     b) School-based
   school definitions of 'numeracy': cognitive skills eg NNS eg tests
   eg metacognitive awareness eg 'two-ness', place value (relation to	

metalinguistic awareness?) modes of representation.

conceptions of numeracy embedded in school/ home relations

eg

homework eg schemes (Impact)

School and National policies towards numeracy curriculum

and

pedagogy linear, hierarchical, absolutist Explanations for
achievement in maths

c Teacher-based

Teacher conception of maths; relation to policy and school
versions. notions of importance, valued. Selection. Roles and
social relations. Purposes, contexts

Teachers' numeracy pedagogical practices. Explanations for
achievement in maths

Teacher images of home maths practices, carers' & children's
experiences at home what they use maths for at home. How

they

see carers' roles in "teach" children maths at home

Teacher's perception of children's responses to maths

Teacher images of home as context for numeracy practices eg

deficit constructing relations with carers - discipline, 'cosy'

Researcher-based models: *Emerging from/ synthesis of the
observations and analysis of models of parties above - research,
mathematicians, school, teacher, carer, child: re our prior
expectations/ models*

Separate strands for descriptive purposes?

Comparison for analytic purposes eg 'matrix' of parties' positions?

Home numeracy practices and schooled numeracy practices

Salience/visibility axis; eg 'mobilisation/ resistance

Contrasts of practices within and between homes and schools

Modes of representation eg reformulations/ switching between oral/ written; notation, sign, words; visual, objects Switching between home and schooled numeracy practices **Key concepts emerging from data:** dis/continuities; barriers/links support/ tensions consonant/ dissonant; compensate/ complement dis/engagement; mis/trust; value, valorise; accept/ reject mis/communicate; identities; insiders outsiders status, authority, relations	

Numeracy Practices: 'Framework 2'
(note)

For working purposes we begin observations with some of the conceptions of numeracy practices listed above, held by different parties, noting the differences that each set generates. We started with school and research based, moved into classrooms and thence to homes, moving backwards and forwards between this empirical work and the theoretical and research literature. The model of 'numeracy practices' is thus not an ontological claim to a given but is constructed out of description of different models held by different parties. We might follow through the implications of each position/ view for how we observe/ make sense of the activities of home and school and their relationship eg how far does one party take account of views of others eg on 'homework' eg what are relationships between different parties' models - does one 'determine/ influence' another, are they independent, which has authority? We might then begin to develop/ refine our own model as a way of delimiting the field of enquiry with respect to the research questions raised by the project. This model too is a construct not a given, but its validity/ value will rest on its ability to help us observe what might otherwise be missed and to begin to offer explanations (eg for 'success'/ underachievement) that are not apparent from other perspectives. The framework can provide a basis for observation and interview schedules and to make explicit what is taken for granted in the situations we describe. Team discussions of data will lead to occasional revisions of this framework.

BS 19.10.01

APPENDIX B

LEVERHULME NUMERACY PROGRAMME
FOCUS 4: SCHOOL AND COMMUNITY NUMERACIES

Checklist for conversations with parents/ carers

<u>Home practices</u>

Uses of numeracy/ number /maths practices at home? for example helping around the house, setting the table, games, TV, video, mobile phone, shopping, pocket money, dates, time, behaviour? data handling e.g. labels on videos, computer discs. How important is it at home?

'*Relationships'* of carer/ child around NP e.g. negotiable? control? home/ outside agendas?

Varied uses of number/ numeracy eg numbers on video/ buses/ that could functionally be letters; measurement, estimation, range, interval etc.

Smith's books - does carer buy/ use commercial books to help child's numeracy? which ones? in what ways does carer/ another adult work with them?

Engagement: distinction between things (real and imaginary) that do and do not engage child's intentions and attention ie not distinction between 'everyday' and 'abstract' maths but what engages them.

Home practices taken into school

Does child take number activities into school from home eg times, calendars, festivals, problems, puzzles, games, dice, Pokemon?

School practices taken into homes.

Homework does child bring home work set in class, (eg learning tables), does carer help, how long do they spend on it, do they have opinions about children doing homework? Do they help him/her? Does she/he use SNP at home? eg puzzles, games, problems. when? why/why not? Does carer model school practices at home? eg naming and practising on clock eg numbering steps as child goes up/ down

Complementing/ compensating: in what ways do carers represent their engagement in maths activities at home with child? eg as complementing what school does? as compensating for gaps in what school does? relate to those of school?

Literacy: there is a book bag for literacy but is there any equivalent for numeracy sent home? Do they see literacy as different from numeracy from the point of view of the child's learning and of what the school does?

Home/school sharing of experiences/information

Does carer know about what goes on in school? how, when where? Do they get letters/ information home from school - general/ re numeracy? Do teachers ask what goes on at home (or only communicate when there are problems?). Do they have a role in child's education/ numeracy or is that just for the school? How different is HNP and SNP? Why? What changes in the relationship to school have they noticed from R to Year 1? eg distancing of parents at school door eg child's maths work less familiar to parents/ carers?

Parents' concepts of numeracy

Views of HNP

What is carer's own history, views etc about numeracy? Do they use it? context, How important is it at home? Why? What are the implications of their own maths history for their child's numeracy? What counts as maths? what remains 'invisible'? Views of child's maths?

Views of SNP

Value of SNP why?. What content of SNP are important? why, who decides?.

Views of numeracy teaching and learning

best ways of teaching/ learning it? why do some children do well others not? What do they hope child will get from school numeracy?

Links with other institutions

Do they have contacts/ get help from e.g. Sure Start; Play Link; EAZ; Hill View; etc.?

APPENDIX C

LEVERHULME NUMERACY PROGRAMME

FOCUS 4: SCHOOL AND COMMUNITY NUMERACIES

CHECKLIST FOR CLASSROOM VISITS

Reference Framework 2 for school's or teacher's explanation for numeracy achievement eg School-based: a. policy b teacher; eg Home/school relations as context for perceptions of numeracy practices

Home/school

- What is the teacher's view of NP at home?

- relationship of homework (if any) to classroom activities eg whether homework grows out of class activities, includes writing/setting of homework, as well as aftermath. her perceptions of purposes value role of HW is there evidence of drawing on home NP and experience in the classroom? eg non-teacher led use of home approaches/experiences. : Does T know about/ make use of NP that children use at home? eg puzzles, games, problems? Does T ask parents to help children with numeracy at home eg naming and practising on clock eg numbering steps as child goes up/ down.

- parents/carers arriving with children – in playground/allowed in class?

- any evidence of relationships of F4 parents/carers with teacher. Communication and access. Separation. Beliefs about roles parents can play, mobilising? Role of documents parents evenings and meetings; tensions or conflicts with parents' purposes and roles of homework. Perceptions of cultural resources of homes and children

Classroom & school

focus on numeracy

- Displays of children's work; role play changes; table layouts etc e.g. role play re 'topic' maths. Relevant school displays e.g. photos *Schooled NP:* numeracy work - content and form; relation to NC and school programmes of work; eg number, shape, eg counting in twos, odd /even, measuring weighing and time;, number bonds; Purposes of numeracy activities: educational; embedded in other tasks, e.g. school meals, register, games, contexts for SNP; values and social relations

School numeracy

Building blocks of what we might then analyse as schooled numeracy practices. aspects to do with school vision towards numeracy, what things are valued selected stressed etc. How they relate to NNS and NC and Pandas. School vision towards numeracy pedagogy. Does it set?

Numeracy work: teacher focus
- Teacher's pedagogical practices in maths;
- role of the teacher/ children in classroom
- relation to maths insider outsider
- intended learning outcomes, e.g. from teacher's plan, as told to children, or interpreted by researcher, including specialised vocabulary
- relation to national curriculum, NNS, schemes of work, where known
- values towards maths - correctness debate, autonomous, sitedness
- relationship of literacy work to numeracy
- mediating devices, procedures, techniques, technologies, tools, objects
- classroom organisation e.g. whole class, mat, small groups, does school/ teacher set? children volunteer to answer questions or called upon etc, individual worksheets
- whole class and individual 'engagement' including sanctions, 'noise'
- classroom language eg modality, narrative, vocabulary, interpersonal styles
- role of LSAs, SEN support staff, speech therapists etc eg how teacher/LSA/researcher time is distributed among children e.g. whether children usually work with same adult eg differences between LSAs
- beliefs about learning in pedagogical practices, building of children's experiences
- Reactions to Pandas and other data
- Teacher's explanations for achievement in maths; Teachers perceptions of different roles status; social relations;

- Teacher images of home eg constructing relations with parents - discipline, 'cosy'; deficit; compensating complementing

Numeracy work: focus on children

- children's choices (where they have any), e.g. choices of numeracy work, who to sit with
- social relations around numeracy work e.g. sharing, competition, friends; who they ask for help
- detail of 'what happens' in particular work: mediating devices, procedures, literacy issues, talking
- dis/engagement in numeracy tasks
- any evidence of dis/continuities with home experiences, or relating of classroom and home experiences

Wolcott's framework for analysing field data:

The framework suggested by Wolcott, for representing research data involves dividing the account into: Description (mainly accounts of data eg literacy events); Interpretation (mainly insights, knowledge you bring to bear from elsewhere, theoretical perspectives); and Analysis (in his terms this means doing systematic trawls through Description in relation to Interpretation, to check whether you can validate/ support your insights: this forces you to be selective, i.e. to recognise that interesting though some insights are, you can't actually follow them up sufficiently to make valid and sustainable claims in the outside world...). The categories are, of course, not water tight and they are contestable, but the framework provides a starting point for discussion of the issue involved in doing qualitative research. I will provide an example of how I have tried to work this through in relation to my own current research on home/ school numeracy practices. My methodological questions are - what goes in the 'Analysis' column and how does it relate to the other two? Does this approach/ procedure help/ what are its limitations?

Wolcott,H 1994 Transforming Qualitative Data: Description, Analysis and Interpretation Sage: CA esp chapter 2 'Description, Analysis and Interpretation in Qualitative Inquiry' pp. 9-53

APPENDIX D; Layout for Recording Classroom Data

Leverhulme Numeracy programme: F4 'School and Community Numeracies'

Brian Street Report on Mountford home visits: Mar 14th 2000
Lenny in Pamela's Class (Reception). Mother (M) and Sister (Z).

DESCRIPTION	INTERPRETATION	ANALYSIS	
Lenny is in Pamela's reception Class at Mountford. First visited March 00. Spring child. He is in the top band according to the teacher's baseline. Lives with Mother (Mrs W), Sister (Samantha; in year 7 at F Secondary School, 11 years old). Grandfather (G) often present and helps out e.g. buying computer e.g. supporting Lenny in maths work.			
Met M and Lenny at school and went to the house in her car, Lenny had only just returned to school yesterday after two weeks off following having his adenoids out. His mother hoped that his nasal passages would be unblocked and he could breathe through his nose not just his mouth and thereby speak more clearly. He had been a little subdued in class and wasn't quite so hyped up at home as before. They had bought a new computer with lots of educational games and software so that when he came out of hospital he had plenty to do and also to contribute to his educational development.			

DESCRIPTION	INTERPRETATION	ANALYSIS
New computer game - Encyclopaedia of Nature: Dorling Kindersley, typical quality of picture from their books with computer graphics, moving images, hot spots etc... They had only played with it once or twice so were learning the keys and the procedures. Lenny in charge of mouse and keys, M and Z watching and asking/advising/ cajoling. He opened up a nature information piece, with fish swimming around an a po-faced American voices in 'scientific' register framing the video with pieces of 'knowledge' e.g. 'flat fish as they move across the ocean bed allow the water to flow over their fins and a gap beneath allows them to sweep up small creatures which are their food'. He then scanned a world map and from it opened up pictures of a Rain Forest in S. America and then found a way of individually magnifying the animals/ plants depicted there (this procedure was new as we went along and his M and Z remarked on this, they had not done it last time they opened the programme). He moved around the forest space focusing upon individual objects/ animals and his M and Z tried to encourage him to then find out information on them by clicking: it took him a while to find the way to do this (outside the magnification, by double clicking - he had at first tried a small complex window with arrows and images that was hard to focus on or to link to the larger picture). He then occasionally responded to their requests and brought up text or other images and sometimes a moving image was available or a sound. M was highly impressed and said she loved this kind of activity and information - she had bought a Human Body CD for herself and hoped now to apply to it some of	On a different plane from classroom activities, including classroom computer (old BBC with simple tasks e.g. click on numbers, get them right, a clown dances). Need to establish links between children's home activities and those of school? Lenny's M keen to offer him support and has bought the computer and software with this in mind. But she has no idea what goes on in school and how her home activities relate. For him the excitement of the high quality graphics and moving images and control are light years ahead of the school computing. But at present he just surfs about clicking and jumping images, without much structure or direction: meanwhile, the school activity has structure and direction but lacks the excitement and sheer visual and image excitement or pupil control. Mother keen to help child - how can school build on this e.g. Teachers to be trained in what children are doing at home e.g. re computers. Teachers could send home activities e.g. number line, bonds, that parents could practice via the computer games or via everyday activities. But teachers afraid 'a little knowledge is a dangerous thing' (A. in staff room)	check out other examples of home/ school practices around computers interview teacher/ parent re pedagogies associated with computer use Policy implications - follow up

the procedures she had learned this afternoon. She kept asking me whether this activity was 'educational' and how. I occasionally commented on what Lenny might be 'learning' e.g. manipulating computer mouse and procedures e.g. bits of information about the world e.g. routes to knowledge e.g. different discourses associated with 'knowledge' in the world.

ie don't trust parents with this level of complexity. meanwhile parents out of touch with school activity so go for 'educational' books and software but children jump around in them without structure and without clear link/ cohesion with what is happening in class.

Shirley Heath in a meeting on Fri comment on the 'frames of knowledge' that she identified urban youths deploying and bringing to school. She was concerned that schools ignore these/ have no conceptual framework for recognising them and has prepared TT materials to bridge this gap. Thinking of Lenny on his computer one might identify emerging frames of knowledge regarding computer representations of knowledge (e.g. the 'scientific voice'), perhaps some maths context, certainly some serendipitous knowledge of the natural world that might hook into more structured knowledge later. The pedagogic implications of all of this are enormous but the school's interest is mainly in inculcating the children into its routines and into fairly limited discourses/ voices. How far should we pursue these policy questions at this stage?

ANNEX 1

CORE PROJECT: TRACKING NUMERACY

The aim of the core project of the Leverhulme Numeracy Research Programme was to obtain large-scale longitudinal value-added data on numeracy to:
- inform knowledge about the progression in pupils' learning of numeracy throughout the primary years, and
- assess relative contributions to gains in numeracy of the different factors to be investigated in the programme.

Our objectives were:
- to assess longitudinally the numeracy attainment of two overlapping cohorts of primary pupils so that a picture of year-on-year achievement in a variety of schools was obtained from Year 1 (pupils aged 5-6 years) up to Year 6 (pupils aged 10-11 years), with some limited extension both into Reception (pupils aged 4-5 years) and into Year 7 (pupils aged 11-12 years)
- to match the year-on-year value-added attainment data against data relating to *classroom practice*, including, but not limited to, teaching method, teaching organisation, and curriculum in order to investigate the influence of these factors on attainment
- to match the year-on-year value-added attainment data against data relating to each *teacher*, in particular to teachers' subject knowledge and expectations, as well as other factors, in order to investigate the influence of these factors on attainment
- to match the year-on-year value-added attainment data against data relating to each *school,* in particular to data on the existence of clear policies and agreed practices, as well as other factors (such as the experience of the headteacher and the mathematics co-ordinator), in order to investigate the effect of these factors on attainment
- to match the year-on-year value-added attainment data against data relating to individual *pupils* (in particular social class), in order to investigate the effects of these factors on attainment at different stages of schooling
- to generate hypotheses from large-scale quantitative analyses which can be further explored in the Focus Projects, in particular in Focus Project: *Case Studies of Pupil Progress*, and in addition to provide data which will allow hypotheses which arise from case study samples in the focused projects to be validated on a larger scale.

No longitudinal data is available in the United Kingdom to indicate the ways, or the rate, at which primary pupils develop over time the understanding and skills which together constitute competence in numeracy, nor of how this is related to a broader range of school and other factors.

The long-term nature of the Leverhulme Numeracy Research Programme gave an opportunity to track the progress of pupils in numeracy over five years. By selecting two overlapping cohorts, the first starting with Reception (pupils aged 4-5 years) and the second with Year 4 (pupils aged 8-9 years), this covered the full primary age range and allowed one group to be followed through to Year 7 in secondary school as shown in Table A.1.1. This provided for the first time a unique set of longitudinal year-on-year data on a large primary sample.

Table A.1.1. The two cohorts

	1997-1998	1998-1999	1999-2000	2000-2001	2001-2002
Cohort 1	Reception	Y1	Y2	Y3	Y4
Cohort 2	Y4	Y5	Y6	Y7	

The fact that Year 4 data was available for both the second cohort in 1997/98 and from the first in 2001/02 has also made it possible to evaluate the effect of the National Numeracy Strategy which was implemented across all years in all primary schools in the UK during 1999/2000.

By selecting a sample which was relatively large and covered schools drawing pupils from a variety of different social backgrounds, with differences in teaching style and organisation, it was possible to determine the effects of the different factors listed below (and the interactions between them), together with others which were later suggested.

Classroom practice factors
    (a) teaching methods
    (b) teaching organisation
    (c) curriculum
Teacher factors
    (d) teacher subject knowledge
    (e) low teacher expectations
School factors
    (f) school leadership
Social context factors
    (g) home contexts

One important feature of the relatively long time-span of the project was that it enabled hypotheses which arose from the analysis of early rounds of data to be investigated further.

The 40 schools that took part in the longitudinal study were chosen from four Local Education Authorities, and the 10 schools in each of them included inner city schools in deprived areas, racially mixed schools and schools in pleasant suburbs with expensive housing. Two authorities were from the London area; the other two authorities were both large counties, one in the South East of England and the second in the North of England. In the North of England authority, some of the schools were in an urban area with a large population of South Asian origin. Some schools in one of the Local Education Authorities in the sample had been involved in the National Numeracy Project (See Introduction).

School sample

Within each of these Local Education Authorities the selection of 10 schools was made with the assistance of the professional advisory staff and the available performance and intake data. In this programme the focus was on the effect of particular factors and therefore a quota rather than a representative or random sample was appropriate. The aim within each Local Education Authority was to choose 10 primary schools so that they included:
- relative to the socio-economic circumstances of the population in each Local Education Authority, at least two schools from relatively advantaged, two from intermediate and two from less advantaged catchment areas
- at least two church schools
- relative to the balance within the Local Education Authority, at least two large and two small schools
- at least three schools which were identified (according to available value-added data) to be effective in teaching numeracy, together with at least two which were identified as average and two weak
- in addition to primary schools (ages 4-11 years), some linked infant (ages 4-7 years) and junior (ages 7-11 years) schools where these were a common form of school organisation within a Local Education Authority.

At the point at which the older cohort of pupils in the study transferred into secondary schools at age 11, there was no attempt to trace the progress of all the pupils. However, at least one secondary school in each Local Education Authority which received a substantial number of the pupils in the cohort, including some from different primary schools, was selected and agreed to collaborate in the study, providing some information on the achievements of the pupils at the end of the first year of secondary school. In one of the two Local Education Authorities in London, two further secondary schools were also included, and in the other one additional school was selected, making a total of seven secondary schools in the study, with over 180 pupils. It was believed that these seven schools constituted a reasonable range of types of secondary school.

37 out of the original 40 primary schools (seven of which were linked infant and junior schools) remained as participants in the project over this five year period. There was less attrition than expected, especially given the pressures on primary schools and teachers over the years 1997-2002 which included the introduction of both the National Literacy and National Numeracy Strategies (see Introduction). This meant that with students joining and leaving schools over the five years, there were more than 2000 pupils on the database for each of the two cohorts. However, in any one year, at least 1300 pupils in over 70 classes had taken part for each of the two cohorts.

Data Sources and Instruments

Pupil Data: Numeracy assessment. To enable progress in each year to be measured, pupils in the two cohorts were tested at the beginning and end of each year between Year 1 and Year 6, using a class test of numeracy. There was no formal testing in the Reception year, although results of baseline and other tests were collected.

Children were tested towards the beginning and end of each school year, within a designated two weeks towards the end of October and the beginning of June. A sequence of tests, one for each year group, was used which were derived from instruments developed from earlier research by members of the team (Hart (Ed.), 1981; Denvir & Brown, 1986; Askew et al., 1997). The items had in almost all cases been designed for one-on-one diagnostic interviews and based on reviews of related research; Denvir and Bibby (2002) have updated in a format usable by teachers and teaching assistants a diagnostic interview for low attaining primary pupils from which many of the items were drawn. These items were later adapted for whole class settings, and were thus extensively trialled in both formats. The reliability (using Cronbach's alpha) was found to be very high (of the order of 0.94). Denvir and Brown (1987) had earlier compared pupils performance on interviews and class tests using many of the items. Items were designed to assess conceptual understanding and cognitively based skills. They include contextual as well as purely numerical items. Most items required short open responses but a small number were in multiple choice format. Many items were linked with others assessing similar concepts/skills but often of varying facility. The same test was used at the start and end of the year, and was orally administered by teachers from a provided script with pupils answering in specially designed booklets. The emphasis was on mental rather than written processes. For some cases teachers were asked to display a poster for a fixed number of seconds. The number of items in the test varied from 41 in Year 1 to over 80 in older age groups.

The tests were designed both to contain a large number of common items from one year to the next (including three items which were assessed in each year from Year 1 to Year 6), and to have the same uniform distribution of facility within each test. This means that equal numerical gains were made by children at different attainment levels.

The inclusion of common items has allowed the facilities across several years of the primary school to be plotted for each item and compared for the linked sets of items. An index of difficulty has been calculated for each item which indicates the estimated age at which 50% of the cohort can succeed on it. The Rasch procedure allows children to then be assigned a 'numeracy age' for each sitting of the test.

The test was given orally by the teacher to avoid reading problems and to enable a time limit on some questions to focus on mental numeracy skills and prevent pupils from using ineffective methods. The test had been successful in differentiating within year groups and was clearly appropriate in the level of attainment it tested.

A problem solving task was developed and trialled and was administered to Year 4 pupils in the first year. However as it was found in the assessment that pupils' strategies were heavily influenced by their teachers, it was decided that the data was not sufficiently valid or reliable to justify the considerable marking costs in later years.

The Year 6 test was repeated at the end of Year 7 in the seven secondary schools included in the study.

Pupil Data: Other sources. In addition to numeracy assessment, we collected additional data on pupils in the sample. This included:

- national test data on mathematics and English for Year 2 pupils (aged 6-7 years) and Year 6 pupils (aged 10-11 years); in some cases results of nationally set tests were also available in Year 4
- reading age data where available
- baseline data where available (for pupils aged 4-5 years at the start of Reception class
- social class data (using post-code analysis as a proxy)
- gender and ethnicity data
- any relevant data from the seven secondary schools e.g. mathematics sets allocated.

These data assisted especially with the exploration of factors relating to pupil social background.

School data: interviews and school statistics. We visited each school in each year of the project, for a minimum of one day, and more than this in the case of larger schools. In the first year we interviewed the headteacher and the mathematics co-ordinator, collected relevant school data on the size and characteristics on the school population and relevant documents including curriculum policies for mathematics. This gave some information on factor (f) school leadership, in particular, clear policies and agreed practices for numeracy teaching. It also provided information on factor (e) of low teacher expectation. In later years brief interviews were held with the head teacher and co-ordinator to update information. In the final year there were again longer interviews with the headteacher and co-ordinator. Only one year-group was involved in primary schools for the fourth and fifth year of the study (Cohort 2 had by that time moved into secondary school). In the fourth year, visits were made to each of the three selected secondary schools in each Local Education Authority, to interview the head of the mathematics department.

Classroom data: observations. Lessons were observed in the classrooms of the pupils in each year of the two cohorts, starting with Reception and Year 4 classes in 1997/98. Aspects of classroom organisation, resources and teaching methods, and also brief conversations with pupils were recorded in fieldnotes. In the fourth year, visits were made to each of the seven secondary schools to observe one or more Year 7 lessons.

Teacher data: questionnaires. Over the five years, each teacher of a class in either cohort was also asked to provide brief data relating to several other factors under investigation, and where possible, this was triangulated with data from field observations. These data included:

- range of teaching methods
- classroom organisation
- curriculum materials
- assessment and recording methods

- own mathematical experience, qualifications and training (initial and in-service).

As well as information on the above factors this also included brief items on teachers' beliefs and priorities in teaching numeracy. There was about an 80% return each year on teacher questionnaires.

Teacher data: interviews. Teachers of the classes in both cohorts, starting with Reception and Year 4 in 1997/98, were interviewed each year. Interviews were semi-structured and were tape-recorded and transcribed. Protocols for teacher interviews were modified each year to take account of national developments, like the National Numeracy Strategy and targetting.

Data analysis

Tests were marked centrally by students onto optical mark reading forms which were scanned into the computer. All questions were marked simply as correct, wrong or omitted, using a marking schedule. Various checks were made on the reliability of this process. Data analyses were undertaken using Excel and Datadesk.

The responses to the closed questionnaire items were also coded for optical mark reading, and joined with manually keyed in open questionnaire items and the other data, in order to provide the most comprehensive possible dataset.

Transcripts of interviews and other qualitative data were also stored in a database. Classroom observations were in the form of fieldnotes taken either longhand or entered into an electronic notebook.

Several methods of analysing both quantitative and qualitative data were developed. Where relevant these are described in the main text.

Askew, M., Brown, M., Rhodes, V., Johnson, D., & Wiliam, D. (1997). *Effective Teachers of Numeracy. Final Report.* London: King's College.

Denvir, B. ,& Brown, M. (1986). Understanding of number concepts in low attaining 7-9 year olds: parts 1 & 2. *Educational Studies in Mathematics. 17*, 15-36 and 143-164.

Denvir, B., & Brown, M. (1987). The feasibility of class-administered diagnostic assessment in primary mathematics. *Educational Research, 29(2),* 95-107.

Denvir, H., & Bibby, T. (2002). *Diagnostic Interviews in Number Sense.* London: BEAM Publications.

Hart, K. (Ed.) (1981). *Children's Understanding of Mathematics: 11-16.* London: John Murray.

FOCUS PROJECT: TEACHERS' KNOWLEDGE, CONCEPTIONS AND PRACTICES

This project was part of the Leverhulme Numeracy Research Programme funded by The Leverhulme Trust at the School of Education, King's College London. The aim of this project was to investigate the relationship between teachers' beliefs about, knowledge of and practices in teaching numeracy and whether changes in beliefs, knowledge and/or practices raise standards. Our objectives were:
- To understand and document the effect of the National Numeracy Strategy's programme of five day training in terms of changes in teachers' beliefs, knowledge and practices in teaching numeracy
- To examine the impact of any changes in beliefs, knowledge and practice upon pupil attainment
- To further develop understanding of which aspects of teachers' beliefs, knowledge and practices are most salient in promoting effective teaching of numeracy and raising standards.

The research tracked a group of 12 teachers and their pupils over a two year period (spanning three school years) in order to identify changes over time in teacher beliefs and practices, pupil attainment and possible reasons for changes occurring.

The schools were selected from the cohort of schools identified by the Local Education Authorities as taking part in the National Numeracy Strategy Five-day training that took place in the second year of the implementation of the Numeracy Strategy (2000/01). Hence the schools fell outside the set of schools identified as requiring intensive support within the first year of implementation of the National Numeracy Strategy but nevertheless had been identified as being capable of improving their standards (as measured by national test results) in mathematics.

Within that overall cohort of schools, the four schools, two in the north of England and two in the south, were selected to represent a range in terms of pupil intake (see Table A.2.1). In each of the four schools, we opted to work with the two teachers who would be undergoing the National Numeracy Strategy Five-day training in 2000-2001, and a third teacher within the school who would not be directly engaged in the training. Three of this latter group of four teachers subsequently undertook the training the following year (see Table A.2.2).

Table A.2.1. Details of the schools involved in the research 1999-2002

School	Characteristics of school
School 1	One form entry, outer urban, high level unemployment and social deprivation, 10% pupil mobility, FSM 45%, EAL 0%
School 2	One and a half form entry, outer urban, varied socio-economic conditions, many parents on temporary contracts or from army base, 33% pupils have experience of several schools, FSM 8%, EAL 14%
School 3	One and a half form entry, outer urban, mainly social housing, below average socio-economic background, FSM 41%, EAL 22%
School 4	One form entry, inner urban, high level social deprivation, 25% pupil mobility at Key Stage 2 (ages 7-11), FSM 63%, EAL 40%

Note. FSM denotes free school meals; EAL denotes English as an additional language

Table A.2.2 Details of the teachers involved in the research 1999-2002

Teacher	Teachers' mathematics qualification and teaching experience
Sam	GCSE mathematics. Experience: 2 years, pupils aged 7-11 years
Chris	GCE 'O' Level mathematics. Experience: 12 years, pupils aged 4-7 years
Jules	GCSE mathematics. Experience: 3 years, pupils aged 7-11 years
Jo	GCE 'O' Level mathematics. Experience: more than 10 years, pupils aged 3-7 and 11-16 years
Andy	GCE 'O' Level mathematics. Experience: over 20 years, pupils aged 7-11, 11-16 years
Pat	GCE 'O' Level mathematics, studied physics to 'A' Level. Experience: 20 years, pupils aged 7-13 years
Jess	GCE 'O' Level mathematics. Experience: 7 years, pupils aged 4-7 years
Frankie	GCSE mathematics. Studied mathematics for an additional year post 16. Experience: 3 years, pupils aged 7-11 years. Mathematics Co-ordinator
Charlie	GCE 'O' Level mathematics. Teaching experience: 9 years, pupils aged 7-11 years
Clare	GCSE mathematics. Experience: 4 years, pupils aged 7-11 years. Mathematics Co-ordinator
Toni	Access mathematics course to higher education as a mature student. Experience: 2 years, pupils aged 5-7 and 7-11 years
Jenny	No mathematics qualification. Experience: 23 years, mainly pupils aged 4-7 years; two terms with pupils aged 8-9 years

Note. The post-16 qualification was known as General Certificate of Education (GCE) 'O' Level until 1985, then as the General Certificate of Secondary Education (GCSE). The post 18 qualification is known as Advanced ('A') Level.

	Denotes teachers who attended the Five-day course in 2000/01
	Denotes teachers who attended the Five-day course in 2001/02

The teachers were selected for the training by their headteachers. One teacher not initially engaged in the training was replaced early on in the project by the teacher who took over her class. One of the eight teachers engaged in the training in 2000-2001 did not take part in the final interview as she had left the school.

Table A.2.3. Details of the data sources

Interviews	Focus of interview
1. June/July 2000 (for the majority of teachers)	Teaching experience; experience of mathematics; description of own practice. Changes in practice since the introduction of the National Numeracy Strategy. Understanding of aspects of the National Numeracy Strategy. Knowledge of whole-school approach to mathematics
2. June/July 2000 (for the majority of teachers)	Understanding of selected aspects of mathematics through working through examples. Responses to pupils' misconceptions. Conceptions and beliefs about the teaching and learning of mathematics
3. September/ October 2000	Pre-course interview. Expectations of the course (omitted for the four teachers not attending the course)
4. November 2000	Post-course interview. Impressions and responses immediately following the course
5. June/July 2001	Responses to the course over time. Details of current practice and any changes noted
6. November 2001	Views of mathematics as a subject, both as a learner and as a teacher. Contrasting mathematics with other subjects in the curriculum
7. March 2002	Overview of changes in practice, beliefs and understanding over the course of two years. Return to selected mathematics questions from Interview 2. Return to conceptions of teaching and learning mathematics. This interview was missed for the teacher who left towards the end of the research
Observations	**Details of observations**
June 2000; March 2001; June 2001; November 2001; March 2002.	Lesson observations were recorded on video camera and supported by fieldnotes: The first observation was missed for the replacement teacher. The last observation missed for the teacher who left towards the end of the research
Tests	**Details of test administrations**
October 2000, June 2001; October 2001, June 2002	Administration by the class teacher of the Leverhulme Numeracy Research Programme assessments (see Introduction) for the appropriate year group at the beginning and end of the school year

In June or September 2000, baseline data was gathered on the 12 teachers in terms of profiles of their beliefs, knowledge and practices, prior to the training. Using methods developed in previous research at Kings' College (Askew et al., 1997) extended interviews and classroom observations probed teachers' understandings and beliefs. Each of the 12 teachers was interviewed twice (Interviews 1 and 2): once to explore their beliefs and practices, and once to elicit their understanding of aspects of mathematics. (This data was collected one term later for the replacement teacher.) The teachers were also observed teaching mathematics to establish teaching methods, styles of teaching organisation and curriculum emphases prior to the National Numeracy Strategy training. Given the increased emphasis within the National Numeracy Strategy of aspects of mathematics that are based around understanding of multiplicative reasoning – ratio and proportion, rational numbers, models of multiplication and division – for the current study we chose to present to teachers specific mathematical problems related to these aspects. Sources for these problems were from previous research (for example, Ma, 1999) taken in conjunction with an analysis of key aspects of the National Numeracy Strategy Framework for Teaching Mathematics from Reception to Year 6 (Department for Education and Employment, 1999).

Each mathematical problem was presented to the teachers on a separate piece of paper and the teachers were asked for their initial reaction to it. They were then encouraged to try and work out the solution and talk through what they were doing. Calculators were available and the teachers were free to record whatever they wished on the paper. The extent to which the interviewer probed a teacher on their methods, particularly where these were incorrect, depended partly upon the judgement of the interviewer of the extent to which the teacher perceived the questions as stressful. Although the main emphasis in the questions was on the teachers' understanding of the mathematics, in some of the questions the teachers were also asked to comment on the ways in which they might introduce the ideas to the pupils. The interviews were recorded and later transcribed.

Seven interviews were conducted with the teachers over the course of two school years, and video recordings were made of their practice on five occasions over that time. Details of the data sources are given in Table A.2.3. All interviews were recorded and transcribed. They were analysed in conjunction with the video-recordings of lessons around several themes:

- current classroom practice
- subject matter knowledge
- pedagogic content knowledge
- responses to the Five-day course of training
- conceptions and beliefs about mathematics as a subject
- conceptions and beliefs about the teaching of mathematics
- changes in classroom practice.

Pupils in the classes of nine teachers (Reception age pupils, 4-5 years, were not tested) completed the appropriate numeracy assessments developed for the Core longitudinal project of the Leverhulme Numeracy Research Programme (see Introduction), at the beginning and end of the school years 2000/01, 2001/02.

Askew, M., Brown, M., Rhodes, V., Johnson, D., & Wiliam, D. (1997). *Effective teachers of numeracy: Final report.* London: King's College.

Department for Education and Employment. (1999). *The National Numeracy Strategy: Framework for Teaching Mathematics from Reception to Year 6.* London: Department for Education and Employment.

Ma, L. (1999). *Knowing and teaching mathematics: teachers' understanding of fundamental mathematics in China and the United States.* Mahwah, NJ: Lawrence Erlbaum Associates.

ANNEX 3

FOCUS PROJECT: WHOLE SCHOOL ACTION ON NUMERACY

Whole School Action on Numeracy (1997-2001) was one of six projects in the major research programme carried out at King's College London - the Leverhulme Numeracy Research Programme (1997-2002). The overall aim of the project was to identify whole-school and individual teacher factors, which appeared to facilitate or inhibit the development of strategies for raising attainment in numeracy.

Whole School Action on Numeracy focused on six schools as they prepared for, experienced and followed up an Office for Standards in Education (Ofsted) inspection, and continued for a total period of four years (See Table A.3.1).

Table A.3.1. Details of the six schools involved in the research 1997-2001

School	Size	Characteristics
1. Woodbury	600 pupils 3-form entry 21 classes	Suburban, mixed socio-economic, average special needs, above average free school meals, ethnic minorities
2. The Grove	70 pupils 0.5-form entry 3 classes	Rural, Low special needs, very low eligibility for free school meals, very low pupils from ethnic minorities
3. Maple	200 pupils 1 form entry 7 classes	Suburban, mixed socio-economic, average free school meals, above average pupils from ethnic minorities
4. Pennington	340 pupils 1.5-form entry 10 classes, Nursery	New town, high unemployment. About average special needs, free school meals. Few pupils from ethnic minorities
5. Sandmere	340 pupils 1.5- form entry 10 classes, Nursery	Outer urban, high special needs, high free school meals, substantial Asian and African-Caribbean minorities
6. Wolverton	200 pupils 1 form entry 7 classes, Nursery	Inner urban. High levels of pupil mobility, well above average free school meals, above average special needs and pupils from ethnic minorities

The schools (Schools 1-6, given the names Woodbury, The Grove, Maple, Pennington, Sandmere, Wolverton) were chosen to provide a range of contexts. Two schools experiencing inspection or re-inspection were added to the project each term, so that at the end of the first year work had begun in all six schools.

The schools varied in size; they were situated in inner urban, outer urban, suburban and rural environments; their populations had varied levels of economic status and spoke a range of languages other than English; their recent histories exhibited turbulence, moderate disturbance and stability; they were at different stages in their experience of development planning and self-evaluation. However they shared a concern that they had themselves established - the need to develop their mathematics and, in particular, certain aspects of numeracy. In five out of the six schools, mathematics was on the school development plan before the inspection and in the sixth school it was due for priority action during the term following inspection. Interviews with key informants in the schools revealed that all were concerned about raising attainment in mathematics. Some of this concern stemmed specifically from recent poor national test results at ages 7 and 11.

Table A.3.2. The data set 1997-2001

Year	School visits	Interviews	Observations
1997-98	46	6 headteacher 10 co-ordinator 13 class teacher 1 governor	23 classrooms 12 meetings
1998-99	49	6 headteacher 9 co-ordinator 16 class teacher 1 governor	25 classrooms 19 meetings
1999-2000	29	7 headteacher 11 co-ordinator 11 class teacher	9 classrooms 10 meetings
2000-2001	13	6 headteacher 10 co-ordinator 3 class teacher	1 classroom 2 meetings

Data for the research included interviews with teachers, mathematics co-ordinators or subject leaders, headteachers and school governors (school board members), observations of the teaching of mathematics in selected classrooms and notes taken at whole-school and group meetings and in-service training (Inset), both in school and out, related to mathematics/numeracy (See Table A.3.2). School documents were also collected.

Data was collected on:
• Views about, and practice of, mathematics/numeracy prior to the inspection
• Intended development as identified in the School Development Plan
• Interpretations of the requirements of Ofsted
• Preparations made by the school prior to the inspection
• Reactions to the inspection report translated into preparations for the action plan
• Strategies identified for the development of numeracy
• Ways in which these strategies were implemented
• Changes in practice or beliefs (perceived and observed)
• Pupil levels of achievement (at ages 7 and 11 and non-statutory assessments)
• Interaction with the pressures of statutory assessment and the impact of new government emphases, in particular the National Numeracy Strategy.

During the course of 1998, each school experienced an Ofsted inspection and a national initiative on literacy. In September 1999 the National Numeracy Strategy was introduced (See Introduction). One school received intensive numeracy support during this year, the remaining five received this help the following year (2000/01).

Interviews were transcribed, and the transcripts returned to interviewees for validation. Observations were written up from fieldnotes and tape recordings (not transcribed) and also returned to classroom teachers; meetings were recorded in fieldnotes. Interview transcripts and observation notes were coded to identify key categories. These categories were subject to continuous interrogation and revision using the constant comparative method (Strauss, 1987). Interviews were analysed to compare and contrast perceptions within and across schools. Data collection and analysis were contiguous and on-going to enable the feedback of analysis into data collection. Data reduction techniques and memo-ing (Miles & Huberman, 1994) were used in the building up of constructs.

Miles, M. B., & Huberman, A. M. (1994). *Qualitative data analysis: an expanded sourcebook* (2nd ed.). Thousand Oaks, CA: Sage.

Strauss, A. L. (1987). *Qualitative analysis for social scientists*. Cambridge, UK: Cambridge University Press.

FOCUS PROJECT: COGNITIVE ACCELERATION IN MATHEMATICS EDUCATION IN THE PRIMARY SCHOOL (P-CAME)

The aim of this project was to investigate the effectiveness of an intervention programme with children aged 9-10 and 10-11 years (Years 5 and 6 of primary school). The programme consists of a series of mathematics lessons conducted over two consecutive years to the same classes by their own teachers. The lessons were to be designed around key cognitive challenges across the main conceptual strands of the mathematics curriculum. The classroom conduct by the teacher was to be structured to encourage verbal interactions and metacognitive activity in whole-class and various small group arrangements of children.

The main goals of the project were to:
- provide evidence on the effect of the programme on children's cognitive development and mathematical achievement
- create and describe a model of intervention-style teaching in primary school mathematics to serve as a basis for teachers' continuous professional development.

The implementation was carried out in two overlapping phases, each with specified personnel and tasks (see Table A.4.1). Minor pragmatic modifications were needed, mainly in enlarging the role of the teacher researchers and the elaboration of the professional development methodology.

Phase 1 continued throughout the three years by the full team comprised of teacher-researchers, the Local Education Authority maths adviser, three university researchers and an attached research student. The intensity of contact within the research team was at its greatest in the first year – 20 full day whole group formal meetings plus a similar number of school visits by researchers in various combinations. In the following two years this was nearly halved to 12 days a year, including the time allotted to the main study professional development sessions.

Table A.4.1. P-CAME research implementation

Tasks	Year 1	Year 2	Year 3
Phase 1 Development of lessons Support material Lesson observations Assessment instruments Revising materials Quantitative data	Full research team working with 2 Y5 and 2 Y6 classes in 2 lab schools) • Pre-tests in lab schools	Full research team working with 2 Y5 and 2 Y6 classes in 2 lab schools Post tests in lab schools Pre-tests in main study schools	Full research team working in main study schools and two additional lab schools Post tests in main study schools KS2 tests
Phase 2 Main research: lesson and Professional Development observations [Development of the Professional development methodology]		19 teachers in 9 main study schools Y5 classes only King's researchers and LEA adviser Teacher-researchers as peer tutors	19 teachers in 9 schools Y6 classes only King's researchers and LEA adviser Teacher-researchers as peer tutors

One teacher-researcher went on maternity-leave at the end of the first year, did not return to teaching, and was replaced by two teachers from different main study schools at the end of Year 2 of the project. The two teacher researchers in the other laboratory school became Local Education Authority numeracy consultants, one at the end of Year 1, the other during the second year, but both continued their involvement in the project voluntarily up to the present. It was felt that, despite the personnel and position changes, the research team was the strongest component of the project. That helped to compensate for large-scale staff turnover in the main study (Phase 2) cohort of teachers, and also helped to generate important theoretical and practical innovations in the approach.

Phase 2 started in the summer of the first year, with the introduction of main study teachers to the approach. Over the following six terms there were 12 formal half-day professional development sessions, and three times that number of in-class observations and tutorial support in various formal and informal arrangements, including team teaching and peer tutoring.

In total 24 lessons (out of the 34 considered) were fully developed and offered to the main study teachers, at a regular rate of four lessons a term. They addressed concepts and reasoning patterns in number and algebra, shape and space, and handling data, but with emphasis on number relations. On average 17 lessons were conducted in the main study classes.

PROFESSIONAL DEVELOPMENT IN PRIMARY MATHEMATICS

Additional work funded by Kings' College related to Primary CAME: Research Student Jeremy Hodgen

This additional research was funded as a research studentship by King's College London in order to investigate more fully the professional development aspects of the Primary CAME intervention. The initial aim of this attached project was to investigate the professional change of classroom teachers as they participated in the Primary CAME Professional Development programme.

As the project developed, the emphasis of the research shifted to focus more specifically on the teacher-researchers in the research and development team as practitioner teacher educators. The research explored the teacher-researchers' own knowledge and practice in primary mathematics and the tutoring relationship between the teacher-researchers and the classroom teachers. An additional, but secondary, aspect to the research was the teacher-researchers' involvement in the National Numeracy Strategy. Two teacher-researchers became numeracy consultants, whilst the others had led both Local Education Authority and in-school numeracy training sessions.

Early work emphasised the importance of collaboration and reflection with teacher change. A further aspect was an identification of some philosophical challenges that primary teachers faced in relation to school mathematics. The research explored ways in which these teacher-researchers' beliefs and understandings of big mathematical ideas had evolved. A major focus was on the impact of the teacher-researchers' engagement with the research and development activities of Primary CAME and subsequently through a consideration of their roles as consultants/tutors in the National Numeracy Strategy.

REFERENCES

Abreu, G de, 1995 "Understanding how Children Experience the Relationship between Home and School Mathematics" *Mind Culture and Activity* **2** (2) pp 119-142

Abreu, G. de., & Cline, T. (1998). *Studying social representations of mathematics learning in multiethnic primary schools*: work in progress. *Papers on social representation*, 7(1-2), 1-20.

Abreu, G. de., Cline, T., & Shamsi, A. (1999). *Mathematics Learning in Multiethnic Primary Schools* (ESRC). Luton: University of Luton, Dept. of Psychology.

Agar,M 1996 *The Professional Stranger: an informal introduction to ethnography* 2nd edition. Academic Press: NY. especially new chapter 1 "Ethnography Reconstructed: the Stranger at Fifteen". pp. 1-51

Alexander, R 2000 *Culture and pedagogy: International Comparisons in primary Education* Oxford: Blackwell

Alexander, Robin 1996 "Other Primary Schools and Ours: Hazards of International Comparison" CREPE Occasional papers, Warwick;

Aubrey, C, Godfrey, R & Dahl, S 2000 "Boosting the Boosted": evaluations of Key Stage 3 Numeracy Project" presented at *BERA Conference, Sept. 2000* Cardiff: BERA

Aubrey, Carol 1997 "Children's early learning of number in school and out" in I. Thompson, (Ed.), Teaching and Learning Early Number (pp. 20-30). Milton Keynes: Open University Press

Aubrey, Carol, 1997 *Mathematics teaching in the early years*: An Investigation of Teachers" Subject Knowledge. London: The Falmer Press.

Baker D A (1996) "Children's Formal and Informal School Numeracy Practice" in D Baker, J Clay & C Fox (Eds*.) Challenging Ways of Knowing in English Maths and Science.* London: Falmer

Baker D A (1998) "Numeracy as Social Practice; and adult education context in South Africa", *Journal of Literacy and Numeracy Studies* Vol. 8, No. 1, pp. 37-50.Sydney, Australia.

Baker D A and Street B V (1996) "Literacy and Numeracy Models" in *The International Encyclopaedia of Adult Education and Training,* Oxford, Elsevier Science, pp 79-85

Baker D A Street B V (submitted) "Navigating schooled numeracies: explanations from the UK for the low achievement in math of children from a low SES background" in *Special Issue of Mathematical Thinking and Learning on Parents' Perceptions of the Children's Mathematics Education: Considerations of Race, Class, Equity, and Social Justice.* Allexsaht-Snider M (Ed), Brisbane: Queensland University of Technology

Baker D A with B Street and A Tomlin (2000a) "Schooled and Community numeracies; understanding social factors and "under-achievement" in numeracy." in the *Proceedings of the Mathematics Education and Society Conference* Algarve Portugal

Baker D A with B Street and A Tomlin (2000b) "Understanding the social in maths and "under-attainment" in numeracy" in *Proceedings of the 2th 4 Annual Conference of the International Group for the Psychology of Mathematics Education,* Hiroshima (July 2000) Vol. 2 p 49

Baker, D & Street, B 2004 "Mathematics as Social" *For the Learning of Mathematics* 24,2 (July) pp. 19-21, Ontario, Canada

Bartlett, L and Holland D (2002) "Theorising the Space of Literacy Practices." *Ways of Knowing Journal* Vol. 2 (1) Brighton; University of Brighton

Barton, David & Hamilton, M & Ivanic, R (eds.) 1999 *Situated Literacies: reading and writing in context* Routledge: London

Barton, David & Hamilton, M 1998 "Local Literacies: reading and writing in one community" Routledge: London

Basic Skills Agency. *Count and figure it out together: A magazine for parents and children aged 3-5* [.pdf file]. Retrieved 10 Sept., 2002, from the World Wide Web: http://www.basic-skills.co.uk/_media/documents/cf1.pdf

Baynham, M 1995 *Literacy Practices* Longman: London

Bennett N et al 1976 *Teaching styles and pupil progress* London: Open Books

Bernstein, B 1 1996 *Pedagogy, Symbolic Control and Identity: theory, research, critique* Taylor & Francis: London

Blackledge, A 2000 *Literacy, Power and Social Justice* Trentham Books: Staffs

Bloch, C, P Stein. & M. Prinsloo. 2001 "Progress Report on Children's Early Literacy Learning (CELL) research project in South Africa". *Journal of Early Childhood Literacy* 1(1): 121-122

Boaler, J (2000) (ed.) *Multiple perspectives on mathematics teaching and learning.* Wesport, CT: Ablex

Bottle, G 1999 "A study of Children's Mathematical Experiences in the Home" *Early Years* Vol. 20 no. 1 autumn pp. 53-63

Bourdieu P 1985 "Social Space and the Genesis of Groups" in *Theory and Society* 14:6 p 723 - 744

Bourdieu P 1990 *In other Worlds: Essays towards a reflexive sociology.* Cambridge: Polity Press

Brew,C 2002 "Peer-interactions in the adult mathematics classroom and the flow-on effect to the children of women returning to study mathematics" Occasional Paper La Trobe, Australia

Brilliant-Mills,H 1994 "Becoming a Mathematician: building a situated definition of mathematics" *Linguistics & Education* 5, 301-334 Santa Barabra, UC

Brown M, Askew M, Baker D, Denvir H, Millett 1998 "Is the national numeracy strategy research based?" *British Journal of Education Studies.* Vol. 46 No. 4

Brown, A and Dowling, P (1999) "Parental participation, positioning and pedagogy: a sociological study of the IMPACT primary school mathematics project" in *Collected Original Resources in Education,* Vol. 24, No. 3, 7/A02-11/C09

Brown, T 1997 *Mathematics Education and language: interpreting hermeneutics and poststructuralism.* Kluwer Academic publishers, Dordrecht: Holland

Bruner, J (1960)(2nd edition (1977) *The Process of Education,* Cambridge, Mass.: Harvard University Press. 97 + xxvi pages.

Bruner, J. (1990) *Acts of Meaning* Cambridge, MA: Harvard University Press.

Burkhardt, H. (1981). *The Real World and Mathematics.* Glasgow: Blackie and Son.

Cairney T H (1997) "Acknowledging Diversity in Home Literacy Practices: Moving Towards Partnership with parents". *Early Child Development and Care* Vol. 127-128 pp 61-73

Carraher, T Schliemann A Carraher D (1988) "Mathematical Concepts in Everyday Life". In G Saxe and M Gearhart (Eds) *Children's Mathematics New Directions in Child Development.* SF: Jossey-Bass

Carraher, T., Carraher, D., & Schleimer, A. (1985). "Mathematics in the streets and in schools". *British Journal of Developmental Psychology, 3,* 21-29.

CASE (Centre for Analysis of Social Exclusion). (1999*). Persistent Poverty and Lifetime Inequality: The Evidence* (5). London: London School of Economics.

Chall, J. S., Jacobs, V & Baldwin, L 1990 *The Reading Crisis: why poor children fall behind* Cambridge MA: Harvard UP

Civil, M. & Quintos, B. 2002 *Uncovering Mothers' perceptions about the Teaching and Learning of Mathematics* Univ of Arizona, Tucson

Clarke, Julia; Edwards, Richard; Harrison, Roger & Reeve, Fiona (2002) "Why don't you give the money back? Questions of accounting and accountability in three accounts of educational research" *International Journal for Qualitative Studies in Education,* Vol 15 No.5 ISSN 0951-8398

Cobb, P & Bowers, J 1999 "Cognitive and Situated Learning perspectives in Theory and Practice" *Educational Researcher* vol. 28, no. 2, March pp 4-15).

Coben, D (2000). "Mathematics or common sense? Researching invisible mathematics through adults' mathematics life histories". In J. O. D. Diana Coben, and Gail E. FitzSimons (Ed.), *Perspectives on Adults Learning Mathematics: Research and Practice* (pp. 53-66). Dordrecht, The Netherlands: Kluwer Academic Publishers

Coben, Diana, O'Donoghue, John, & FitzSimons, Gail E. (editors) (2000) *Perspectives on Adults Learning Mathematics: Research and Practice.* Mathematics Education Library Vol.21, Series Editor: Alan Bishop. Dordrecht, The Netherlands: Kluwer Academic Publishers. ISBN: 0-7923-6415-5

Cooper, B. and Dunne, M. (2000). *Assessing Children's mathematical Knowledge: Social class, sex and problem-solving.* Buckingham, Open University Press.

de Acosta, M and Volk, D 1999 "Literacy Policy and Literacy in the Classroom: what ethnography teaches us" paper at *Oxford Ethnography and Education Conference,* Sept 1999.

Department for Education and Employment (1999) *The National Numeracy Strategy* Sudbury, Suffolk: DFEE

Department for Education and Employment (1999) *The National Numeracy Strategy: Mathematics Vocabulary* London, DfEE.

Dewey J (1998) "School and Society". *In Dewey on Education*. New York: Teachers College Press. (Original Work published in 1899)

Dienes Z P 1970 *The six stages in the process of learning mathematics* Windsor NFER

Dienes,Z. 1960 *Building Up Mathematics* Hutchinson Educational: London

Dowling, P. (1998). *The Sociology of Mathematics Education: Mathematical Myths/Pedagogic Texts.* London, The Falmer Press.

Edwards, R., & Alldred, P. (2000). Children's Understandings of Home-school Relations. *Education 3-13*(October 2000), 41-45.

Evans, J (2000) *Adults' Mathematical Thinking and Emotions* London: Routledge

Evans, J and Tsatsaroni, A 2000 "Mathematics and its publics: texts, contexts and users" in *Social Epistemology* vol. 14, no. 1 pp. 55-68

Feinstein, L. (2003) "Inequality in the early cognitive development of British children in the 1970 Cohort". *Economica 70* (277) pp 73 - 107

FitzSimons, G.E & Godden, G.L. (2000) "Review of research on adults learning mathematics" in: D. Coben, J. O"Donoghue and G.E FitzSimons (eds*)* *Perspectives on Adults Learning Mathematics; research and practice.* Mathematics Education Library, Vol.21. Dordrecht, Boston, London: Kluwer Academic Publishers, pp13-45 32

Freebody, P Ludwig, C et al *Everyday literacy practices in and out of schools in low Socio-Economic urban communities.* Vol. 1 Brisbane; DEET

Galton M, Gray J and Rudduck Jean (1999) *The impact of school transitions and transfers on pupil progress and attainment* London: Department for Education and Employment

Galton, M. Simon B. and Croll P (1980) *Inside the primary classroom* London: Routledge and Kegan Paul

Gates P (2001) *Issues in Mathematics Teaching* London: Routledge

Gee, J 2003 *What Video Games Have to Teach Us about Learning and Literacy.* New York: Palgrave/St. Martin's

Gee,J 2001 "Reading, Language Abilities and Semiotic resources: beyond limited perspectives on reading" in Larson, J ed. *Literacy as Snake Oil* New York: Peter Lang

Gerdes, P. (1986) "How to Recognise Hidden Geometric Thinking: A Contribution to the development of Anthropological Mathematics" *For the Learning Of Maths* 6 (3)

Gerofsky S. (1996). "A Linguistic and Narrative View of Word Problems in Mathematics Education". *For the Learning of Mathematics, 16*(2), 36-45.

Gerofsky, S. (1999). "Genre analysis as a way of understanding pedagogy in mathematics education." *For the Learning of Mathematics* 19(3): 36-46.

Gewirtz, S 2001 "Cloning the Blairs: New Labour's programme for the re-socialising of working parents" in *Journal of Educational Policy* vol. 16, no. 4; 365-378

Ginsberg H P Choi Y Em, Lopez S L, Netley R, Chao-Yuan C 1997 "Happy Birthday to you: Early Mathematical Thinking of Asian, South American and Us Children" in *Learning and Teaching Mathematics An International Perspective.* T Nunes P Bryant (Eds.) Hove UK: Psychology Press

Gipps, et.al. 2000 *What makes a good primary school teacher? Expert Classroom Struggles* London and NY: Routledge, Falmer

Gold E and Mordecai-Phillips R, 2003 "Learning in Multiple Worlds: An Examination of the Intersection of Home and School Mathematics Practices" Presented at the *American Educational Research Association (AERA) Annual Meeting, Chicago*, April 2003 Philadelphia: PA Research for Action

Green, J and Bloome, D. (1997) "Ethnography and ethnographers of and in education: a situated perspective" in Flood, J., Heath, S and Lapp, D (eds.), *A handbook of research on teaching literacy through the communicative and visual arts* (pp 181-202) New York, Simon and Shuster Macmillan

Gregory, E & Williams, A 2000 *City Literacies* Routledge: London

Gregory, E 1993 "What counts as reading in the early years" classroom?" in *British Journal of Educational Psychology* 63: 214-230

Gregory, E 1997 *One Child, Many Worlds: early learning in multicultural communities* London: David Fulton

Gregory, E Williams A, Baker D, Street B 2004 "Introducing Literacy to four year olds: Creating classroom cultures in three schools". *Journal of Early Childhood* Literacy 4(1) pp 85 - 108 Sage ISSN 1468-7984

Grenfell M, James, D with P. Hodkinson, D. Reay, & D. Robbins (1998), *Bourdieu and Education: Acts of Practical Theory* (pp. 55-71). London: Falmer Press.

Grenfell,M 2003 "Bourdieu in the Classroom" *Centre for Language in Education: Occasional paper No. 62*, Southampton, UK: University of Southampton

Hammersley ,M 1992 *What's Wrong with Ethnography?*, London: Routledge

Hannon,P 1998 "How Can We Foster Children's Early Literacy Development Through Parental Involvement" in S. Neuman & K. Rozkos (eds.) *Children Achieving: instructional practices in early literacy* Newark DE: International reading Association pp. 121-143

Heath, S. B. and Wolf, S 2004 *Visual Learning in the Community School* London: Creative Partnerships:

Heath, S. B.. and Mangiola, l 1991 *Children of Promise: literate activity in linguistically and culturally diverse classrooms* NEA School restructuring series: Washington DC

Heath, S.B. 1983 *Ways with Words* Cambridge: CUP

Heath,S.B. 1982 "Questioning at Home and School: a comparative study" in G. Spindler ed. *Doing the Ethnography of Schooling: Educational Anthropology in Action* pp. 102-131 New York: Holt, Rinehart and Winston

HM Treasury March 99 *The modernisation of the British Tax and Benefit System. No. 4 Tackling Poverty and Extending Opportunity.* London HM Treasury. Available from http://www.hm-treasury.gov.uk

Hobcraft, J. (1998). *Intergenerational and Life-Course Transmission of Social Exclusion: Influences of childhood poverty, family disruption, and contact with police.* London: CASE (Centre for Analysis of Social Exclusion), LSE.

Holland D, Lachicotte Jr W. Skinner D Cain C (2001) *Identity and Agency in Cultural Worlds* Cambridge: Mass: Harvard University Press

Holland, D & Lave, J 2001 (eds.) *History in Person: enduring struggles, contentious practice, intimate identities* Santa Fe: SAR Press

Hoyles, C., Noss, R. & Pozzi, 2001 S. "Proportional Reasoning in Nursing Practice". *Journal for Research in Mathematics Education* 32, 1, 4-27.

Hughes M 1986 *Children and Number* Oxford: Blackwell.

Hughes M 1992 *Mathematical Thinking in very young children: the origins of written representation.* BSRLM ms available from the author Bristol Univ. UK

Hughes M, Greenhough P 1998 "Moving between Communities of Practice: Children linking mathematical activities at home and at school" in *Situated Cognition and the Learning of Mathematics* ed. A Watson pp 127-142 Oxford: Centre for Maths Education Research

Hughes M., Desforges C., Michell C, 2000 *Numeracy and Beyond. Applying mathematics in the primary school* Buckingham: Open Univ Press

Hughes, M. and Greenhough, P. (1998) Moving between communities of practice: Children linking mathematical activities at home and school. In A. Watson, (ed) Situated Cognition and the Learning of Mathematics, 127-141, University of Oxford: Centre for Mathematics Education Research

Jenkins R 1992 *Pierre Bourdieu* London; Routledge

Jones L, 1995 *Linking School and Community Numeracy Practices: A family numeracy project base in London.* London: Goldsmiths University of London.

Jones, K. & M. Martin-Jones eds. 2000 *Multilingual Literacies: comparative perspectives on research and practice* Amsterdam: J. Benjamins:

Kleifgen, Jo Anne and Patricia Frenz-Belkin 1997 "Assembling Knowledge: International and Transcultural Studies" in *Research on Language and Social Interaction.* 30(2), 157 –192.Teachers College, Columbia University

Knijnik, G. (2000) "Ethnomathematics and political struggles" in: D. Coben, J. O'Donoghue and G.E. FitzSimons (eds) *Perspectives on Adults Learning Mathematics: research and practice.* Mathematics Education Library, Vol.21.Dordrecht, Boston, London: Kluwer Academic Publishers, pp119-133

Kress, G & van Leeuwen, T 1996 *Reading Images: the Grammar of Visual Design* London: Routledge

Kress, G 2002 *Literacy in the New Media Age* Routledge: London

Labov, W 1972 *Language in the Inner City: studies of Black English Vernacular,* Philadelphia: U. of Pennsylvania press

Lave, J 1994 *Cognition in Practice* CUP

Lave, J. (1992). "Word problems: A microcosm of theories of learning". *Context and cognition: Ways of learning and knowing.* P. Light and G. Butterworth. New York, Harvester Wheatsheaf.: 74-92.

Lee, V & Burkham,D 2002 *Inequality at the Starting Gate: social background and achievement at Kindergarten entry* Michigan: Univ of Michigan

Lemke, J 2003 "Across the Scales of Time: Artefacts, Activities and Meanings in Ecosocial Systems" http:/www-personal.umich.edu/~jaylemke/webs/time/MCA-intro.htm

Lerman, S (2000) "The Social Turn in Maths Education research" in Boaler J (ed.) *Multiple Perspectives in Mathematics teaching and L earning.* Westport Connecticut: Ablex

Levin B (1999) *Va lue for money in the National Literacy And Numeracy Strategies.* Toronto: OISIE (Ontario Institute for Studies in Education), University of Toronto, November 1999

Luke, A 1993 "Genres of Power?" in *Literacy & Society* ed. R. Hasan & G. Williams. Longmans: London

Machin S (1999) "Childhood Disadvantage and Intergenerational Transmission of Economic Status" in *CASE Report 5 Persistent Poverty and Lifetime inequality: The Evidence,* London: LSE

Masingila, J. O. Davidenko, S. and Prus-Wisniowska E, 1996 "Mathematics Learning and Practice In and Out of School: a framework for connecting these experiences" *Educational Studies in Mathematics* vol, 31 p 175-200

McDermott, R "When is math or science?" in *Thinking practices.* Edited by J. Greeno and S. Goldman

McNamara, O. (1999?). "Your Country Needs You": mobilising the "informed consumer" as an "active partner" in *School-home relations* pp. 14 Manchester: Manchester Metropolitan University.

Mitchell, J 1984 "Typicality and the Case Study" pp. 238-241 in R.F. Ellen (ed.) *Ethnographic Research: a guide to conduct* Academic Press: New York

Moll L. Amanti C, Neff D and Gonzalez N, (1992) "Funds of Knowledge for Teaching: using a qualitative approach to connect homes and classrooms", in *Theory into practice,* XXXI (2) p 131-141

Morgan C (1998) *Writing Mathematically. The discourse of Investigation.* London: Routledge

Muijs, D Reynolds D 2001 *Effective teaching: evidence and practice* London: Paul Chapman

Mundaschenk,N & Foley,R 1994 "Collaborative Relations between School and Home: implications for Service Delivery" in *Preventing School Failure* Washington: Heldref Pubications

Noss R (1997) "New Cultures, New Numeracies" Inaugural Professorial Lecture, Instutue of education, University of London.

Nunes T Schliemann A Carraher D (1993) Street Mathematics and School Mathematics. Cambridge: CUP

Office for Standards in Education. (2000). *Inspection Report, "Tarnside".* London

Oldham,J, Parker,D, MacCabe,C,Marshall,B and Street,B *2001Report on Literacy & Media Research Project*: British Film Institute/King's College, King's College London, Centre For Research On Literacy and The Media London, October 1997 - November 2000.

Osborn,M, McNess,E, Broadfoot,P with Pollard,A & Triggs,P 2000 *What teachers Do: changing policy and practice in primary education* London: Continuum

Pahl, K. (2002a) "Habitus and the home: texts and practices in families" pp. 45 – 53 *Ways of Knowing Journal.* Vol. 2 No 1 May 2002

Pahl, K. (2002b) "Ephemera, Mess and Miscellaneous Piles: Texts and Practices in Families". pp. 145 – 165 *Journal of Early Childhood Literacy.* Vol. 2 No 2 August 2002

Pahl, K. and Rowsell, J. (2005) *Literacy and Education: Understanding the New Literacy Studies in the Classroom.* London: Paul Chapman Publishing

Parekh, B 2000 *Rethinking Multiculturalism - cultural diversity and political theory* London: Palgrave, Macmillan Press.

Parekh, B. 2000 *The Future of Multi-Ethnic Britain* London: Runnymede Trust and Profile Books

Parker J (2000, 9 Sept.) "Shared learning schemes help parents and children to cope with homework: why parents must not play teacher. The Sunday Times

Peterson,D 1989 "Parent Involvement in the Education Process" *ERIC documents no ED312776*

Philips, S 1972 "Participant Structure and Communicative Competence: Warm Springs Children in Community and Classroom" in Cazden,J & Hymes,D *Functions of Language in the Classroom* pp. 370-94 New Yor: Teachers College Press

Pimm D 1995 *Symbols and meanings in school mathematic*s London: Routledge

Pimm, D (1987) *Speaking Mathematically: Communication in Mathematics Classrooms.* London; Routledge Kegan Paul

Pollard, A with Filer, A. 2000 *The social worlds of pupil career: strategic biographies through primary school* London: Cassell

Purcell-Gates,V, L"Allier,S & Smith,D 1995 "Literacy at the Harts and the Larsons: diversity among poor inner-city families" in *The Reading Teacher* vol. 48, no.7

Radford, L 2002 "Symbolic Thinking" *Proceedings of PME* 27; pp. 81-88

Raz,I.A. & Bryant,P 1990 "Social Background, phonological awareness and children"s reading" *British Journal of development Psychology* 8, 209-225

Reay D (1998) Class Work: Mothers involvement in their Children's Schooling. London: UCL Press.

Reay, D(1998). "Rethinking Social Class: Qualitative Perspectives on Class and Gender." *Sociology* 32(2): 259 - 276

Reay, D. (1998). "Cultural Reproduction: Mothers' Involvement in Their Children's Primary Schooling". In M. Grenfel, D. James, with P. Hodkinson, D. Reay, & D. Robbins (Eds.), *Bourdieu and Education: Acts of Practical Theory* (pp. 55-71). London: Falmer Press.

Reay, D. (1999). "Linguistic Capital and Home-School Relationships: Mothers' Interactions with their Children"s Primary School Teachers". *Acta Sociologic 1999, 42,* 159-168.

Reay,D and Lucey,H 2000 "I Don't Really Like it Here But I Don't Want to be Anywhere Else": *Children and inner city Council Estates,* Antipode 32:4 pp. 410-428

Rees,M 1999 *Just Six Numbers: the deep forces that shape the universe* Wiedenfeld & Nicolson: London

Rogoff B (2003) *The Cultural Nature of Human Development* Oxford: Oxford University Press

Rogoff, B., Paradise, R., Mej a Arauz, R., Correa-Ch vez , M., & Angelillo, C. (2003). "Firsthand learning by intent participation". *Annual Review of Psychology,* 54.

Rogoff, Barbara and Lave, Jean 1984, 1999 *Everyday Cognition: Its Development in social context,* Harvard. chapters by Michael Cole, Sylivia Scribner, Jean Lave and Barbara Rogoff:

Rowlands, S. (1999, 27 February 1999). "Have socioculturists turned Vyotsky on his head?" *Paper presented at the BSRLM Day Conference,* Open University.

Saxe G 1988 "Candy Selling and maths learning" *Educational Researcher* 17, 14 - 21

Saxena,M 1994 "Literacies Among Punjabis in Southall" in *Worlds of Literacy* ed. M. Hamilton, D. Barton & R. Ivanic. Multilingual Matters: Clevedon pp. 195-214

Setati M, Adler J, Reed Y, and Bapoo A. (2002) "Code Switching and other language practices in mathematics, science and English language classrooms in South Africa" in J Adler, Y Reed (Eds.) *Challenge of Teacher Development* Pretoria: Van Schaik

Sheridan D., Street,B and Bloome D 2000. *Ordinary People Writing: Literacy Practices and Identity in the Mass-Observation Project,* Hampton Press, Cresskill NJ

Silverman,D 1993 *Interpreting Qualitative Data* esp. chapter 3 "Observation: the ethnographic tradition" and chapter 4 "Texts: ethnographic analysis" Sage: London

Singh, Jagjit 1954 *Mathematical Ideas: their nature and use* London: Hutchinson

Skovsmose,O 1994 "Critique and education" Chapter 1 of *Critical Maths Education* Dortrecht: Kluwer Academic

Slavin, R. E., N. L. Karweit, et al. (1989). *Effective Programs for Students at Risk.* Boston, Allyn and Bacon.

Smith (2004) Making Maths Count: The Report of Professor Adrian Smith"s

Smith A 2004 *Making Mathematics Count: Inquiry into Post-14 Mathematics Education* London: DFES

Smith Adrian (2004) *Making Maths Count: The Report of Professor Adrian Smith's Inquiry into Post-14 Mathematics Education* London: DFES

Snow, C, Burns, M S & Griffin, P (eds.) *1998 Preventing Reading Difficulties in Young Children* Washington DC: National Academy Press

Street 1984 *Literacy in Theory and Practice* Cambridge; CUP

Street 1993 *Cross Cultural Approaches to Literacy* Cambridge; CUP;

Street, B (2000) "Literacy Events and Literacy Practices" in *Multilingual Literacies: Comparative Perspectives on Research and Practice* ed. K. Jones & M. Martin-Jones. Jason Benjamin"s; Amsterdam pp. 17-29

Street, B (2004) "Applying New Literacy Studies to Numeracy As Social Practice" in Urban Literacy: communication, identity and learning in urban contexts edited Alan Rogers UIE Hamburg

Street,B 1988 "Literacy Practices and Literacy Myths", in *The Written Word: Studies in Literate Thought and Action* ed. R. Saljo, Vol. 23 of Language and Communication Series, Springer-Verlag Press, Heidelberg.pp. 59-72

Street,B 1994 "Literacy and Power?" *Balid Bulletin* Vol. 10, no. 1 pp. 33-36

Street,B ed (2004) *Literacies across Educational Contexts*; mediating learning and teaching ed. Caslon Press: Phila.

Thompson P 1993 "Notations Conventions and Constraints: Contributions to effective use of concrete materials in elementary mathematics". *Journal for Research in Mathematics Education* 23(2) NCTM USA.

Tizard, B., & Hughes, M. (1984). *Young Children Learning*. London: Fontana.

Tizard, B., Blatchford, P., Burke, J., Farquhar, C., & Plewis, I. (1982). *Young children at school in the inner city*. Lawrence Erlbaum Associates: Hove, Sussex

Verran,H 1999 "Staying True to the Laughter in Nigerian Classrooms" in *Actor Network Theory and After* ed. J. Law & J. Howard. (Special Issue of *The Sociological Review*) Blackwell: Oxford pp. 136-155

Verschaffel, L., B. Greer, et al. (2000). *Making Sense of Word Problems*. Abingdon, Swets & Zeitlinger.

Walkerdine V (ed) 2001 *Challenging subjects : critical psychology for a new millennium* New York ; Houndmills : Palgrave

Walkerdine, V (1988) *The Mastery of Reason* London: Routledge

Zevenbergen,R "Language, social class and underachievement in school mathematics" in Gates, P 2001 ed. *Issues in Mathematics Teaching* Routledge: London pp. 38-50